Maker Innovations Series

Jump start your path to discovery with the Apress Maker Innovations series! From the basics of electricity and components through to the most advanced options in robotics, Machine Learning, and even the metaverse, you'll forge a path to building ingenious hardware and controlling it with cutting-edge software. All while gaining new skills and experience with common toolsets you can take to new projects or even into a whole new career.

The Apress Maker Innovations series offers project-based learning with a strong foundation in theory and best practices. So you get hands-on experience while also learning the key concepts, terminology, and creative processes that professionals such as entrepreneurs, inventors, and engineers, use when developing and executing hardware projects. You can learn to design circuits, program AI, create IoT systems for your home or even city, or build immersive environments for the Metaverse. Each book provides the building blocks to bring your ideas to life, and so much more!

Whether you're a beginning hobbyist or a seasoned entrepreneur working out of your basement or garage, you'll scale up your skillset to become a hardware design and engineering pro. And often using low-cost and open-source software such as Raspberry Pi, Arduino, PIC microcontroller, and Robot Operating System (ROS). Programmers and software engineers will also find opportunities to expand their skills, as many projects use popular languages and operating systems like Python and Linux.

If you want to build a robot, set up a smart home, assemble a weather-ready meteorology system, create a brand-new circuit using breadboards and design software, or even build anything with LEGO, this series has all that and more! Written by creative and seasoned Makers, every book tackles both tested and leading-edge approaches and technologies, for bringing your visions and projects to life.

More information about this series at `https://link.springer.com/bookseries/17311`.

Performance Modeling of Computer Systems

A Comprehensive Guide to Microarchitectural Simulation

Ananya Pareek

Apress®

Performance Modeling of Computer Systems: A Comprehensive Guide to Microarchitectural Simulation

Ananya Pareek
SUNNYVALE, CA, USA

ISBN-13 (pbk): 979-8-8688-2475-3
ISBN-13 (electronic): 979-8-8688-2476-0
https://doi.org/10.1007/979-8-8688-2476-0

Managing Director, Apress Media LLC: Welmoed Spahr
Acquisitions Editor: Miriam Haidara
Editorial Project Manager: Marina Engler

Cover designed by eStudioCalamar

Distributed to the book trade worldwide by Springer Science+Business Media New York, 1 New York Plaza, New York, NY 10004. Phone 1-800-SPRINGER, fax (201) 348-4505, e-mail orders-ny@springer-sbm.com, or visit www.springeronline.com. Apress Media, LLC is a Delaware LLC and the sole member (owner) is Springer Science + Business Media Finance Inc (SSBM Finance Inc). SSBM Finance Inc is a **Delaware** corporation.

For information on translations, please e-mail booktranslations@springernature.com; for reprint, paperback, or audio rights, please e-mail bookpermissions@springernature.com.

Apress titles may be purchased in bulk for academic, corporate, or promotional use. eBook versions and licenses are also available for most titles. For more information, reference our Print and eBook Bulk Sales web page at http://www.apress.com/bulk-sales.

Any source code or other supplementary material referenced by the author in this book is available to readers on GitHub. For more detailed information, please visit https://www.apress.com/gp/services/source-code.

If disposing of this product, please recycle the paper

For my parents.

Table of Contents

About the Author xxiii

About the Technical Reviewer xxv

Acknowledgments xxvii

Introduction xxix

Part I: Foundations 1

Chapter 1: Introduction to Performance Modeling 3

Prerequisites 4

1.1 The Role of Performance Modeling 4

1.1.1 Why We Cannot Just Build and Test 5

1.1.2 Use Cases for Performance Modeling 6

1.1.3 A Brief Note on History 7

1.2 The Spectrum of Modeling Approaches 7

1.2.1 Analytical Models 7

1.2.2 Transaction Level Models (TLM) 8

1.2.3 Cycle-Accurate Simulation 9

1.3 Accuracy, Speed, and Flexibility Tradeoffs 10

1.3.1 The Fundamental Tradeoffs 10

1.3.2 Accuracy vs. Speed 11

1.3.3 Flexibility vs. Accuracy 11

1.3.4 Fit for Purpose 11

1.3.5 Case Study: Prefetcher Evaluation 12

1.4 Open-Source Simulation Tools 14
1.4.1 The Toolkit 15
1.4.2 ChampSim 15
1.4.3 gem5 16
1.4.4 Accel-Sim 16
1.4.5 SCALE-Sim 17
1.4.6 Supporting Tools 18
1.5 Summary 18
Review Questions 19

Chapter 2: Architecture Through the Modeler's Lens 21

2.1 The Compute-Memory Balance 22
2.1.1 The Fundamental Relationship 22
2.1.2 Operational Intensity 23
2.1.3 Compute Resources 24
2.1.4 Memory Resources 25
2.1.5 Cross-Platform Comparison 26
2.2 Bandwidth and Latency 27
2.2.1 Bandwidth Constraints 27
2.2.2 Latency Constraints 28
2.3 Parallelism 30
2.3.1 Instruction-Level Parallelism (ILP) 30
2.3.2 Thread-Level Parallelism (TLP) 32
2.3.3 Data-Level Parallelism (DLP) 33
2.3.4 Platform Comparison 34
2.4 Summary 36
Review Questions 37
Further Reading 37

Chapter 3: Workload Selection and Experimental Validity 39

3.1 The Generalization Problem 40

3.1.1 From Sample to Population 40

3.1.2 Representativeness Failures 41

3.1.3 Claims and Applicability 43

3.1.4 Evidence Requirements by Claim Strength 44

3.1.5 Working Backward from Claims 44

3.1.6 Example: Cache Replacement Study 45

3.2 Workload Characterization 46

3.2.1 Purpose of Workload Characterization 46

3.2.2 Using Hardware Performance Counters 47

3.2.3 Characterizing Operational Intensity 48

3.2.4 Characterizing Memory Access Patterns 49

3.2.5 Characterizing with Clustering and Visualization 50

3.3 Standard Benchmark Suites 51

3.3.1 CPU Benchmarks 51

3.3.2 GPU and Accelerator Workloads 52

3.3.3 Server and Cloud Workloads 53

3.3.4 Limitations 54

3.4 Practical Aspects of Workload Selection 55

3.4.1 Common Workload Sources 55

3.4.2 Selection in Practice 56

3.4.3 Pragmatic Considerations 56

3.5 Summary 57

Review Questions 58

Further Reading 58

Chapter 4: Simulator in a Nutshell 61
4.1 From Trace to Statistics 61
4.2 Path of a Memory Access 63
Further Reading 66

Part II: The Simulation Pipeline 67

Chapter 5: Trace Collection and Management 69
Tool Setup 70
5.1 What Traces Capture 72
5.1.1 Trace Contents 72
5.1.2 What Traces Omit 73
5.1.3 Trace Formats 74
5.2 Choosing a Collection Approach 76
5.2.1 When to Use Which Approach 77
5.3 Dynamic Binary Instrumentation Using Pin 79
5.3.1 How Pin Works 79
5.3.2 Starting with Pin 80
5.3.3 Pintools 80
5.4 Generating ChampSim Traces 81
5.4.1 Building the Tracer 81
5.4.2 Collecting a Trace 81
5.4.3 Trace Compression 83
5.5 Trace Validation 83
5.5.1 Sanity Checks 83
5.5.2 Instruction Mix Analysis 84
5.5.3 Hardware Counter Validation 85
5.5.4 End-to-End Validation 86

5.6 Trace Organization and Management 86
5.6.1 Naming Conventions 87
5.6.2 Metadata Documentation 87
5.6.3 Storage Considerations 88
5.6.4 Version Control and Artifact Management 88
5.7 Trace Fidelity Limitations 89
5.7.1 The User-Kernel Gap 90
5.7.2 Missing Wrong-Path Execution 90
5.8 Summary 91
Review Questions 92
Exercises 93
Further Reading 93

Chapter 6: Sampling and Simulation Efficiency 95

6.1 Why Sampling Matters 96
6.1.1 Application Behavior 96
6.1.2 Phase Behavior in Steady-State 97
6.2 The SimPoint Methodology 98
6.2.1 Basic Block Vectors 98
6.2.2 Clustering and Representative Intervals 99
6.2.3 SimPoint in the Workflow 100
6.2.4 From SimPoint to Traces 103
6.2.5 Weighted Results 105
6.2.6 Other Sampling Approaches 106
6.3 Warm-Up Strategies 108
6.3.1 Functional Warming 108
6.3.2 Checkpointing 109
6.3.3 Warming Length Guidelines 109

6.4 Common Pitfalls....110
6.4.1 Insufficient Warming....110
6.4.2 Short Intervals....110
6.4.3 Ignoring Low-Weight Points....111
6.4.4 Unweighted Averaging....111
6.5 Summary....111
Review Questions....112
Exercises....113
Further Reading....113
Chapter 7: Understanding Simulation Output....115
7.1 Structure of ChampSim Output....116
7.1.1 The Output Report....116
7.1.2 Output and the Simulation Pipeline....120
7.2 Throughput Metrics....120
7.2.1 Instructions Per Cycle (IPC)....121
7.2.2 CPI and the Stall Budget....122
7.3 Cache Metrics....122
7.3.1 Cache Statistics....122
7.3.2 Cross-Level Cache Analysis....125
7.3.3 Prefetcher Statistics....126
7.4 Branch Predictor Metrics....127
7.5 DRAM Metrics....129
7.6 Comparative Analysis....131
7.6.1 Normalized Speedup....131
7.6.2 Geometric Mean for Multi-workload Studies....132
7.6.3 General Guidelines for Reporting Results....132

7.7 Sanity Checks 133
7.7.1 Internal Consistency Checks 134
7.7.2 Cross-Metric Plausibility Checks..135
7.7.3 Reference Data Comparison..136
7.8 Summary..137
Review Questions 138
Exercises..139
Further Reading 140

Part III: Memory System Modeling 141

Chapter 8: Memory System Architecture 143
8.1 Cache Architecture..143
8.1.1 Set-Associative Organization 144
8.1.2 Cache Miss Classification..146
8.1.3 Replacement Policies 146
8.1.4 Prefetching 147
8.1.5 Write Policies..148
8.1.6 Inclusion Policies..149
8.2 DRAM Architecture..150
8.2.1 DRAM Organization..150
8.2.2 Timing Parameters 151
8.2.3 Refresh Overhead..153
8.3 Memory Controller 153
8.3.1 Address Mapping..154
8.3.2 Scheduling Policies 154
8.3.3 Row Buffer Management..155
8.4 Address Translation and TLBs 155

8.5 Summary....157
Review Questions....157
Further Reading....158
Chapter 9: Cache and Prefetcher Simulation....159
9.1 Simulator Configuration....160
9.1.1 Cache Hierarchy Organization....160
9.1.2 Modifying Parameters....161
9.2 Experimental Design....163
9.2.1 Workload Selection....163
9.2.2 Key Metrics....164
9.2.3 Experimental Process....164
9.2.4 Companion Repository Setup....164
9.3 Cache Replacement Policies....165
9.3.1 Replacement Policy Interface....165
9.3.2 LRU....166
9.3.3 SRRIP....168
9.4 Prefetchers....172
9.4.1 Prefetcher Interface....173
9.4.2 Next-Line Prefetcher....174
9.4.3 Adding a Simple Filter to the Next-Line Prefetcher....178
9.5 Summary....182
Review Questions....182
Exercises....183
Chapter 10: DRAM Simulation....185
10.1 Simulator Configuration....186
10.1.1 DRAM Organization....186
10.1.2 Modifying Parameters....188

10.2 Experimental Design........189
10.2.1 Workload Selection........189
10.2.2 Key Metrics........190
10.2.3 Experimental Process........190
10.2.4 Companion Repository Setup........190
10.3 DRAM Timing........191
10.3.1 The Experiment........191
10.3.2 Results and Explanation........193
10.4 Row Buffer Management........195
10.4.1 The Experiment........197
10.4.2 Results and Explanation........198
10.5 Adaptive Row Buffer Management........200
10.5.1 The Experiment........200
10.5.2 Results and Explanation........203
10.6 Summary........204
Review Questions........205
Exercises........205

Part IV: CPU Core Modeling........207

Chapter 11: CPU Core Architecture........209

11.1 Pipeline Fundamentals........210
11.1.1 Pipeline Organization........210
11.1.2 Depth and Frequency Tradeoff........212
11.2 Front End........213
11.2.1 Fetch and Decode........213
11.2.2 Branch Prediction........214

11.3 Execution Back End 216
11.3.1 Execution Models 217
11.3.2 Rename and Dispatch 217
11.3.3 Reorder Buffer 218
11.3.4 Scheduling and Execution 219
11.3.5 Retirement 221
11.4 Core-Memory Interface 222
11.4.1 Load/Store Queue 222
11.4.2 MSHRs and Memory-Level Parallelism 222
11.4.3 Store Buffer 223
11.5 Multicore Execution 223
11.5.1 Shared Resources and Contention 224
11.5.2 Cache Coherence 224
11.5.3 On-Chip Interconnect 226
11.5.4 Synchronization Cost 227
11.6 Summary 228
Review Questions 229
Further Reading 229
Chapter 12: CPU Simulation 231
Tool Setup 232
12.1 Simulator Configuration 233
12.1.1 CPU Models 233
12.1.2 Configuration Script 234
12.1.3 Default CPU Parameters 236
12.1.4 Pipeline in Code 237
12.2 Experimental Design 239
12.2.1 Workload Selection 240
12.2.2 Key Metrics 241

12.2.3 Experimental Process....242
12.2.4 Companion Repository Setup....242
12.3 ROB Size and the Instruction Window....242
The Experiment....243
Results and Explanation....244
12.4 Execution Unit Bandwidth....245
The Experiment....245
Results and Explanation....247
12.5 Squash Recovery Delay....248
The Experiment....249
Results and Explanation....252
12.6 Summary....253
Review Questions....254
Exercises....254
Chapter 13: Multicore CPU Simulation....255
Tool Setup....256
13.1 Simulator Configuration....257
13.1.1 Classic and Ruby Memory Systems....257
13.1.2 MESI Two-Level Hierarchy....257
13.1.3 Configuration Script....258
13.1.4 Ruby Statistics Output....260
13.2 Experimental Design....262
13.2.1 Workload Selection....262
13.2.2 Key Metrics....264
13.2.3 Experimental Process....264
13.2.4 Companion Repository Setup....265

13.3 Multicore Scaling 265
The Experiment 265
Results and Explanation 267
13.4 False Sharing 268
The Experiment 269
Results and Explanation 270
13.5 Synchronization Cost 271
The Experiment 272
Results and Explanation 274
13.6 Summary 275
Review Questions 276
Exercises 276
Part V: GPU Modeling 277
Chapter 14: GPU Architecture 279
14.1 GPU Execution Model 280
14.1.1 SIMT and Warps 280
14.1.2 Thread Blocks and Grids 281
14.1.3 The Compute Unit 282
14.2 Warp Scheduling 287
14.2.1 Scheduling Mechanics 287
14.2.2 Instruction and Memory Latencies 288
14.2.3 Latency Hiding 289
14.3 Memory Hierarchy 290
14.3.1 Shared Memory and L1 Cache 290
14.3.2 L2 Cache and HBM 291
14.3.3 Memory Coalescing 293
14.3.4 Asynchronous Data Movement 293

14.4 Occupancy and Resource Limits....294
14.4.1 Resource Limits....295
14.5 Performance Pathologies....296
14.5.1 Warp Divergence....297
14.5.2 Uncoalesced Memory Access....297
14.5.3 Bank Conflicts....298
14.5.4 Atomic Contention....298
14.5.5 Execution Throughput Bottlenecks....298
14.6 Summary....299
Review Questions....300
Further Reading....300
Chapter 15: GPU Simulation....303
Tool Setup....304
15.1 Simulator Configuration....305
15.1.1 Accel-Sim Organization....306
15.1.2 Configuration Files....307
15.1.3 Trace Format....308
15.2 Experimental Design....310
15.2.1 Workload Selection....310
15.2.2 Key Metrics....311
15.2.3 Experimental Process....311
15.2.4 Companion Repository Setup....311
15.3 Memory Coalescing....312
The Experiment....312
Results and Explanation....314
15.4 Warp Divergence....315
The Experiment....315
Results and Explanation....316

15.5 Latency Tolerance 317
The Experiment 317
Results and Explanation 321
15.6 Summary 322
Review Questions 322
Exercises 323

Part VI: Accelerator Modeling 325

Chapter 16: Tensor Accelerator Architecture 327
16.1 The Case for Tensor Accelerators 328
16.2 The Systolic Array 329
16.2.1 Array Organization 329
16.2.2 Data Movement Through the Array 330
16.2.3 The TPU Example 331
16.3 Dataflow Choices 332
16.4 Memory Hierarchy on Accelerators 333
16.4.1 Scratchpad Hierarchy 333
16.4.2 Software-Managed Data Movement 334
16.5 Mapping and Performance Bottlenecks 335
16.6 Summary 336
Review Questions 337
Further Reading 338

Chapter 17: Accelerator Simulation 339
Tool Setup 340
17.1 Simulator Configuration 341
17.1.1 SCALE-Sim Architecture Model 342
17.1.2 Configuration File 342
17.1.3 Topology File 344

17.1.4 Layout File 345
17.2 Experimental Design 345
17.2.1 Workload Selection 346
17.2.2 Key Metrics 346
17.2.3 Experimental Process 347
17.2.4 Companion Repository Setup 347
17.3 Dataflow Comparison 347
The Experiment 348
Results and Explanation 349
17.4 Array Size and Mapping Efficiency 349
The Experiment 350
Results and Explanation 351
17.5 Sparsity 352
The Experiment 352
Results and Explanation 353
17.6 Summary 354
Review Questions 354
Exercises 355

Part VII: Power Modeling 357

Chapter 18: Power Modeling – A Walkthrough 359
18.1 Why Model Power 359
18.2 CPU Power with McPAT 360
18.3 GPU Power with AccelWattch 361
18.4 Looking Further 362

Closing Thoughts 365

Index 367

About the Author

Ananya Pareek is a senior engineer specializing in computer hardware performance modeling and architecture. With over 15 years of industry experience across firms such as Google, Apple, Samsung, and AMD, he brings exceptional expertise in microarchitectural simulation and performance analysis across diverse computing domains. Over the years, he has worked on multiple well-known products, developing cutting-edge simulation techniques and frameworks spanning full systems, CPUs, GPUs, etc. He holds a B. Tech in Electrical Engineering from the Indian Institute of Technology (IIT) Kanpur and an MS in Electrical and Computer Engineering from the University of Rochester.

He has also delivered lectures and talks on hardware performance with an audience ranging from new undergraduate students to experienced academics.

About the Technical Reviewer

Massimo Nardone has more than 30 years of experience in security, web/mobile development, and cloud and IT/OT/IoT architecture. His true passions are security and Android. He has been programming and teaching how to program with Android, Perl, PHP, Java, VB, Python, C/C++, and MySQL for more than 30 years. He holds a Master of Science degree in Computing Science from the University of Salerno, Italy. He has worked as Chief Information Security Officer (CISO), software engineer, chief security architect, security executive, and OT/IoT/IIoT security leader and architect for many years. He currently works as VP, OT Security, for SSH Communications Security.

Acknowledgments

I am grateful to the researchers and maintainers behind the projects used in this book, including, but not limited to, ChampSim, gem5, Accel-Sim and GPGPU-Sim, SCALE-Sim, and SimPoint. This book would not exist without the open-source simulation community. Its chapters and experiments are built directly on tools created and maintained by others.

I would also like to thank Apress, especially Shobana Srinivasan and Miriam Haidara, for providing support and keeping everything on track throughout the project.

Introduction

Performance modeling is one of the most important stages of hardware IP design. Long before a chip is taped out, architects evaluate thousands of design alternatives and commit to the handful that go into production. Simulation makes these informed, data-backed decisions possible, and every processor that reaches the market, along with every generational gain we have come to expect, quietly rests on this work.

This book teaches performance modeling and simulation for modern computer architecture, covering CPUs, GPUs, accelerators, and memory systems. Essential concepts behind each component are paired with hands-on experiments, using open-source simulators commonly used in academia and industry.

The aim of the book is strictly practical. By the end, you should be able to choose a modeling approach, run a well-designed experiment, and reason about the results obtained from the architectural perspective.

Book Organization

The book is organized into seven parts. Part I (Chapters 1–4) lays the foundations, including the motivation, basic architectural principles, workload selection, and a brief peek into the simulator code. Part II (Chapters 5–7) covers essential experimental methodology, including collecting traces, sampling key regions, and analyzing outputs. Part III (Chapters 8–10) turns to real experiments on the memory system. It sets the architectural foundations and continues with hands-on exercises using ChampSim. Part IV (Chapters 11–13), Part V (Chapters 14 and 15), and Part VI (Chapters 16 and 17) follow the same pattern applied to CPUs, GPUs, and accelerators, using gem5, Accel-Sim, and SCALE-Sim, respectively. Part VII (Chapter 18) offers a brief walkthrough of power modeling to point the reader in the right direction for further exploration.

Prerequisites

The book assumes familiarity with general computer architecture concepts, basic C++ and Python programming languages, and the ability to use POSIX-compliant Linux shells such as bash.

The hands-on chapters assume an x86-64 Linux machine (Ubuntu 22.04 or 24.04) with around 50 GB of free disk space, a working C++17 toolchain, and python3x installed.

Companion Repository

The hands-on chapters are supported by a companion repository that should be downloaded before starting Part II. Each experiment-oriented chapter has a corresponding top-level folder containing useful artifacts, including a README.md and a subset of

- configs/: Configuration files for the chapter's experiments
- listing-files/: Simulator source files modified in the chapter, supplied in their original form and as the finished version for each experiment
- traces/ or workloads/: Precollected instruction traces or workload source/binaries
- results/: The directory experiments write their output to, as unpopulated placeholders

The repository does not include the simulators; each chapter provides instructions for obtaining them as needed.

PART I

Foundations

CHAPTER 1

Introduction to Performance Modeling

Designing computing chips, such as CPUs, system-on-a-chip, GPUs, and others, is a daunting task at every level.

Companies must meet tight deadlines; commit to the architecture, i.e., the chip structure and design, months to years in advance; and consistently monitor the development through its lifecycle. Moreover, in a highly competitive industry, staying up to date with the state of the art and anticipating what the landscape may look like in a few generations is crucial. All these factors, combined with tight budget constraints, necessitate a need to iterate on and make hundreds of critical architectural decisions before final tape-out (the point at which the chip design is finalized for manufacturing). Even small mistakes and missed targets can cost a company a considerable amount of money and damage its reputation.

To address these challenges, performance modeling offers a path to evaluate design and architectural choices at varying levels of detail, from back-of-the-envelope estimates to detailed high-fidelity simulations. These modeling techniques enable bottleneck identification, tradeoff decisions, understanding the art of the possible, and defining targets well in advance.

A. Pareek, *Performance Modeling of Computer Systems*, Maker Innovations Series,
https://doi.org/10.1007/979-8-8688-2476-0_1

What This Book Covers: This book covers performance modeling of major IPs of a computing chip, namely CPUs, GPUs, accelerators, and memory systems. You will learn to apply common techniques and concepts while working with specific tools and their nuances. You will develop a consistent mindset for choosing the best approach for each system, balancing accuracy, effort, and timeliness.

Prerequisites

- A standard computer architecture course (or equivalent knowledge) covering concepts like pipelining, caching, memory systems, etc. The book provides refreshers as needed along the relevant chapters.
- C++ and Python programming skills for practical exercises with simulation tools.
- Basic statistical concepts are helpful, but they will be introduced as needed.

Let's now examine why performance modeling is essential and how it fits in the development process.

1.1 The Role of Performance Modeling

To illustrate modeling's pivotal place in development, this section examines how performance modeling fits into the computing systems development lifecycle. It walks through the field's historical evolution, diverse use cases, and the economic and practical aspects that make modeling essential.

1.1.1 Why We Cannot Just Build and Test

Building a chip all the way to tape-out for testing is obviously prohibitively expensive, intractable, and incredibly time-consuming. One may think that the RTL (Register Transfer Level) is a good place to start experimenting. But consider a scenario: does an 8-core processor with faster cores outperform a 16-core processor with slower cores? Running these two experiments on RTL may take multiple days. Once these are done, one may develop balancing strategies, such as doubling the cache size in the slower configuration. This would lead to another few days of running the RTL code and analyzing the results. What if the power consumption turns out to be higher now? As you can see, this gets really slow and difficult to track very quickly. This is exacerbated by the fact that RTL development must follow set protocols, validations, and so on to be ready for use.

Performance models make this problem manageable. Using computational representations (mathematical and software-based approximations) of processor behavior, one can evaluate multiple configurations in a fraction of the time. It also eliminates the need to wait for the RTL design to be ready close enough to the actual design. Instead of waiting for the RTL, these models could instead be used to guide the direction while it is being built. Moreover, depending on the level of confidence needed, one can start very early in the product lifecycle, even one or two generations ahead.

Modeling Perspective: Actionable insight is the primary goal, not necessarily perfect accuracy. A model churning out 90% accurate data in 1 hour may be more suited to the needs of the moment than one that is 99.9% accurate but takes 6 months. One of the main skills a performance modeler needs to cultivate is choosing the right level of detail needed for the task at hand.

1.1.2 Use Cases for Performance Modeling

Since performance modeling generally offers trade-offs between speed and accuracy, as we will learn throughout this book, it can serve multiple purposes in industry and academia. We will explore some of these next:

Processor (or Any Computing Unit) Development in the Industry

The domain where modeling is highly applicable. Performance models carry the project throughout the development lifecycle. Starting with analytical models for feasibility studies, which provide low-fidelity yet highly valuable directional data, all the way to detailed cycle-by-cycle simulation to verify implementation choices and validate the design before tape-out. Modeling also enables companies to look multiple generations ahead, even before the product enters the build phase.

System Optimization and Capacity Planning

At a higher level of abstraction, modeling computer systems as queuing systems enables datacenter architects to determine optimal server counts, identify areas for infrastructure investment, and optimize configurations.

Performance Debugging

Developers can use models to identify performance problems in software, as they can systematically guide them to where the problems lie: the processor, the memory system, or the application design itself. Compiler writers can similarly determine optimizations such as loop unrolling and vectorization, just using models.

Academic Research

Researchers do not always have access to modifiable production chips. Modeling tools offer a practical testbed for experiments. Modeling enables easy evaluation of new cache policies, branch predictor designs, new memory scheduling designs, etc.

1.1.3 A Brief Note on History

Performance modeling has evolved alongside computer architecture itself in many stages. From the early analytical models that focused on simple high-level equations to estimate execution time from instruction count and cycle time, it has progressed through early simulators such as SimpleScalar to modern, sophisticated open-source simulators like gem5, and even web-based simulators for RISC-V.

At each stage of progression, the level of sophistication has directly corresponded to the need of the hour, providing "just enough" detail.

Building on our understanding of why modeling matters, let's now explore the range of approaches available for carrying it out.

1.2 The Spectrum of Modeling Approaches

Modeling approaches lie between the two polarities of fast but approximate and slow but detailed, offering optimal points along the spectrum for various use cases. Let's go over a few examples to understand better.

1.2.1 Analytical Models

Analytical models offer an extremely fast way to evaluate choices across large design spaces, running into thousands of configurations. The main utility lies in higher-level analysis using mathematical equations to calculate performance metrics from system parameters. This approach lets modelers ignore finer-level details until higher-order effects have been used to navigate down the design space search path.

Some examples of such models are listed below:

Queuing Theory helps model systems that involve requests waiting for service from various components. Memory access queues (buffers holding pending read or write memory operations), instruction buffers (storage for instructions awaiting processing), and cache-miss handlers (logic managing situations when requested data is not in the cache) are examples of such systems. A simple way to model these systems is by using Little's Law, which states that the average number of requests in a system (Q) equals the arrival rate (λ, the number of items entering the queue per unit time) multiplied by the average time in the system (W).

$$Q = \lambda \times W$$

The Roofline Model, developed by Williams, Waterman, and Patterson in 2009, uses the following equation to find performance bounds based on peak computational throughput (π, measured in operations per second) and peak memory bandwidth (β, measured in bytes per second). For a workload with operational intensity (I, the ratio of operations to bytes moved):

$$\text{Performance} = \min(\pi, I * \beta)$$

It effectively determines, at a high level, if a workload is bound by computation or by memory access.

Modeling Perspective: Being higher-level doesn't mean less important, by any means. These models force one to articulate assumptions explicitly and comprehend why performance behaves as it does. Lower-level simulation alone doesn't offer this easily.

1.2.2 Transaction Level Models (TLM)

TLM focuses on transactions within a system and models hardware communication at that level, largely ignoring internal or lower-level details. Instead of modeling all clock edges and wire toggles, TLM represents data transfer between components via function calls that move the payload between the sender and receiver. The communication infrastructure (such as buses and interconnects that link chip components) can be modeled and refined independently of other computational components. TLM is standardized through the SystemC TLM-2.0 library, a set of C++ classes supporting this modeling style.

1.2.3 Cycle-Accurate Simulation

At the most detailed end of the spectrum, cycle-accurate models simulate every single clock cycle of hardware execution. These may include very low-level details, such as pipeline stages, queues, buffers, and functional units, and the data movement through them in simulated time, cycle by cycle. Using these models, you can examine subtle aspects and ultra-fine-grained details. These include structural hazards, out-of-order scheduling, exact timing of cache operations, memory controller operation, and interactions between threads.

Cycle-accurate simulation can be performed either using an "execution-driven" methodology, where the simulator actually executes the instructions of the workload, or using a "trace-driven" methodology, which typically involves capturing program instruction flow and replaying it with timing. While an execution-driven approach is great for observing the effects of phenomena such as wrong-path executions, the trace-driven approach offers a much faster alternative when these effects are not highly important, increasing iteration and search space exploration speed by orders of magnitude.

In this book, we will primarily focus on these simulation-based methods, as they form the backbone of most architectural research and design work in academia and industry alike.

Building on these different levels of modeling fidelity and applicability, the following section systematically examines fundamental tradeoffs to help determine the best tools for the job at hand.

1.3 Accuracy, Speed, and Flexibility Tradeoffs

Understanding the tradeoffs between various modeling approaches and abstractions is very important to ensure that "important enough" details are accounted for. In this section, we will review the key dimensions, examine their relationships, and develop a framework for selecting the most appropriate approaches for different purposes.

1.3.1 The Fundamental Tradeoffs

The three main dimensions that steer modeling approach selection are accuracy, speed, and flexibility (i.e., ease of iterating on the modeling infrastructure). Unfortunately, none of the approaches excels at all three. As shown in Table 1-1, we must choose based on what we can compromise on and what we value most. Note that the error margins mentioned in the table are typical ranges. The exact numbers depend on the configuration and simulators used, among other things.

Table 1-1. *Modeling Approach Tradeoffs*

Approach	Speed	Accuracy (Error Margin)	Flexibility	Suited For
Analytical models	Very Fast	Order of magnitude	Very high	Early exploration, boundedness
Transaction-Level Modeling (TLM)	Fast	About 10–20%	High	System-level research, software development
Cycle-accurate (execution-driven)	Very Slow	About 5%	Low	Microarchitecture research, validation
Cycle-accurate (trace-driven)	Slow	About 5–10%	Medium	Design space exploration

1.3.2 Accuracy vs. Speed

The amount of detail in a model directly relates to how long it takes to simulate. This essentially means that the faster the model simulates, the more detail it ignores in the modeled hardware. From analytical models to cycle-accurate simulation, runtime can increase by orders of magnitude, from a few seconds to days or even weeks.

1.3.3 Flexibility vs. Accuracy

Cycle-accurate simulators, while able to capture the highest level of detail, are the least flexible for changing architectural units or dataflow, as a single change can potentially trigger a cascade of accommodating modifications throughout the tightly coupled components of the system.

Consequently, analytical models, being highly flexible, allow changing the details fairly easily at the cost of accuracy.

Modeling Perspective: Practically, this tradeoff will impact how you match your research question to what type of model (simple analytical or cycle-accurate) is most appropriate for your work. For example, if you want to compare various cache replacement policies, you don't need to include extensive details about the CPU pipeline. Conversely, studying the effects of out-of-order execution requires those details.

1.3.4 Fit for Purpose

To reiterate one of the main points of our discussion, there's no universally superior modeling approach. It has to match the question the modeler is trying to answer. A basic walkthrough is outlined below.

Exploring the Design Space: At this stage, the objective is to develop an understanding of the design possibilities. How do varying numbers of processor cores impact performance? Is there a cache size that provides sufficient capacity? Are memory bandwidth limitations a constraint?

Because these are relative comparisons rather than exact measurements, they may be evaluated using analytical models or rapid simulations (or a combination of these) to develop an intuitive feel for the design, which will guide further exploration.

Refining the Design: Once design decisions begin to take on a definitive nature (e.g., replacement policy, number of entries in the Branch Target Buffer (BTB), fetch width), more precision is required as the design narrows to specific options. To evaluate numerous configuration combinations during this phase, transaction-level and cycle-accurate simulations provide sufficient accuracy.

Validation of Performance Before Tape-Out: With a multi-million-dollar tape-out at stake, architects require extreme confidence that their performance objectives have been satisfied. As such, this phase requires the most detailed simulation possible, preferably one that has been extensively validated against real hardware. Due to the fact that the configuration space is minimal (i.e., the design under consideration and its immediate variations), simulation time is somewhat less restrictive. Cycle-accurate simulations, preferably execution-driven, fit the best here.

Publication of Research Results: For academic research to be credible and reproducible, publication-quality results from widely used, extensible modeling tools are essential. Ad hoc models are often subject to criticism for their methodology, as they are harder to reproduce and document well enough to offer a clear understanding of how they work. The level of accuracy depends on the concepts being researched, as we have discussed earlier.

1.3.5 Case Study: Prefetcher Evaluation

A design team had to choose a prefetcher for a new microprocessor core. There were two possible alternatives: (a) a conservative prefetcher based on stride patterns that issues a prefetch when it finds a pattern in the way accesses are made; (b) an advanced but aggressive prefetcher based on multiple lookahead and complex patterns that issues four prefetches as soon as a pattern has been identified (hypothetical case; details don't matter here).

Phase 1 - Analytical Reasoning:

The memory subsystem had enough bandwidth to support 25 GB/s, and the target workloads demanded an average of 12 GB/s, leaving 13 GB/s available for the prefetcher or other system components. However, this bandwidth would be wasted unless the prefetches issued were correct. Incorrect prefetches would consume bandwidth, pollute the cache, and could actually reduce overall system performance compared to not using the prefetcher.

Phase 2 - Rapid Exploration:

ChampSim (a trace-based performance simulator) was run against 15 different traces to evaluate the impact of both prefetchers. On average, the advanced prefetcher improved performance by 18%. However, three of the traces resulted in a 5–12% decrease in performance. The conservative prefetcher resulted in a 9% average performance increase and did not cause any performance reduction. Coverage metrics indicated that the advanced prefetcher achieved 80% coverage, but its accuracy was only 40%. The conservative prefetcher achieved lower coverage (55%) but much higher accuracy (90%).

Phase 3 - Detailed Confirmation:

gem5 (a detailed cycle-accurate simulator) was run on the three traces that showed regression with the advanced prefetcher to determine the cause. It was determined that the regression was due to pointer-chasing access patterns, in which the advanced prefetcher incorrectly predicted and prefetched future accesses, leading to useful data being evicted from the L2 cache.

Phase 4 - Recommendation:

The modeler recommended implementing the advanced prefetcher with a confidence threshold. This would require it to identify five consecutive confirmations before entering multi-lookahead mode.

Rerunning the traces showed that this hybrid prefetcher improved performance by an average of 15% and resulted in regressions of less than 2%, effectively capturing all the benefits of the aggressive prefetcher while reducing the likelihood of worst-case behavior.

This combination of analytical reasoning, rapid exploration, detailed confirmation, and refinement illustrates a commonly employed methodology that integrates several approaches to reach a decision that yields superior results compared to relying on a single method to do it all.

Modeling Perspective: This example used ChampSim and gem5, both for illustrative purposes. It is often not necessary to switch between simulators. Many well-known simulators offer fast or detailed simulation methods with varying levels of accuracy applicable to this kind of task.

Having a collection of tools to address varying needs in developing end-to-end modeling methodologies, as in the example, is extremely important. To this end, the next section provides an overview of open-source simulation tools and where they fit.

1.4 Open-Source Simulation Tools

The plethora of open-source simulation tools has truly democratized the modeling landscape. One can quickly get started on frameworks that have been in development for decades and provide valuable insights and conduct deep research and development, which in turn can feed back into the frameworks. This convenience comes with the risk of being overwhelmed by choices when starting out. To help with this, we will go over a curated collection of tools best suited to the topics covered in this book. This section presents these tools, explains the rationale for their selection, and outlines where they best fit within the modeling spectrum.

1.4.1 The Toolkit

The tools curated for this book cover all aspects of performance modeling we will touch on while minimizing the effort required to learn them. The basis for the selection was as follows:

- Active development and community support
- Non-overlapping capabilities to the best possible extent
- Progressive complexity in learning and development
- Transferability of learned skills into real-world professional experience

The selected tools are briefly summarized in Table 1-2.

Table 1-2. *Selected Tools*

Tool	Domain	Approach	Complexity
ChampSim	CPU caches, prefetchers, branch predictors	Trace-driven	Low
gem5	Full CPU systems	Trace/Execution-driven	High
Accel-Sim	GPU architectures	Trace/Execution-driven	Medium-High
SCALE-Sim	ML accelerators (Systolic Arrays)	Analytical/Cycle Accurate	Low-Medium

1.4.2 ChampSim

As a trace-driven simulator optimized for memory hierarchy studies, it provides a strong starting point. The codebase is neither too heavy nor too complex, enabling easier learning and fast iterations. It has been used in many peer-reviewed competitions over the years, including the Cache

Replacement Championship. Additionally, it supports modular extensions and component replacements, such as the cache system and prefetchers, providing a gentler learning curve and immediate usability.

1.4.3 gem5

After learning trace-driven simulation with ChampSim, you will be able to move on to more detailed simulation with gem5. It is one of the most widely used academic CPU simulators, capable of simulating multiple Instruction Set Architectures (ISAs) (x86, ARM, RISC-V). It includes a range of CPU models, from a simple functional CPU model to an OOO (out-of-order) core, with a level of detail that supports speculative execution, register renaming, and related features.

For modeling the memory system, its Ruby memory model provides support for configurable cache hierarchies, replacement policies, and coherence protocols. Depending on the fidelity needed, it supports internal DRAM models and integration with external DRAM simulators, such as DRAMSim3 and Ramulator.

The learning curve for this tool is steep. However, the time invested will be worthwhile. It is widely used across the research community, enabling researchers to easily compare their results in a reproducible manner. Additionally, skills learned while using gem5 can be transferred to the industry, as similar tools are used by many companies worldwide.

1.4.4 Accel-Sim

Accel-Sim is one of the most widely used frameworks for tackling the challenges that GPU modeling poses compared to CPU-based modeling. It combines a validated timing model (GPGPU-Sim 4.0) with a flexible front-end for either trace-driven or execution-driven simulations.

Accel-Sim excels at capturing key aspects of GPU performance, including SIMT (single instruction, multiple threads), warp scheduling, memory coalescing, the GPU memory hierarchy, including L1/shared memory, and L2 caches.

It offers two simulation modes:

Execution-driven (PTX): PTX is the intermediate representation used by NVIDIA. As a result, execution-driven simulation allows functional execution of CUDA programs. This is useful when trace collection is not feasible.

Trace-driven (SASS): SASS refers to NVIDIA's native GPU assembly instructions that are collected from real hardware using NVBit (NVIDIA's dynamic binary instrumentation framework).

Accel-Sim offers validated configurations for multiple generations of released NVIDIA architectures (Pascal, Volta, Ampere, etc.). Combined with automatic validation tools that compare simulated results to real hardware, it has secured a prominent position in recent GPU-architecture research.

1.4.5 SCALE-Sim

Machine-learning accelerators (e.g., systolic arrays, dataflow architectures, domain-specific processors) require a modeling paradigm that differs from general-purpose CPUs and GPUs. One of the primary reasons for this differentiation is that the computations performed by ML workloads are highly regular: the same operation is repeatedly executed across large datasets. Such regularity enables analytical approaches to offer strong predictive capabilities.

SCALE-Sim is one such framework that focuses on systolic arrays. It uses a combination of a hardware description (array dimensions, on-chip SRAM sizes, memory bandwidth, dataflow choice) and a workload description (dimensions and structure of neural network layers or GEMM shapes) to determine how the computation will map onto hardware resources and provides cycle-accurate timing estimates.

1.4.6 Supporting Tools

Pin (Intel): Pin is a dynamic binary instrumentation framework for collecting traces from programs. It gathers execution information (instruction addresses, memory accesses, branch outcomes) as a program runs. The resulting traces can be fed into trace-driven simulators such as ChampSim.

DRAM Simulators: External DRAM simulators are often used when detailed DRAM timing is required beyond what gem5's built-in DRAM models provide. For such cases, DRAMSim3 and Ramulator can be used with it as plugins. They offer support for specific needs, such as modeling accurate timing and row-buffer management, as well as broader support for memory technologies (including DRAM, HBM, etc.).

Having described the basic components of the simulation toolkit, the next section will give you an overview of how this book is structured and how to use it based on your interests.

1.5 Summary

In this chapter, we discussed the foundations of performance modeling and surveyed a range of tools and methodologies relevant to modern computer architecture research. To summarize, let's go over the key conclusions this chapter draws.

First, performance modeling is indispensable. It enables the evaluation of a multitude of configurations during various design phases. This, in turn, helps reduce development costs and risks.

Second, a wide spectrum of modeling approaches exists. The whole gamut ranges from analytical models that complete in seconds to week-long cycle-accurate simulations. Each offers a trade-off between accuracy and speed and implies the relative effort needed to adapt to a particular scenario.

Third, the principle of "fit for purpose" should guide the choice of modeling approach. In early exploratory phases, speed of evaluation is often preferred over accuracy, whereas in later validation phases, accuracy is preferred over speed. One must strategically combine multiple approaches.

Finally, the availability of a wide range of open-source frameworks has democratized access to performance modeling and research. Tools like ChampSim, gem5, Accel-Sim, and SCALE-Sim enable the capability of simulating CPUs, GPUs, and accelerators using a range of methodologies from trace-driven to analytical.

Next up, Chapter 2 reviews architectural concepts common to all forms of computing relevant to performance modeling. Chapter 3 addresses an important question: what workload(s) should you model?

Review Questions

1. What are the common issues with just building the hardware and testing it directly? What problems does performance modeling solve?
2. How do analytical models and cycle-accurate simulations differ?
3. What is the difference between trace-driven and execution-driven simulations?
4. Why is it important to select the right modeling approach for the research question at hand?

CHAPTER 2

Architecture Through the Modeler's Lens

This chapter introduces general computer architecture concepts commonly found in many textbooks and courses. However, here we will approach these differently through the lens of performance modeling. This shift in perspective changes the type of questions we ask. Hardware designers focus on how structures are built and how they interact, but performance modelers focus on what must be captured to represent the system behavior faithfully. They care about the design aspects that influence the metrics that are important to a system's performance. For a performance modeler, identifying the details that can be ignored is as important as understanding which ones are essential.

This chapter builds architectural intuition to help think in terms of modeling-oriented questions, such as: Where does execution time go? What limits the throughput? What can be ignored? Instead of treating CPUs, GPUs, and machine learning accelerators as separate domains, we illustrate how concepts such as latency, bandwidth, and parallelism manifest differently across these. We will also highlight why such distinctions matter for modeling decisions.

By the end of the chapter, you will not only learn the basic principles of computer architecture often found in textbooks but also gain the ability to see them through the perspective of performance modeling.

A. Pareek, *Performance Modeling of Computer Systems*, Maker Innovations Series,
https://doi.org/10.1007/979-8-8688-2476-0_2

Let's begin with the most fundamental constraint: the balance between compute and memory.

2.1 The Compute-Memory Balance

Performance modeling starts off with a seemingly easy-to-answer question: how is execution time really spent? Every cycle, the program either does useful work or stalls. At the most fundamental level, identifying these two categories and understanding what each depends upon is the basis for all types of performance analysis. To ground further discussion, this section explores the essential compute-memory balance that governs performance in all computing systems.

2.1.1 The Fundamental Relationship

Performance is fundamentally defined by the equation:

$$\text{Time} = \text{Work} / \text{Rate}$$

"Work" refers to the set of activities an application must perform to complete its task. This includes every instruction executed, each computation performed, and all data moved within the system. In performance modeling, it is important to remember that "work" is not only about processor instructions but also about memory operations and data transfers, which are fundamental to system behavior.

"Rate" defines the speed at which the hardware can produce that work.

Therefore, the first question you should ask as a modeler is "What resource is limiting the rate at which useful work is produced?"

There are two competing types of resources that influence the useful work rate:

> **Compute**: The hardware's ability to execute operations, e.g., ALU, FPU, tensor cores, or multiply-accumulate arrays.
>
> **Memory**: The hardware's ability to supply data to compute units. This includes cache bandwidth, main memory (e.g., DRAM) throughput, and on-chip buffering capability.

Because few applications require similar amounts of compute and memory, they tend to stress these resources unequally: either compute units are frequently idle while waiting for data (memory-bound), or memory can supply data faster than compute units can process it (compute-bound). Identifying a workload's regime before detailed simulations lets the modeler focus efforts for maximum impact.

2.1.2 Operational Intensity

Operational intensity is a metric that quantifies the ratio of computational work performed to data transferred by a workload, or part of a workload. Specifically, it measures the number of operations performed per byte of data moved between memory and compute units. This ratio is important for understanding which system resource-compute or memory-is likely to limit performance.

Operational Intensity = Operations Performed / Bytes Transferred

For example, matrix multiplication has a high operational intensity because each data element loaded is reused many times, which results in multiple arithmetic operations for each byte of data moved. Vector addition is an example of low operational intensity, since it performs a small number of operations per element of data moved.

The balance point of a hardware system - the peak compute throughput divided by peak memory bandwidth - is where a workload shifts from memory-bound to compute-bound on that hardware in terms of its operational intensity. For example, with 1 TFLOPS compute and 100 GB/s memory bandwidth, the balance point is 10 floating-point operations per byte. Workloads below this threshold are likely memory-bound; those above are likely compute-bound.

Numerical Example: The operation count for a dot-product between two 1,000-element vectors is 2,000 (1000 multiply-accumulates), and it reads in 8,000 bytes (2 * 1,000 * 4 bytes per floating-point number vector). Hence, ignoring the negligible cost of storing the result, operational intensity = 2,000 / 8,000 = 0.25 ops/byte. In a system with a compute-memory balance point of 10 ops/byte, this workload is very memory-bound, and the computation unit will largely be idle.

The roofline model formalizes the relationships among operational intensity, peak compute rate, and memory bandwidth. By plotting your application's intensity against hardware limits, you can spot bottlenecks without simulations. For more details, you are encouraged to follow the Williams et al. reference in the Further Reading section.

Operational intensity as a concept applies universally across domains, for example, CPU code, GPU kernels, etc. The hardware and workload may vary, but its applicability remains consistent.

2.1.3 Compute Resources

The execution time of compute-bound workloads is determined by the speed at which a system's computational resources perform operations.

Modern processors contain numerous execution units that operate in parallel. For example, a single CPU core could have four integer Arithmetic Logic Units (ALUs), two floating-point units (FPUs), and two load/store units. A GPU Streaming Multiprocessor (SM) has dozens more CUDA cores (basic parallel processors in NVIDIA GPUs) plus tensor cores; a machine learning accelerator could have thousands of multiply-accumulate units.

Collectively, these resources influence how fast compute operations execute through the system. The maximum rate that can be achieved, or the peak computational throughput, is defined by the following equation:

Throughput = functional units × max operations per cycle per functional unit × clock frequency

If all units cannot find enough independent operations to constantly occupy their cycles, the potential peak throughput will never be realized. Stalls can occur when there are dependencies between the instructions, branch mispredictions that flush the pipeline and structural hazards that force serialization of instructions. These can prevent computational units from processing as many operations as possible. The difference between actual and peak throughput can illustrate how well both the application and the microarchitecture use the available resources.

In addition to functional stalls, clock frequency directly influences throughput by defining the rate of operations across the chip. However, increasing frequency results in a higher power consumption. Since most processors adjust their frequency to meet thermal and power constraints, care must be taken to consider the impact on throughput. This matters when detailed energy consumption needs to be modeled. For first-order performance modeling, it may be ignored.

2.1.4 Memory Resources

When memory-bound, a workload's execution time is primarily determined by how quickly and frequently data reaches the computation unit. For such scenarios, two primary attributes determine the execution time. These are bandwidth (how much data can be delivered per unit time) and latency (how long it takes for individual memory accesses to complete). Both require distinct modeling approaches. We will examine these in more detail in Section 2.2.

2.1.5 Cross-Platform Comparison

The computing platforms covered in this book use varied strategies to address the compute-memory balance. Table 2-1 summarizes the ways in which CPUs, GPUs, and ML accelerators approach this challenge. These are example ranges, and may change over time.

Table 2-1. *Compute-Memory Balance Across Platforms*

Aspect	CPU	GPU	ML Accelerator
Compute resources	Tens to 200 powerful cores, wide superscalar execution	Many simple cores (thousands), SIMT execution (32 threads/warp)	Massive MAC (multiply-accumulate) arrays (thousands), often systolic dataflow
Peak throughput	100s of GFLOPs up to 10s of TFLOPs (varies with precision)	100s of TFLOPs up to PFLOPs (varies with precision)	100s of TFLOPs up to PFLOPs (varies with precision)
Memory strategy	Deep cache hierarchy, hardware prefetching	High bandwidth (HBM), latency tolerance via threading	Explicit buffer management, compiler-scheduled data movement
Memory bandwidth	Hundreds of GB/s	Multiple TB/s	Multiple TB/s (varies widely)
Bottleneck tendency	Often memory-latency-bound	Often memory-bandwidth-bound	Depends on layer shape and mapping

Examining the compute-memory balance is a great first step in understanding the workloads and systems. Building on this, the next section will examine memory behavior in more detail. For most modern workloads, the memory system centrally impacts performance and deserves closer attention.

2.2 Bandwidth and Latency

Bandwidth and latency limits may seem similar, but they show different symptoms and require different architectural approaches. Let's focus on the distinct characteristics and modeling considerations of each.

2.2.1 Bandwidth Constraints

Memory bandwidth is the rate at which bytes flow from memory into computing units. For a bandwidth-bound workload, the compute units can process data faster than the memory system can deliver it. Hence, achieving high compute utilization is difficult regardless of how well the code is optimized.

The following factors influence the peak bandwidth that a system can provide:

Memory Technology Type and Generation: Memory technology imposes a bandwidth ceiling. Modern DDR5 can deliver tens of gigabytes per second per channel, while GDDR6 and HBM-based systems can provide aggregate bandwidth from hundreds of gigabytes per second to multiple terabytes per second per device.

Number of Channels: Memory channels increase bandwidth proportionally by providing parallel paths for data movement. For example, an 8-channel DDR5 server system may achieve several hundred gigabytes per second of aggregate bandwidth, and a GPU with multiple HBM stacks may go over 2 TB/s.

Bus Width: Wider buses (the width of the physical data path) allow more data to be moved per transfer. For example, HBM (high bandwidth memory)'s 1024-bit bus (2048-bit in HBM4) contributes significantly to its bandwidth advantage.

To reach peak bandwidth, the workload must keep all channels engaged. This is largely influenced by the workload's memory access patterns. If the request size for a given channel is small and the transfer is spread out (i.e., the channel is idle frequently), the overall effective bandwidth will be lower than it could have been if larger, sequential transfers were made through that channel (e.g., in matrix multiplication or convolution).

Modeling Bandwidth-Bound Workload: Models should include an accurate representation of both bandwidth limits and memory access patterns to effectively model bandwidth-bound workloads. It may be sufficient to build a simple model with the correct peak bandwidth and some reasonable queuing behavior rather than requiring detailed cycle-accurate timing for the DRAM. Emphasis should be placed on how efficiently a workload can use available bandwidth rather than on faithfully reproducing every internal detail, such as bank scheduling.

Numerical Example: A GPU has a total HBM bandwidth of 900 GB/s and processes a kernel that requires 400 MB of data. At peak bandwidth, reading the 400 MB dataset should take 0.44 milliseconds. If, in reality, it takes 2 milliseconds to read, then only about 22% of the available memory bandwidth is being utilized. Because the bandwidth is not at capacity (i.e., the workload is not bandwidth-limited), there is no advantage to increasing the memory bandwidth. Some other factor, such as compute, latency, or synchronization, could be limiting the system's performance.

2.2.2 Latency Constraints

Latency is the time between a request and the arrival of the data from the memory. Typically, in a latency-bound workload, the compute unit frequently stalls while waiting for memory accesses to complete, regardless of available bandwidth.

The following factors influence latency:

Physical Distance: Just being further away can increase latency due to the sheer limits of physics. For example, off-chip DRAM, being physically distant from the processor, will have higher latency than on-chip SRAM, such as registers.

Access Mechanics: Accessing memory occurs in steps, regardless of the type of memory. For example, DRAM accesses involve activating the row, reading column data, and precharging the row for the next access. That process will take some time, regardless of how quickly the request reaches the memory itself.

Cache Hierarchy: The cache hierarchy influences latency by keeping frequently used data closer to the compute unit. A request will experience a considerable variation in latency depending on whether it hits in L1, L2, L3, or DRAM.

As an example, pointer chasing is an extreme case in which each load must wait for the previous one to complete. This linearizes the accesses and renders any available bandwidth or even compute capacity obsolete. This type of access pattern solely depends on latency and is often used to measure it in real hardware systems.

Modeling Latency-Bound Workloads: In scenarios where latency is the bottleneck, simulation models may need to progressively include more detailed, faithful representations of the cache, such as replacement policies, prefetcher behavior, and, in some cases, memory timing.

We will dive deeper into cache, DRAM, and memory controller modeling in subsequent chapters.

Modeling Perspective: Identify whether your application is bandwidth-bound or latency-bound before deciding on a memory model. If the application exhibits very high memory bandwidth usage when it stalls, it suggests being more bandwidth-bound. Conversely, if the application has low memory bandwidth usage with a lot of stalls, there's an indication of it being latency-bound (the processor can't generate enough concurrent memory accesses to keep the pipeline full) – typically because of dependencies between memory accesses.

In this section, we focused on the limitations that memory systems can impose on performance. In the next section, we will cover one of the primary strategies for tolerating these limits: parallelism.

2.3 Parallelism

Parallelism is an effective strategy for tolerating latency by increasing throughput. However, as we have seen, nothing comes for free in the world of performance. There are trade-offs that must be made to obtain the advantages it offers. Throughout the years, different hardware platforms have emphasized different aspects of parallelism, or combinations thereof, and understanding these enables a holistic view of the best form suited to a given platform.

2.3.1 Instruction-Level Parallelism (ILP)

This is parallelism at the lowest level, i.e., instruction stream. Essentially, the hardware finds independent instructions in the stream and executes them in parallel to the greatest extent possible. Note that the commit still happens serially, and, for the outside world (i.e., the program and the rest of the system), it still appears to be a perfectly serial execution of the instruction stream. Since most introductory courses and texts on computer architecture cover these principles adequately, we will only touch on them as a quick refresher.

Hardware Mechanisms for ILP:

Pipelining: Pipelining achieves parallelism by breaking instruction execution into well-defined steps and overlapping them. For example, a CPU may fetch the next batch of instructions while the current batch is being decoded. Note that there is no change to the execution time or steps for any instruction on its own, but in aggregate, there is an increased throughput in the processing of the instruction stream. For example, one instruction could take many cycles, but we may be able to commit one each cycle.

Superscalar Execution: By increasing the number of execution units, the processor can issue independent instructions simultaneously in a given cycle, depending on resource availability. There is no change in the order of execution, just more than one at the same time.

Out-of-Order Execution: Instead of executing instructions in program order, the processor can identify independent streams of instructions that do not have mutual dependencies. These can then be executed as soon as their dependencies are ready, rather than sequentially waiting for their turn. The final commit still goes in the program order, but the execution deviates if possible.

Speculation: Building on previous techniques, this mechanism "runs ahead" of the instruction stream by predicting branch outcomes before they are definitively resolved. Correct predictions help eliminate cycles spent waiting to determine branch outcomes and targets, whereas errors require complex mechanisms to handle replays and flushes.

True dependencies between instructions create serialization points that cannot be evaded with these techniques. The extra structures needed to enable these techniques come at the cost of power, area, and complexity. Furthermore, these structures are still limited in number, and structural hazards can create choke points that limit their usefulness.

Modeling Perspective: Efficiently implementing ILP techniques is a balancing act that requires accurate modeling of a compute unit's intricacies. This significantly increases development and runtime. While trace-based simulation is a common middle ground that covers the techniques mentioned, highly accurate speculative modeling can only be achieved with execution-based techniques (which may introduce significant complexity in the simulator).

2.3.2 Thread-Level Parallelism (TLP)

TLP, as the name suggests, relies on executing multiple independent threads in parallel. The instruction stream is not shared. Since this is generally at the application level, the programmer explicitly specifies what to parallelize and how. This adds an additional layer of complexity in finding optimal regions for parallel execution and managing coordination between them.

Hardware Mechanisms for TLP

1. **Multiple Cores:** In modern multi-core processors, different cores can be assigned to run specific threads of an application. Memory bandwidth and synchronization should be carefully considered to determine the optimal number of parallel threads to launch.

2. **Simultaneous Multithreading (SMT):** Also known as hyperthreading, this approach enhances the microarchitecture of a single core to be able to run multiple independent streams of instructions (abstracted as threads in the application) by adding or partitioning resources within. Complexities to be handled here include managing multiple contexts (the machine state unique to the incoming thread) and finding "just enough" structures to partition and/or replicate.

No amount of parallelism will speed up the serial portions of a program, which inevitably exist, and impose a fundamental limitation on the amount of achievable gains. Other limited resources, such as memory bandwidth, are not infinitely scalable with the number of parallel threads. Cache coherence and synchronization overheads start taking over and diminishing possible gains if not managed properly.

Modeling Perspective: To model TLP, it is necessary to account for the interactions between threads. Doing this adds significant complexity to the modeling codebase, especially with SMT. Usually, modelers rely on finding reliable "proxies" to capture the effects of these complexities, such as simulating only certain parts of the processor or using the simplest representative instruction/thread mixes to reliably identify bottlenecks.

2.3.3 Data-Level Parallelism (DLP)

Data-level parallelism refers to applying the same operation to every element of a data set simultaneously. DLP is the most structured type of parallelism and the most effective when the workload fits its structure.

Hardware Mechanisms for DLP:

SIMD Instructions (CPUs): Vector instructions enable CPUs to apply the same operation to multiple data elements in a single instruction. For example, AVX-512 can operate on 512 bits (or 16 floats) of data at once, which could achieve 16 times the performance of scalar code if it were perfectly utilized.

Warp Execution (GPUs): In a warp or a wave, a set number of threads (32, 64, etc.) can run the same instruction simultaneously using their own data elements. This results in extremely high parallelism, significantly improving throughput. Multiple warps can be switched in or out depending on stalls, allowing latency to be hidden with throughput, to a certain extent.

DLP relies on the regularity of the workload, requiring that each data element undergo the same operation. Divergence and synchronization can significantly reduce efficiency. Irregularity in memory access patterns can also negate the benefits quickly by increasing memory latencies.

Modeling Perspective: Data-level parallelism is relatively easy to model (even at the analytical level) compared to ILP and TLP since the parallelism is explicitly structured. Important questions to be answered include effective resource utilization and efficient data movement. These types of questions lend themselves well to analytical models.

2.3.4 Platform Comparison

The most common approaches taken by computing systems are best highlighted side-by-side. Table 2-2 compares these for CPU and GPU.

Table 2-2. *Parallelism Emphasis Across Platforms*

Platform	Primary Parallelism	Secondary Parallelism	Modeling Priority
CPU	ILP (within core)	TLP (across cores), DLP (SIMD)	Pipeline hazards, branch prediction, cache coherence, etc.
GPU	DLP (warp execution)	Massive concurrency (latency hiding)	Warp scheduling, divergence, memory coalescing, etc.

Accelerators are omitted from this table (and the section) because they can be designed based on a wide variety of principles. Some examples include spatial dataflow arrays (similar to TPU), reconfigurable logic (such as FPGAs), and other pipelines optimized for specific operations. Thus, the ILP/TLP/DLP classification system, created to characterize general-purpose processor performance, cannot be easily applied to the variety of accelerator designs. Chapters 16 and 17 specifically address ML-based accelerator architectures and modeling.

Parallelism can greatly affect performance. Let's go over a few examples that showcase how parallelism-friendly workloads perform better at the different levels discussed, and how these strategies can be ineffective against less amenable workloads.

ILP on CPU: Consider elementwise addition of two arrays. The additions are independent, so a superscalar CPU, whether in-order or out-of-order, can execute many of them simultaneously. Conversely, when computing a Fibonacci sequence, each number depends on the two preceding numbers, and thus, execution must be sequential.

If we have a four-wide superscalar processor and execute an array addition of length 1000, the processor may issue up to four operations per cycle. In contrast, computing the first 1000 terms of the Fibonacci sequence will force a largely sequential execution regardless of the processor's issue width.

Even though the machine is designed to find and exploit opportunities for instruction-level parallelism, if the problem is inherently sequential, it adds no value.

TLP on Multi-core: Resizing 1,000 images independently is trivially parallelizable, with little or no coordination required among processors. An eight-processor system could potentially deliver almost 8x speedup over a single-core processor. Sorting a large array is an example of a task that requires significant inter-process coordination, which would likely yield much less improvement in performance with the same eight processors.

Thus, the ability to achieve TLP depends heavily on how easily the work divides and how often the units of work need to communicate with each other.

DLP on GPU: Making the same brightness adjustment to every pixel in an image is perfect for DLP, as thousands of threads can perform identical operations on different pixels. However, applying a different operation to each pixel based on a condition (e.g., brightening some pixels while darkening others) introduces divergence, in which multiple threads in a warp take different execution paths. This can cause serialization.

If 50% of the pixels follow each possible path, the GPU's overall throughput can drop by approximately 50%. As the degree of divergence increases (i.e., fewer threads follow the same execution path), the GPU's throughput will continue to decrease.

When workloads fit the DLP model perfectly (i.e., all operations are uniform and applied to regular data, as in color space conversion or per-pixel transformations), even simple analytical models can accurately predict GPU performance.

Modeling Perspective: Determine the level of detail for modeling parallelism based on your target hardware. For example, CPU models will need detailed ILP modeling (such as out-of-order execution, speculative execution); GPU models will need detailed modeling of warp behavior (including divergence and scheduling). Modeling an incorrect level of detail will not provide much value.

2.4 Summary

In this chapter, we looked at essential aspects of computer architecture through the lens of performance modeling. The intention was to avoid listing computer architecture facts and instead offer a perspective on where execution time goes and what factors affect it. To that end, three concepts matter most:

First, the compute-memory balance governs performance at a fundamental level. High operational intensity indicates a compute-bound workload, whereas a low operational intensity suggests a memory-bound workload. Performance modeling should be focused on one or the other, depending on this diagnosis.

Second, bandwidth and latency represent two distinct performance constraints with their own unique solutions. Throughput of streaming workloads is limited by available bandwidth, while dependent operation sequences are limited by latency. Confusing these may lead to misdirected modeling efforts.

Third, parallelism forms vary among different architectures. CPUs emphasize ILP within cores, GPUs emphasize DLP across thousands of threads, and accelerators usually offer a combination, which may vary widely by niche and design philosophy. Each method of parallelism has its own strengths and weaknesses that guide the development of the performance model.

Although this chapter covered architectural details at a high level and intentionally avoided going deeper, the following chapters do cover them when the context is clear: CPU microarchitecture in Chapter 11, GPU in Chapter 14, and accelerator-related concepts in Chapter 16.

The next chapter will address another important foundational aspect: the role of workloads, how to select them appropriately, and how the selection dictates the conclusions that can be drawn from them.

Review Questions

1. What is the difference between compute-bound and memory-bound workloads? What role does operational intensity play in determining which one applies?
2. How do bandwidth-limited and latency-limited behaviors differ?
3. Why would the same workload be able to run very differently on a GPU vs. a CPU?

Further Reading

J. L. Hennessy, D. A. Patterson, and C. Kozyrakis, *Computer Architecture: A Quantitative Approach*, 7th Edition. A complete source of further information about any subject that has been covered here.

W. Hwu, D. Kirk, and I. El Hajj, *Programming Massively Parallel Processors*, 5th Edition. Information about GPU architectures from a programming standpoint.

The original GPGPU-Sim paper (Bakhoda et al., ISPASS 2009) and Accel-Sim (Khairy et al., ISCA 2020) for learning GPU simulation models in detail.

V. Sze et al., "Efficient Processing of Deep Neural Networks: A Tutorial and Survey," *Proceedings of the IEEE*, 2017. This article introduces concepts related to accelerator architectures.

A. Parashar et al., "Timeloop: A Systematic Approach to DNN Accelerator Evaluation," *ISPASS*, 2019. This article describes an analytical modeling approach to evaluate accelerators.

S. Williams, A. Waterman, and D. Patterson, "Roofline: An Insightful Visual Performance Model for Multicore Architectures," *Communications of the ACM*, 2009. This is the seminal article about using a compute/memory performance model.

B. Gregg, *Systems Performance*, 2nd Edition. Methodology for analyzing performance that can be applied outside of simulation.

CHAPTER 3

Workload Selection and Experimental Validity

In Chapter 2, we explored computer architecture from a performance modeling perspective and covered design tradeoffs, including compute-memory balance, bandwidth versus latency, and parallelism. However, hardware alone is only part of the story; choosing appropriate workloads is an equally important part and, if not done carefully, can undermine modeling conclusions seriously.

Consider a researcher who proposes a new hardware prefetcher, tests it on general benchmarks, and reports an average improvement of 20%. Later, a different group finds no benefit in their graph analytics workload; in fact, performance declines. Reason: the benchmarks did not represent key memory access patterns, making the prefetcher ineffective for the latter workloads.

This is not a hypothetical example. Published results have frequently been undermined by errors in workload selection throughout the history of computer architecture research. Benchmark overfitting is a common pitfall in performance studies. This issue often goes unnoticed until later because no explicit error is raised anywhere in the process when the selected benchmarks do not represent the study's domain. Only careful planning and analysis reveals the problem.

A. Pareek, *Performance Modeling of Computer Systems*, Maker Innovations Series,
https://doi.org/10.1007/979-8-8688-2476-0_3

Building on these concerns, this chapter presents workload selection as an important aspect of performance modeling. Since a modeling study evaluates specific programs, it is important to assess the claims that can legitimately be made about the broader class of workloads those programs represent. This chapter discusses how to match workloads to research claims, how to characterize workload behavior before committing to a detailed simulation, and what standard benchmark suites offer, including their limitations.

For this chapter (and elsewhere in the text), the term "workload" denotes a program with its inputs and execution context. Benchmarks denote standardized workloads provided by benchmark suites and should be treated as a subset of workloads.

3.1 The Generalization Problem

Most performance studies evaluate a certain set of workloads yet make claims for broader classes. This section examines the appropriateness of making these claims and when they may be justifiably made.

3.1.1 From Sample to Population

There is an implicit structure in most performance modeling studies. Performance is observed and measured on a selected set of workloads, and the findings are extrapolated to claim their applicability to a larger class. The validity of this assertion depends on how well the selected workloads represent the target class.

This framework is analogous to a statistical sampling problem:

- **Population**: The complete class of workloads to which conclusions are intended to apply (e.g., all server applications or ML training workloads)

- **Sample**: The specific set of programs or workloads measured in the study (e.g., the Geekbench 6 suite)
- **Representativeness**: The extent to which sample characteristics accurately reflect those of the defined population

Standard benchmark suites offer convenient samples, i.e., collections of readily available, runnable programs. However, these must be carefully mixed and matched to suffice as representative samples of a defined population. The conclusions made should be weighted by the representativeness. Let's examine some common pitfalls that lead to suboptimal representativeness and their mitigations.

3.1.2 Representativeness Failures

There are several types of representativeness failures. Each type has its own warning signs and remedies:

Coverage Gaps: The selected workloads do not exercise the behaviors aligned with the research question. An example we discussed earlier, a prefetcher evaluated only on streaming workloads, will provide no information about how it would behave for pointer-chase-dominant workloads.

Remedy: Before selecting workloads, analyze candidate workloads for the specific behavioral traits your research question addresses. Ensure the chosen workloads exercise key behaviors relevant to your evaluation goals.

Selection Bias: Workloads favoring proposed techniques are over-represented, usually because they continue to be used for evaluation after being used during development.

Remedy: Select workloads prior to reviewing experimental results to guard against unintentional bias. Intentionally include workloads unlikely to showcase the benefits of the proposed technique. Analyze and report both success and failure cases. When feasible, rely on standardized benchmark suites over custom-built workloads, and document the rationale for every workload choice.

Temporal Mismatch: Benchmark characteristics lag behind updates and are no longer consistent with the target applications' characteristics. For example, the working set size of the current target applications may have ballooned over time, but the benchmarks still use smaller sizes.

Remedy: Only use the most relevant version of the benchmarks. Scale up input sizes to better reflect updates to the target application and supplement your study with recent workloads.

Scale Mismatch: The input size for benchmarks differs significantly from that of the target production-scale applications. For example, a database benchmark using 1 GB of data may behave very differently if the input data size is changed to 1 TB.

Remedy: Ensure the input sizes produce characteristics representative of the target applications.

Over-Representation of Benchmarks: An excessive number of benchmarks are run without considering relevance. This dilutes research and wastes effort.

Remedy: Choose a small group of workloads based on clear reasoning rather than a large group of workloads with little to no reasoning behind them.

Neglecting Phases: Incorrect phases are used to evaluate a feature's efficacy. This leads to wrong results and misguided proposals. Applications generally have phases with distinct characteristics, for example, initialization, warm-up, steady-state, and checkpointing. Avoid making general assertions using the wrong phase.

Remedy: Properly identify and evaluate relevant phases. We will cover sampling methodologies to identify representative phases in Chapter 6.

It is not uncommon for any of these mistakes to creep into a project and nullify months of research, resulting in missed timelines and wasted resources. All the failures discussed have one thing in common: a mismatch between the measured workloads and the conclusions drawn from them. To solve this issue, we need to explicitly reason about the scope of the benchmarks used, i.e., the class of workloads they represent.

3.1.3 Claims and Applicability

The representativeness issues discussed above affect the applicability of study claims. While claims denote the assertions to be made in a study, scope defines where those claims apply. Scope implicitly gets constrained by workload selection. For example, using SPEC CPU2017 implies that the study is geared towards general-purpose CPU performance and probably won't provide meaningful insights into parallel scientific computing or neural network inference. Well-defined, focused claims with clear scope are far more useful than overreaching claims based on murky assumptions.

Table 3-1 shows examples of suitable and unsuitable workload choices for various research questions.

Table 3-1. *Research Questions and Appropriate Workload Classes*

Research Question	Appropriate Workload Class	Inappropriate Workload Choice
Cache replacement policy	Memory-intensive workloads with diverse access patterns	Compute-bound workloads with minimal cache misses
Branch predictor design	Control-flow-intensive workloads with varied branch behavior	Streaming workloads with minimal branching
GPU memory coalescing	Kernels with varied access patterns, including irregular	Perfectly coalesced synthetic benchmarks
Accelerator buffer sizing	Neural network layers spanning small to large dimensions	Layers that fit the proposed buffer size

3.1.4 Evidence Requirements by Claim Strength

The strength of research claims derived from a performance modeling study can vary, and the evidence requirement changes accordingly.

Narrow claims make assertions about very specific and limited outcomes; e.g., "Technique X improved performance on SPEC CPU2017 integer benchmarks by 8%." These claims can be supported sufficiently by the cited benchmarks. In other words, the claim is exactly what was being measured.

Domain claims assert an applicability to a certain class or category of workload; e.g., "Technique X improves server application performance." These claims require evidence that the measured workloads are representative of the entire class (e.g., server applications).

General claims assert applicability to a wide range of workloads; e.g., "Technique X improves memory system performance." These claims require evidence demonstrating applicability across multiple classes of workloads, and often an explicit analysis or description of when the technique will and will not be applicable.

Modeling Perspective: The quality of research depends on strong evidence for claims. A narrow, well-supported claim can be more valuable than a broad, weakly supported one.

3.1.5 Working Backward from Claims

Choosing a good set of workloads starts with the claims you are trying to make. A systematic way to do so is illustrated below. It is the reverse of the fallacy of selecting convenient benchmarks and then determining what claims they support.

State the Claim: What is your claim? What statement should the research make?

State the Target Population: Which class of workloads will your claim be about?

State Relevant Characteristics: How do various workload properties impact the aspect we want to study?

Choose Workloads for Coverage: Select workloads that span all the relevant characteristics.

Verify Workload Alignment: Verify that the workloads you have chosen exhibit the same characteristics found in the target population.

Let's look at an example to clarify.

3.1.6 Example: Cache Replacement Study

A new cache replacement policy is to be proposed. From the above guidelines, here's how the analysis proceeds:

Research Study Claim: "The proposed caching strategy will result in lower LLC miss rates for memory-intensive server workloads."

Target Application Population: "Memory-intensive server applications—databases, key-value stores, web servers operating under full load."

Stating Relevant Characteristics: Working set size relative to cache size; access pattern regularity; reuse distance distribution; multi-threaded sharing patterns.

Selecting Representative Workloads:

- SPEC benchmarks that are memory-intensive (mcf, lbm, omnetpp) for Baseline Coverage
- PARSEC benchmarks with shared-memory behavior (e.g., *canneal, dedup*)
- Database workloads (TPC-C, TPC-H) for server representativeness
- Microbenchmarks with controlled reuse patterns aligned with the specific mechanism of the study

Validating Workload Alignment: Use metrics from prior research on server workloads to characterize each workload you selected for study. This validation confirms whether the key characteristics (miss rates, working set sizes, access patterns) are consistent with those observed in production servers.

Modeling Perspective: Document your rationale for selecting the workloads to be evaluated. Providing explicit justification for selecting specific workloads enhances the credibility of your methodology and facilitates reproduction of the study.

As we have seen, quantitative measurement of workloads is essential for multiple steps in the process. The next section presents some techniques for doing so.

3.2 Workload Characterization

Understanding and measuring workload behavior is essential in enabling proper selection and meaningful simulation. This section presents some characterization techniques and illustrates their application to selection decisions, modeling choices, and interpretation of results.

3.2.1 Purpose of Workload Characterization

Primary purposes of characterization in performance modeling methodology are listed below:

Enabling Selection Guidance: Characterization enables informed selection by highlighting which behavioral regions are covered by which workloads.

Enabling Bottleneck Identification: Determining workload boundedness (compute-bound, memory-bandwidth bound, etc.) helps guide modeling decisions as illustrated in Chapter 2.

Enabling Proper Result Interpretation: Characterization enables a deep understanding of workload behavior, which in turn provides context to establish a causal connection to why performance changed the way it did, given the workloads used.

Enabling Validation: Characterization helps validate simulation runs, as observed metrics can be correlated with expected directional performance changes and bottlenecks.

3.2.2 Using Hardware Performance Counters

Modern systems make a variety of hardware performance counters available to users. These counters enable direct measurement of architectural events during execution. Thus, they can be used to conduct workload characterization on a given system.

For example, in Linux systems, the perf tool provides access to common counters. Some examples of using it are illustrated below.

perf stat -e cycles,instructions,cache-references,cache-misses,branches,branch-misses ./workload

This command displays the following information:

- cycles, instructions: IPC = instructions / cycles. A low IPC indicates stalls.
- cache-references, cache-misses: Miss Rate = misses / references. A high miss rate indicates memory pressure.
- branches, branch-misses: Misprediction Rate = misses / branches. A high misprediction rate indicates control-flow complexity (which the predictor may not be handling well).

perf stat -e L1-dcache-loads,L1-dcache-load-misses,LLC-loads, LLC-load-misses ./workload

This provides additional details about cache behavior at various hierarchy levels.

Significant differences in miss rates between the L1 and LLC caches indicate effective intermediate caching, while similar miss rates (if high) across the two cache levels suggest that the working set size exceeds the cache capacity.

Performance counters can be used to gauge how close key system resources are to their maximum capacity. This, in turn, helps identify the resources that limit performance, i.e., the system bottlenecks. Let's discuss the two most important utilization metrics, namely memory and compute.

Memory Bandwidth Utilization: Measured as a fraction of achieved bandwidth relative to peak and measurable through memory controller counters or other tools (such as the Intel Memory Latency Checker). A high memory bandwidth utilization indicates that the workload is memory-bandwidth-bound. Low memory bandwidth utilization warrants looking at other data to determine what may be going on.

Compute Utilization: Operations per second as a ratio of peak. For Nvidia GPUs, tools such as Nsight show it directly. For CPUs, finding utilization is not straightforward: Usually, we count different types of operations individually (e.g., floating-point operations via counters like fp_arith_inst_retired) and compare them against their maximum rates.

The combination of utilization metrics (such as memory bandwidth and compute utilization), along with IPC and miss rates, shows whether the workload is compute-bound, memory bandwidth-bound, or memory latency-bound. This information helps determine the appropriate model abstraction to use.

3.2.3 Characterizing Operational Intensity

For CPUs, operational intensity (defined in Section 2.1.2) can be estimated as follows:

$$\text{Operational Intensity} \approx \text{Number of Operations} / (\text{LLC\_misses} \times \text{Cache\_line\_size})$$

Note that the number of operations depends on the workload class. For floating-point-heavy workloads, FLOPs can be used, and for integer-heavy workloads, the number of integer ops is a good estimate. In certain situations, the sum of both may make more sense.

For GPUs, profiling tools such as NVIDIA's Nsight Compute measure both FLOPS and memory throughput, allowing direct calculation of the workload's operational intensity.

Analogous to GPUs, operational intensity for accelerator workloads is calculated based on layer specifications. As an example:

$$\text{Convolution Operations} = 2 \times N \times H \times W \times C\_in \times C\_out \times K\_h \times K\_w$$

$$\text{Data Movement} = \text{input bytes} + \text{weights bytes} + \text{output bytes}$$

The ratio between these two represents theoretical operational intensity. The actual operational intensity will depend on how well the mapping allows for data reuse.

3.2.4 Characterizing Memory Access Patterns

In addition to aggregate statistics, characterizing a workload's memory access patterns provides insight into how the cache and memory system will likely behave. Some common forms of analysis to achieve this are discussed below.

Stride Analysis: Sequential access (stride-1) is optimal for achieving high bandwidth and effectively using prefetchers. Higher stride access allows for partial bandwidth utilization (still good). However, random access eliminates prefetchers' ability to assist, resulting in the full penalty of the access latencies.

Working Set Estimation: A working set is the total amount of data actively used by a workload. A small working set that fits within the cache size produces high hit rates; however, when a working set exceeds the cache size by several orders of magnitude, it results in many capacity misses.

Reuse Distance Analysis: Reuse distance measures the number of unique addresses accessed between two consecutive accesses to the same address. A short reuse distance indicates that most accesses result in cache hits; a long reuse distance indicates that many accesses result in cache misses. Reuse distance distributions can be computed with tools such as Pin and DynamoRIO.

Phase Behavior: Many workloads exhibit distinct phases of activity with different memory access characteristics during execution (e.g., initialization, computation, cleanup). Aggregate statistics can mask important information when phases change meaningfully in a short time. This necessitates the importance of classifying memory accesses with respect to phase information.

3.2.5 Characterizing with Clustering and Visualization

If we think of each characterization metric as a single coordinate, all the metrics together define a point in an n-dimensional space, where the dimensions correspond to different types of metrics. Clustering and visualization techniques provide a way to see a workload in this space. This approach to workload design was developed systematically by Eeckhout and colleagues. Their PCA-based methodology for selecting representative benchmark subsets is still widely regarded as the basis for systematic workload selection. Let's touch on some relevant concepts briefly.

Principal Component Analysis (PCA): Reduces the data dimensionality to facilitate visualization of similarities among workloads while preserving most of the original data's variance. Workloads that cluster together in the PCA space tend to exhibit similar microarchitectural behavior and are likely redundant for evaluation purposes.

Clustering: Grouping of workloads by similarity. To ensure broad coverage, benchmarks should be selected from different clusters. Those selected from the same cluster typically do not increase the amount of beneficial information.

Gap Identification: Visualization can also identify areas of the characteristic space that are not covered by any of the benchmarks being considered. This can help indicate which additional workloads may be needed.

Modeling Perspective: Investing time in characterization is necessary prior to investing in simulation. The time investment is small in comparison to the simulation time, and the resulting understanding will guide all subsequent modeling and workload-selection decisions.

With major characterization concepts covered, let's review some commonly used existing benchmark suites in the next section.

3.3 Standard Benchmark Suites

Standard benchmarks enable comparisons across studies, helping ensure reproducibility. In this section, we will briefly survey current standard suites, their uses, and their shortcomings. Since benchmarks keep evolving, users should confirm that the current versions suit their needs before use.

3.3.1 CPU Benchmarks

SPEC CPU 2017 has long been the standard for evaluating single-threaded CPU behavior in architecture research. It comprises two sub-suites: SPECint (benchmarks that stress integer execution, branch prediction, and memory hierarchies) and SPECfp (floating-point execution-based benchmarks with larger memory footprints). The characteristics of these benchmarks are diverse: the memory footprint of each ranges from tens of megabytes to gigabytes, while the instruction per cycle (IPC) ranges from less than 0.5 to greater than 2.0. Note that it requires a paid license to use, which limits its accessibility. Its successor, SPEC CPU 2026, was released in May 2026 with 52 largely new benchmarks across four suites.

The GAP Benchmark Suite includes graph-processing workloads that test irregular memory access patterns, which are not extensively tested by SPEC.

Geekbench 6 provides cross-platform CPU and GPU benchmarks covering a wide variety of workloads, including data compression, machine learning inference, etc. It is widely used for comparing consumer-grade devices. There is support for x86, ARM, and Apple Silicon, with free accessibility tiers. Geekbench AI provides a collection of workloads for evaluating AI performance on client-side (edge) devices, such as NPU and GPU. This suite is less common in academic settings but widely used in the industry.

PARSEC is a traditional multicore benchmark suite (circa 2008) that provides parallel workloads for studies of shared-memory systems. PARSEC is most appropriate when the research focuses on thread interactions, cache coherence, or contention. However, the PARSEC workloads are less representative of modern cloud-native or containerized workloads.

DCPerf (Meta, 2024) is an open-source benchmark suite for evaluating CPU performance in data center environments. In contrast to other traditional benchmark suites, DCPerf captures patterns characteristic of hyperscale workloads, including microservice architecture and multi-process concurrency. DCPerf includes workloads based on Django web serving, video transcoding, and feed ranking, which are not found in desktop-oriented benchmarks.

3.3.2 GPU and Accelerator Workloads

The Rodinia benchmark has historically been a valuable resource in understanding GPU architectures for scientific computing, data mining, and image processing and has supported both CUDA and OpenCL. Since it was last updated in 2015, the workloads have become increasingly unrepresentative of machine learning-dominated production GPU usage, which is rapidly increasing.

TorchBench and MLPerf are two of the most popular and widely accepted GPU and accelerator benchmarks in use today. They can be used for NVIDIA GPUs, Google TPUs, and many other custom ML accelerators.

TorchBench (PyTorch/Meta) provides models across computer vision, natural language processing, recommendation systems, and speech processing. It provides alignment with the state of current deep learning frameworks and a direct interface with PyTorch's performance testing framework.

MLPerf (MLCommons) is another industry-standard benchmarking suite for evaluating ML hardware. It provides separate suites for training and inference. Recent versions of MLPerf include generative AI workloads such as large language models, text-to-image (Stable Diffusion), and mixture-of-experts architectures. MLPerf is updated regularly to reflect rapid changes in AI models; therefore, researchers should always check the current MLPerf round before designing their own experiments.

MLPerf Client extends the MLPerf suite to include edge and on-device inference, something that is getting increasingly important.

In addition to formalized suites, it is quite common to use informal benchmarks such as ResNet-50 and EfficientNet for CNNs and BERT, GPT-2, and Llama variants for transformers.

3.3.3 Server and Cloud Workloads

YCSB (Yahoo Cloud Serving Benchmark) provides a framework for testing and measuring the performance of key-value stores and NoSQL databases using customizable workload mixes. It provides several standard workloads, including read-heavy (95% read) and write-heavy (50% write), along with configurable record counts and access distributions. YCSB is quite useful for memory system research pertaining to cloud-based infrastructure.

TPC benchmarks (TPC-C, TPC-H, TPC-DS) continue to be widely recognized and used standards for databases and transaction processing performance evaluation. TPC-C models online transactional processing (OLTP) workloads, while TPC-H and TPC-DS model decision support query workloads. The three TPC benchmarks each provide a unique way to evaluate different aspects of the memory hierarchy and I/O subsystems compared to the compute-focused benchmarks.

3.3.4 Limitations

There are several inherent limitations to standard suites. Some are highlighted below:

- They are convenience samples and not statistically representative populations.
- They may lag behind recent application releases.
- The input sizes used may not reflect production scales and may be overly naive or atypical.

The difference between benchmarks and production workloads is especially pronounced in datacenter and ML applications, where proprietary workloads drive hardware requirements yet are unavailable to the public. If standard suites fail to meet your needs, you may need to develop custom workloads to address the gaps in the existing standard suites.

Having looked at some commonly available benchmark suites that offer a plethora of choices for a given study across domains, let's now focus on some practical aspects of workload selection.

3.4 Practical Aspects of Workload Selection

So far, we have systematically covered workload representativeness, characterization, and the commonly available pool of standardized workloads (benchmarks). This section emphasizes how workload sets are commonly assembled in practice and the common trade-offs and pitfalls to watch for when choosing them.

3.4.1 Common Workload Sources

Workloads can come from a variety of sources. Each has its strengths and weaknesses. Common sources include standardized benchmarks, real-world applications, scaled variants of existing workloads, and synthetic microbenchmarks. Let's go over some important details to be mindful of when selecting from these sources.

Standardized benchmarks offer high comparability and are easily available with extensive documentation. However, as we discussed in Section 3.3, they must be carefully evaluated for representativeness of the target domain.

Real applications offer direct representational value. The complexity arises due to dependencies, configurations, and reproducibility issues. When using real applications as workload sources, it is essential to accurately document version numbers, configurations, and inputs.

Scaling inputs can help make existing workloads usable by improving their representation. However, it is necessary to ensure that the scaled workloads represent the characteristics of the target domain. Scaling may introduce unexpected changes in workload behavior, such as locality patterns and memory pressure.

Synthetic microbenchmarks enable controlled experiments focused on specific behaviors. They should be used to learn about relevant mechanisms, not to validate claims.

3.4.2 Selection in Practice

In real-world scenarios, often workload selection follows a set of heuristics rather than a rigid procedure.

A coverage-based approach is a common heuristic for selecting workloads. It helps ensure that all relevant behaviors are well captured. As discussed in Section 3.1.5, a comprehensive strategy to achieve this involves identifying the characteristics most relevant to the research question and measuring those for all available workloads. Once done, it is possible to select workloads that together represent the complete range of values across the identified characteristics.

Another common heuristic is sensitivity-based selection. It focuses on workloads most likely to elicit the phenomenon under investigation. For example, workloads with high cache miss rates are used in studies of cache replacement.

Modeling Perspective: Sensitivity-based selection is very different from "cherry-picking," i.e., selecting workloads where your solution works best. Cherry picking adds bias. A good way to think about it: Select based on how sensitive the workload is to the mechanism (i.e., cache behavior) of interest, not how sensitive the workload is to the results (i.e., improvements from the proposed solution).

3.4.3 Pragmatic Considerations

Practical factors impact workload selection: simulation time, trace storage constraints, ability to reproduce results, and licensing fees. If the research builds on previous work, it often requires overlapping workloads to enable direct comparisons. Valid justifications should be made if there is a deviation in this selection.

Workload selection should be documented with enough details to enable reproducibility. This may include benchmark names, versions, sources, input datasets, configuration parameters, and the selection rationale.

Modeling Perspective: Provide explicit documentation for why you chose to include a particular workload. For example, "We selected these ten benchmarks because they represent the full range of memory behaviors we need to examine for cache-related studies and run within our allotted simulation time" is both informative and honest.

3.5 Summary

Workload selection is essential in determining the conclusions a performance study can make and support. Let's summarize the key principles we covered in this chapter below:

First, workload selection is an element of experimental design. The relationship between measured programs and claimed generalized results defines a study's overall validity. Therefore, this relationship must be explicitly justified.

Second, the applicability of claims should match the evidence. Narrow claims can be supported with only the referenced or stated benchmarks. Broader claims require justification that the measured workloads reflect the intended target domain.

Third, characterization precedes selection. Understanding how workloads behave through measurements provides the basis for decision-making and helps interpret results.

Fourth, standard suites are tools, not authorities. Benchmark suites provide common ground for reproducibility and comparison. Representativeness of the target domain cannot be taken for granted and must be carefully justified.

Fifth, coverage is intentional. Effective coverage of relevant workload characteristics requires intentional selection (not an exhaustive inclusion).

Finally, documentation enables proper assessment. Documenting the rationale for workload selection enables readers to assess whether the conclusions drawn are supported.

Having now established workload selection principles, the subsequent parts of the book put them into practice with hands-on simulation experiments. Before moving to the next part, let's take a short detour and understand what happens under-the-hood in common simulators, such as ChampSim.

Review Questions

1. Why is running all available benchmarks not necessarily better than selecting only a subset of them?
2. How would you differentiate between a narrow claim and a general claim?
3. What is selection bias, and how can it be avoided?
4. Why should workload characterization be done before detailed simulation?

Further Reading

SPEC CPU 2017 documentation: *https://www.spec.org/cpu2017/*

DCPerf: "An Open-Source, Battle-Tested Performance Benchmark Suite for Datacenter Workloads," ISCA 2025.

MLPerf documentation: *https://mlcommons.org/benchmarks/*

TorchBench: *https://github.com/pytorch/benchmark*

S. Che et al., "Rodinia: A Benchmark Suite for Heterogeneous Computing," IISWC 2009. The foundational heterogeneous computing benchmark paper.

L. Eeckhout, H. Vandierendonck, and K. De Bosschere, "Workload Design: Selecting Representative Program-Input Pairs," PACT 2002. Foundational work on PCA-based workload selection.

K. Hoste and L. Eeckhout, "Microarchitecture-Independent Workload Characterization," IEEE Micro 2007. General techniques for workload characterization independent of microarchitecture.

S. Kanev et al., "Profiling a Warehouse-Scale Computer," ISCA 2015. An essential read for understanding the behavior of warehouse-scale computer workloads.

L. Eeckhout, "Computer Architecture Performance Evaluation Methods," Synthesis Lectures on Computer Architecture, 2010. A comprehensive resource for evaluation methodologies.

T. Sherwood et al., "Automatically Characterizing Large Scale Program Behavior," ASPLOS 2002. Presents SimPoint that introduces phase-based sampling.

V. J. Reddi et al., "MLPerf Inference Benchmark," ISCA 2020. For learning the design principles behind MLPerf.

CHAPTER 4

Simulator in a Nutshell

So far, we have covered why performance modeling matters, reviewed fundamental architectural concepts from a modeling perspective, and discussed how to select workloads properly. Before we begin collecting traces and running experiments in the remainder of the book, it is worth understanding what happens inside a simulator during a simulation. This chapter provides a brief walkthrough of simulation mechanics using ChampSim as the example. The goal is to develop a mental model of the process so that the content in the rest of the book has a clear context. Hence, we will not go over extensive details.

4.1 From Trace to Statistics

At a high level, a trace-driven simulator reads a recorded sequence of instructions, simulates the microarchitectural effects for each instruction, and records microarchitectural statistics as it progresses. Let's look at each part of this process.

The input to the simulator, or the trace file, contains one record per instruction. Listing 4-1 shows ChampSim's trace entry structure. Each entry contains the instruction address (IP), branch information, register operands, and the memory addresses that are accessed. Chapter 5 will cover how traces are collected.

A. Pareek, *Performance Modeling of Computer Systems*, Maker Innovations Series,
https://doi.org/10.1007/979-8-8688-2476-0_4

Listing 4-1. Trace Entry Structure (from inc/trace_instruction.h)

```
struct input_instr {
    unsigned long long ip;                    // instruction address
    unsigned char is_branch;
    unsigned char branch_taken;
    unsigned char destination_registers[NUM_INSTR_DESTINATIONS];
    unsigned char source_registers[NUM_INSTR_SOURCES];
    unsigned long long destination_memory[NUM_INSTR_DESTINATIONS];
    unsigned long long source_memory[NUM_INSTR_SOURCES];
};
```

The simulator processes these internally, cycle by cycle, in a loop. Each iteration advances the simulated clock one step. Within each step, all the modeled hardware components, such as caches, the DRAM controller, and prefetchers, perform their work. The input injector refills each CPU's input queue from the trace as space becomes available, and the loop continues until each CPU has processed the target number of instructions. Listing 4-2 shows the high-level structure of ChampSim's main loop, simplified for clarity.

Listing 4-2. Main Simulation Loop (simplified from src/champsim.cc)

```
std::vector<bool> phase_complete(num_cpus, false);

while (!std::accumulate(std::begin(phase_complete),
        std::end(phase_complete), true, std::logical_and{})) {
    global_clock.tick(time_quantum);

    // Advance each hardware component by one step
    for (champsim::operable& op : operables) {
        op.operate_on(global_clock);
    }
```

```
    // Refill each CPU input queue from the trace as
    space allows
    for (O3_CPU& cpu : env.cpu_view()) {
        while (!trace.eof() && cpu.input_queue.size() < cpu.
        IN_QUEUE_SIZE) {
            cpu.input_queue.push_back(trace());
        }
    }

    // A CPU is done when it reaches its target
    instruction count
    for (O3_CPU& cpu : env.cpu_view()) {
        phase_complete[cpu.cpu] = (cpu.sim_instr() >= length);
    }
}
```

At each step (or tick), each modeled component updates its state. For example, caches check for hits, the DRAM controller processes its queues, and prefetchers decide whether to issue any requests. The accumulated statistics across all these ticks produce the final simulation metrics, which will be covered in Chapter 7.

Let's see a more concrete example of how a single memory access flows through ChampSim's pipeline.

4.2 Path of a Memory Access

Suppose the trace contains a load instruction that reads from a given address. Simulating this instruction involves the following steps (while stats are collected along the way).

Step 1: Instruction Fetch. The simulator parses the trace entry and places it into a modeled queue that mimics a real processor's front end.

Step 2: L1 Cache Lookup. When the instruction reaches the front of the queue, the simulator finds the cache set from the address given the cache parameters and searches for a matching valid tag. The match determines whether it is a hit or not. Listing 4-3 shows the core of this check.

Listing 4-3. Cache Tag Lookup (simplified from src/cache.cc)

```
auto [set_begin, set_end] = get_set_span(handle_pkt.address);
auto way = std::find_if(set_begin, set_end,
    [matcher = matches_address(handle_pkt.address)](const
    auto& x) {
        return x.valid && matcher(x);
    });
const auto hit = (way != set_end);
```

On a miss, the corresponding cache level sends the request down to the next level, increments the miss counter, and uses an MSHR to track the outstanding access. Listing 4-4 shows the reference code.

Listing 4-4. Forwarding a Miss (simplified from src/cache.cc)

```
bool success = lower_level->add_rq(mshr_pkt.second);
// send to next level

if (mshr_pkt.second.response_requested) {
    MSHR.emplace_back(std::move(mshr_pkt.first));
// track outstanding miss
}

sim_stats.misses.increment({handle_pkt.type, handle_pkt.cpu});
```

Step 3: L2 and LLC Lookup. The miss propagates to the L2 cache, then to the Last Level Cache (LLC) depending on whether it is a hit or miss. The request follows the same tag-matching process at each level.

Step 4: DRAM Access. If the access misses at all cache levels, it is forwarded to DRAM, where the simulator models relevant timing parameters, including precharge (tRP), row-to-column delay (tRCD), column access (tCAS), row-active timing (tRAS), and refresh behavior. Chapter 10 covers these aspects of DRAM modeling.

Step 5: Fill and Update. Data return is also simulated by function calls and state variables, as there is no actual data to return per se. Each level inserts the new block (possibly evicting another), trains its prefetcher, and updates the corresponding statistics. The replacement policy determines which existing block to evict if needed. Common replacement policies are covered in Chapter 9.

Step 6: Simulated Time. The total latency for this access, for example, 4 cycles for the L1 lookup, 12 for L2, 30 for LLC, and 80 for DRAM, contributes to the modeled completion time of the access. It can also overlap with other in-flight work, similar to the hardware unit being modeled.

This walkthrough is intentionally simplified. A real simulator handles many additional details, including multiple outstanding misses, prefetch requests interleaved with demand accesses, and bandwidth contention at various levels of the memory hierarchy. However, the fundamental structure is the core loop that drives common trace-driven simulators. You are encouraged to follow the references in the next section to learn more about commonly used simulators and frameworks in academia and industry.

With a brief high-level understanding of how simulators work, we are ready to work on the simulation pipeline. Chapter 5 starts with the first step, i.e., collecting traces.

Further Reading

Trace-Driven Simulators:

ChampSim: *https://github.com/ChampSim/ChampSim*. A trace-driven simulator for cache, prefetcher, and branch-predictor research.

Execution-Driven Simulators:

gem5: *https://www.gem5.org/*. Cycle-level full-system and syscall-emulation simulator.

ZSim: *https://github.com/s5z/zsim*. A fast execution-driven multicore simulator using Intel Pin for instrumentation.

Sniper: *https://snipersim.org/*. Ghent University's interval-based parallel simulator for multi-core studies.

Modeling Frameworks:

Sparta (MAP): *https://github.com/sparcians/map*. A C++17 modeling framework for constructing, binding, and running full simulations.

SST: *https://sst-simulator.org/*. Sandia's Structural Simulation Toolkit: a modular, parallel, and MPI-capable framework for assembling system simulations.

Memory-System Simulators:

Ramulator 2: *https://github.com/CMU-SAFARI/ramulator2*. SAFARI lab's extensible DRAM simulator.

DRAMsim3: *https://github.com/umd-memsys/DRAMsim3*. A cycle-accurate DRAM simulator from the University of Maryland.

PART II

The Simulation Pipeline

CHAPTER 5

Trace Collection and Management

Part II covers the workflow of turning workload behavior into reliable simulation results. The end-to-end process can be thought of as a simulation pipeline with three stages, namely, trace collection, sampling, and output analysis. We will cover these stages in Chapters 5, 6, and 7. To begin, this chapter explores the first stage: trace collection.

The quality of collected traces directly affects the validity of subsequent simulations. Regardless of the simulator complexity or depth, poorly collected traces will likely produce unreliable results downstream. Understanding the information provided (or not) by traces, and how they are created and validated, will allow you to build a solid foundation for all subsequent phases of the pipeline.

To that end, we will first examine the information contained in and omitted by traces and discuss the three common methods for creating traces. Each method provides different levels of fidelity, overhead, and scope. Next, we delve into the details of dynamic binary instrumentation with Intel Pin, which is the most suitable approach for the simulations used throughout the book. Following this, we cover techniques to catch collection errors early and organizational practices to keep large trace sets manageable. We will also touch on trace fidelity and how errors due to the user-kernel boundary and wrong-path execution can quietly corrupt results.

A. Pareek, *Performance Modeling of Computer Systems*, Maker Innovations Series,
https://doi.org/10.1007/979-8-8688-2476-0_5

Prerequisites

This chapter assumes you are familiar with

- Linux command-line operations
- Basic C/C++ coding
- Concepts related to workload selection as discussed in Chapter 3

Additionally, you will need a Linux x86-64-based machine and about 10-50 GB of free disk space for storing traces.

Tool Setup

This chapter, and the rest of Part II, assumes that you have a working installation of Intel Pin and ChampSim. As we will see in Sections 5.3 and 5.4, Pin is used to collect traces, and ChampSim provides a compatible tracer to generate traces for its specific format. ChampSim will be used more directly in Chapter 6, but preparing both the tools here makes the workflow easier to follow throughout Part II.

To use ChampSim, first download it from the official GitHub page. It contains a README that you are encouraged to follow. We have listed the essential steps in the first part of Listing 5-1. To install Pin, you can download it from Intel's website directly. The steps to install it are provided in the second part of Listing 5-1. Note that we have used a specific version in the example, and the filenames may change depending on your version. Make sure the environment variables are correctly set to follow along the chapters using these tools.

Listing 5-1. Installing ChampSim and Intel Pin

```
# Installing ChampSim
git clone https://github.com/ChampSim/ChampSim.git
```

```
cd ChampSim
git submodule update --init vcpkg
./vcpkg/bootstrap-vcpkg.sh
./vcpkg/vcpkg install
./config.sh champsim_config.json
make

# Set environment variables for ChampSim
export CHAMPSIM_ROOT=$HOME/ChampSim

# Installing Pin
# Download from Intel's Pin downloads page, then unpack
tar -xzf pin-external-4.2-99776-g21d818fa2-gcc-linux.tar.gz

# Set environment variables for Pin
export PIN_ROOT=$HOME/pin-external-4.2-99776-g21d818fa2-
gcc-linux
export PATH=$PIN_ROOT:$PATH

# Verify the installation
pin -version
#If vcpkg reports a cmake issue, follow these steps,
else ignore
# Install a newer CMake locally inside the working directory
curl -fL -o cmake-3.29.2-linux-x86_64.tar.gz \
  https://github.com/Kitware/CMake/releases/download/v3.29.2/
cmake-3.29.2-linux-x86_64.tar.gz
tar -xzf cmake-3.29.2-linux-x86_64.tar.gz
export PATH=$PWD/cmake-3.29.2-linux-x86_64/bin:$PATH
#Retry vcpkg install steps
```

Note If the vcpkg command reports that a suitable version of cmake is not found, install a newer cmake and try again. The recommended steps for version 3.29.2 are shown in Listing 5-1.

With the basic setup complete, we can now explore what execution traces capture and what they ignore.

5.1 What Traces Capture

Before we discuss collection mechanisms, you should know what a trace includes and excludes for better interpretation of results from your simulations.

5.1.1 Trace Contents

For each executed instruction in the program, the trace typically captures the following:

Instruction Address: The memory address from which an instruction is fetched

Instruction Type: Load, Store, Branch, Arithmetic Operation, etc.

Memory Addresses: Virtual addresses of the data loaded or stored

Branch Information: Whether the branch is taken and the target address

Register Operands: Source and destination registers for dependency modeling

The exact information varies with simulators. ChampSim traces, as an example, include the instruction address, register operands, branch behavior, and memory operations per instruction. This format is sufficient for modeling cache hierarchies, prefetchers, and branch predictors.

A Note on ISA Instructions vs. Micro-operations

Modern processor cores break complex instructions into one or more micro-operations (or Uops). These differ from ISA-level instructions (that the program binary comprises), such as ADD, MOV, etc. Within the scope of our interest in studying cache, memory, and prefetcher behavior, ISA-level traces are acceptable, since the memory access patterns we will cover will hold regardless of how the processor decomposes the ISA-level instruction into uops.

However, for studies that evaluate structural port pressure, pipeline scheduling, or backend resource contention, ISA-level traces are insufficient. You would need a trace format that is aware of uops, or an execution-driven simulator, such as gem5, that models the pipeline stage where instructions are decoded into uops (typically the decode stage).

5.1.2 What Traces Omit

Timing: The timing from the original application's execution is not preserved.

Speculative Execution: Traces contain only the instructions that are actually committed by the processor. Instructions speculatively issued on a mispredicted branch path are not included in the trace. These speculative instructions interact with real pipeline resources and can pollute caches, consume bandwidth, and corrupt predictor states. Section 5.7 discusses this omission further.

Kernel Activity: Traces captured using user-space instrumentation tools such as Pin include only user-mode instructions. System activity (i.e., system calls, interrupt handlers, context switches) is not captured by these types of traces. Section 5.7 discusses this in more detail.

Multi-threaded Activity: Traces may not preserve or reproduce the interleaving of threads during multi-threaded execution.

Modeling Perspective: Traces are best suited when the sequence of instructions is largely independent of the microarchitecture timing. This is true for most compute-bound applications and many memory-bound applications but may not apply to synchronization-intensive or I/O-intensive applications. The method you use to collect traces will determine whether any of these omissions will affect your study, as we will discuss in Section 5.2.

With an outline of what traces capture in general, let us focus on the specific formats commonly used in real simulators.

5.1.3 Trace Formats

Simulators typically define their own specific trace formats. Table 5-1 summarizes the most common ones and the contexts where each is used.

Table 5-1. *Common Trace Formats*

Format	Simulator	Key Characteristics	Best For	Not Suitable For
ChampSim trace	ChampSim	Compact binary; correct-path instruction + data addresses	Cache, prefetcher, and basic DRAM studies	Kernel effects, wrong-path execution, timing feedback
gem5 elastic trace	gem5	Timing dependencies and dependency chains (still trace-driven)	Detailed CPU replay modeling	Speculation and OS fidelity depend on how the trace was generated
Intel PT trace	perf/libipt	Low-overhead compressed control-flow packets; kernel-inclusive	Realistic long-running workloads; kernel-inclusive analysis	Data addresses (Intel PEBS provides only sampled addresses, not per-instruction)
Memory trace	Various	Data addresses only	Pure cache/ memory analysis	Control flow, branch prediction
Branch trace	Various	Branch outcomes only	Predictor research	Memory behavior, cache interaction

Note that execution-driven simulation (gem5 in full-system mode) is different from the above: it runs the program directly and models instructions with cycle-level timing without using pre-created traces.

Though this chapter primarily addresses creating traces compatible with ChampSim, the principles apply broadly. The most important step is to match your trace format to the downstream simulation requirements. The first step to that end is choosing the right collection approach.

5.2 Choosing a Collection Approach

Primarily, trace collection is achieved via three widely used approaches. Each has its own tradeoffs in terms of what can be captured, the degree of perturbation to the target workload, and the downstream simulators. Let's cover these three methods briefly.

DBI Tracing (Pin, DynamoRIO)

A software layer collects all the information needed by intercepting each instruction at runtime. This enables the collection of detailed data such as instruction addresses, data addresses, branch outcomes, etc. Note that due to the nature of tracing, only user-space, correct-path instructions are available. The interception introduces a 5-20x slowdown depending on the workload patterns and complexity. Generally, the overhead is not an issue since we trace once and simulate multiple times.

There are two common frameworks for DBI tracing: Pin and DynamoRIO. Both are widely used and well-documented.

Hardware Tracing (Intel PT, ARM CoreSight)

Modern processors have built-in logic that monitors control-flow instructions during program execution. This is done with minimal overhead, usually less than 5%. Intel Processor Trace (PT) and ARM CoreSight are such examples from the x86 and ARM architectures, respectively. Due to the minimal overhead, it is possible to trace production workloads, latency-sensitive applications, and kernel code without significantly altering their behavior. The most important trade-off is that this method captures control flow and not the actual data addresses. PT, for example, records only architecturally retired control flow paths and not the wrong-path instructions. Reconstructing the architectural instruction stream from the trace produced by PT requires combining the trace packets with the original program binary, which can be handled by tools like perf and Intel's libipt.

If you need the data addresses as well as the control flow, you can use additional methods such as Intel PEBS (precise event-based sampling) or ARM SPE (statistical profiling extension). These will give you a sample of the memory addresses the application accesses. These addresses are only statistical samples rather than a complete record of memory accesses, unlike the traces produced by DBI.

Full System Simulation (gem5)

Using execution-driven simulators such as gem5 in full-system mode, you can model the entire application, including the processor, memory system, and operating system. All the instructions (user, kernel, wrong path, etc.) are modeled with cycle-level timing. Performance metrics can also be generated directly, without having to collect them separately. This is the most accurate method for modeling an application, but it is also the slowest, as the simulation can be thousands to millions of times slower than native execution.

5.2.1 When to Use Which Approach

The selection of a collection technique depends on the type of your research question, the characteristics of the workload, and the amount of fidelity you need.

When comparing caches, prefetchers, or replacement policies, DBI tracing with tools like Pin, together with ChampSim, is likely the best approach, as it enables rapid iterations, provides abundant address information, and runs entirely in user space.

When your goal is low-perturbation profiling or kernel-inclusive analysis, trace collection from the hardware (e.g., Intel PT or ARM CoreSight) is more appropriate due to its low overhead and visibility into kernel-space activity. Keep in mind that this approach only tracks control flow information, not data addresses.

When full timing fidelity, OS interaction modeling, or speculation analysis is required, full-system execution-driven simulation (i.e., gem5 in full-system mode) is the preferred option, as it simulates all elements.

When doing a quick, high-level characterization of a workload prior to investing in a more detailed study, hardware counters (via perf stat combined with strace) can provide high-level statistics with essentially no tracing overhead.

Workload-specific characteristics should also guide the selection process. For example, if the workload spends a considerable amount (e.g., more than around 10%) of its time executing within the kernel, Intel PT or gem5 in full-system mode would be more appropriate. Likewise, if the branch misprediction rate is high (e.g., 10 mispredictions per thousand instructions or more), gem5 would be preferable due to its ability to simulate incorrect execution paths. Finally, if data addresses are needed, DBI or gem5 should be chosen, as other approaches may not provide those with enough detail.

PT and DBI tracing are complementary, not competitive. A practical workflow would first use PT to quickly characterize a workload, including the kernel, at low perturbation, then use Pin to obtain a detailed trace of the user-space parts of the workload of interest. PT traces can also serve as a reference for validating DBI traces collected during simulation.

The majority of current cache and prefetcher studies follow the DBI method, where Pin or DynamoRIO is used to generate traces for ChampSim or other simulators. Due to this, we will cover this approach primarily in Parts II and III. Next, we examine the DBI tracing method using Intel Pin in more detail.

5.3 Dynamic Binary Instrumentation Using Pin

Pin is a DBI tool that lets you build custom program analysis tools commonly referred to as Pintools. It works without modifying the target application's source code. Let's cover how it works, how to install it, and the Pintool architecture that the ChampSim tracer is built on.

5.3.1 How Pin Works

At a high level, Pin works as a just-in-time (JIT) compiler and uses the executable as its input. When the application runs under Pin, the following steps occur:

- Pin intercepts and takes control before the target application begins executing.
- For each new region that the execution reaches, Pin's JIT compiler disassembles the original instructions, applies the instrumentation specified through the Pintool, and generates an instrumented copy in a software code cache. From then on, this copy is executed in place of the original application code.
- When the instrumented code runs, the analysis callbacks inserted this way fire at specific points as programmed (e.g., before each instruction, memory access, etc.). This enables data collection (such as addresses and branch outcomes) for the trace to be generated.

Note that Pin has no visibility of kernel space execution (Section 5.7).

5.3.2 Starting with Pin

The Pin framework is bundled with extensive documentation in the doc/ directory and example tools in source/tools/. Additionally, some ready-to-build Pintools for demonstrating common patterns like instruction counting, memory tracing, and call graph generation can be found in the ManualExamples/ and SimpleExamples/ subdirectories. You are encouraged to browse and explore how these are used.

5.3.3 Pintools

A Pintool is a shared library that provides instrumentation and data collection logic for a target application. At runtime, Pin loads a Pintool and applies its instrumentation to the target application. Since it is widely used, simulators such as ChampSim include ready-made Pintools for generating their trace format.

A Pintool defines two types of callback functions:

Instrumentation Callbacks: These are invoked by Pin's JIT compiler when it first encounters a code region. These functions inspect the instructions and insert calls to analysis functions at specified points. An instrumentation callback runs once per code region during JIT compilation and does not run during normal execution of the application.

Analysis Callbacks: These functions collect useful data for creating traces and are called each time the instrumented code region executes. These should be kept as lightweight as possible as they are on the application's critical path.

Through this split, the one-time cost of instrumentation is amortized, allowing Pin to scale to programs executing billions of instructions.

As we wrap up this section with a good understanding of the trace collection mechanism, it should be noted that DynamoRIO is another commonly used DBI framework with different performance characteristics. It can be acquired from `https://dynamorio.org/`.

The concepts discussed in this chapter apply to both frameworks, and only the specific commands and API calls vary. With that in mind, let's now see how actual traces are generated for ChampSim.

5.4 Generating ChampSim Traces

In this section, we will cover the main mechanics of trace collection, namely, building the tracer, running it against applications, and compressing the output for efficient storage. In this process, each step produces artifacts for the downstream stage.

5.4.1 Building the Tracer

A Pin-based tracer is included in the ChampSim repository in the tracer/pin/ subdirectory. Listing 5-2 shows how to build it using the make command after navigating to that directory. Note that the PIN_ROOT environment variable must point to your Pin installation (Listing 5-1).

Listing 5-2. Building the ChampSim Tracer

```
cd $CHAMPSIM_ROOT/tracer/pin
make
```

This produces a shared library at obj-intel64/champsim_tracer.so that Pin loads at runtime.

5.4.2 Collecting a Trace

The built tracer can be used to collect traces from applications. It accepts three parameters: the output file name (-o), the number of instructions to skip before tracing starts (-s), and the number of instructions to be traced (-t). Listing 5-3 illustrates the command, and Table 5-2 describes each parameter concisely. You can use the sample program binary provided in the companion repository (ch05-trace-collection/examples/application) to try it yourself.

Listing 5-3. Collecting a Trace with Pin

```
$PIN_ROOT/pin \
    -t $CHAMPSIM_ROOT/tracer/pin/obj-intel64/champsim_
    tracer.so \
    -o trace.champsimtrace \
    -s 1000000 -t 1000000 \
    -- ./application args
```

Table 5-2. *Trace Collection Parameters*

Parameter	Description
-o trace.champsimtrace	Output file name.
-s N	Skip the first N instructions before tracing begins.
-t N	Trace the next N instructions after the skip window.
-- ./application args	Target application and arguments. The "--" separates Pin/tool arguments from the application.

The skip option (-s) is important because applications typically have an initialization period (loading data, building data structures, etc.) that is not representative of steady-state performance. Hence, skipping this phase results in traces that better model the application's workload. Chapter 6 describes the use of SimPoint analysis to develop a systematic approach to selecting skip points.

5.4.3 Trace Compression

Raw traces can be very large, reaching hundreds of GB when the number of captured instructions approaches billions. As a result, compression is essential for trace management. ChampSim can read compressed traces directly in xz, gzip, and bzip2 formats without the need for decompression before simulation. Listing 5-4 provides the xz command.

Listing 5-4. Compressing a Trace

```
xz -9 -k trace.champsimtrace
```

The compression ratio can vary depending on the content of the traces. Highly repetitive loop-heavy workloads may compress by a factor of 20x or more, while irregular access patterns typically achieve 5-10x.

Once traces are collected, we need to check their quality to ensure they can proceed through the rest of the pipeline.

5.5 Trace Validation

Validating traces assures quality for the entire simulation pipeline. Simulations based on flawed traces can waste weeks of computation and may produce misleading results. In this section, we will cover common steps for validating traces, from simple sanity checks to verification with actual hardware.

5.5.1 Sanity Checks

We can start with basic property checks on the generated files. The commands are shown in Listing 5-5.

Listing 5-5. Basic Trace Sanity Checks

```
# List trace file properties (size, etc.)
ls -lh trace.champsimtrace.xz

# Verify trace file integrity
xz -t trace.champsimtrace.xz && echo 'Trace Integrity OK'
```

Extremely small traces may indicate errors during trace collection if not done intentionally. For example, the number of skipped instructions may mistakenly exceed the number of instructions executed by the application.

5.5.2 Instruction Mix Analysis

The basic instruction mix of the trace should be matched against expectations. For ChampSim, it comprises the fraction of branches (records with is_branch set), loads (records with non-zero source memory addresses), stores (records with non-zero destination memory addresses), and the remainder. Listing 5-6 shows a short Python script that extracts this breakdown from a raw trace. Note that the script assumes a 64-byte instruction record layout, which is present at ChampSim's commit 06de8d3 (November 17, 2025). If your version differs, you may need to adjust the script accordingly.

Listing 5-6. Parsing the Instruction Mix from a ChampSim Trace

```
import struct

with open('trace.champsimtrace', 'rb') as f:
    branches = loads = stores = total = 0
    while (rec := f.read(64)):
        if rec[8]: branches += 1              # is_branch byte
```

```
        if any(struct.unpack_from('4Q', rec, 32)): loads += 1
   # source_memory
        if any(struct.unpack_from('2Q', rec, 16)): stores += 1
  # destination_memory
        total += 1

print(f"Total: {total:,}")
print(f"Branches: {branches/total:.1%}  Loads: {loads/
total:.1%}  Stores: {stores/total:.1%}")
```

Generally, a memory-intensive application, such as data processing, should produce traces with a higher number of load/store instructions. Similarly, a control-heavy workload should show a higher branch ratio.

Any significant deviation from expectations indicates either a problem with the trace collection process or a lack of knowledge about the application being studied and hence should be examined closely before proceeding.

5.5.3 Hardware Counter Validation

For additional confidence, you can compare trace-derived instruction counts and branch behavior (from Listing 5-6) with hardware performance counters derived from workload execution. Listing 5-7 illustrates the steps needed to gather hardware counter data for comparison.

Listing 5-7. Gathering Hardware Counters for Validation

```
perf stat -e instructions:u,branches:u,branch-misses:u
./application
```

The :u suffix restricts counting to user-mode instructions only, as Pin traces do not have visibility into kernel space (Section 5.7).

A trace should have similar instruction counts and branch ratios (but not necessarily identical) to those found in the perf stat output. Any significant deviations warrant investigation before continuing.

You can also use the Intel Processor Trace (PT) trace of the same workload (Section 5.2) and compare the instruction counts between the PT and DBI traces to provide another independent validation source.

5.5.4 End-to-End Validation

The final validation is to run the trace through a downstream simulation and verify that the resulting values are reasonable. For example:

- IPC (instructions per clock cycle) should be greater than 0.0 and usually between 0.1 and 4.0 for a default 4-wide pipeline. The upper bound is determined by the simulated execution width.
- The cache hit rate should be between 0.0 and 1.0.
- The results should be repeatable across multiple simulations of the trace.

If any of these conditions (or similar checks) fail, there is likely a problem with the trace that requires further investigation before it can be used for analysis and research.

Once you have validated your traces, proper organization is the next essential step as the collection grows.

5.6 Trace Organization and Management

Even a single study can yield a large volume of raw trace data from multiple sources. If this data is not properly organized, it can undermine reproducibility, create confusion, and yield unreliable results. To that end, in this section, we will discuss ways to organize trace data using trace naming conventions, trace documentation, and trace storage.

5.6.1 Naming Conventions

You should create a systematic naming convention that includes the information needed to understand and reproduce each trace. An example as a reference is listed below (Listing 5-8).

Listing 5-8. Trace Naming Convention

```
[benchmark]-[input]-[skip]-[length].champsimtrace.xz
```

Example:

```
mcf-ref-10B-100M.champsimtrace.xz
gcc-166-50B-200M.champsimtrace.xz
```

This convention includes the benchmark name, the input set, the number of skipped instructions, and the trace length in millions of instructions.

5.6.2 Metadata Documentation

In addition to having naming conventions, it is also important to keep track of your trace metadata, which is any additional information about your traces that you may want to include. An example is shown in Listing 5-9.

Listing 5-9. Trace Metadata Template

```
{
  "benchmark": "mcf",
  "suite": "SPEC CPU 2017",
  "input": "ref",
  "skip_instructions": 10000000000,
  "trace_instructions": 100000000,
```

```
  "collection_method": "Pin DBI (user-space only)",
  "collection_date": "2024-03-15",
  "pin_version": "4.2",
  "tracer_version": "1.0",
  "host_system": "Intel Xeon Gold, Ubuntu 22.04",
  "kernel_fraction_pct": 1.7,
  "checksum_sha256": "a1b2c3d4e5f6...",
  "notes": "Collected for cache replacement study"
}
```

In this example, the collection_method field allows users to determine the method used to collect the trace. The kernel_fraction_pct field measures the percentage of time the workload spends running in the kernel, as discussed further in Section 5.7. This type of information helps in assessing trace fidelity and applicability when running studies.

5.6.3 Storage Considerations

Trace data can take up a considerable amount of disk space, even with compression, as we discussed earlier. For more optimal management, you can keep actively used traces locally and archive completed studies or less common traces remotely in cloud storage. The locations can be documented in version-controlled manifest files.

5.6.4 Version Control and Artifact Management

Though traces themselves are too large to be used effectively with most version control systems (like Git), we still need proper tracking of their origin and lifetime. There are various tools available to help with this, and some are listed below:

- **DVC (Data Version Control)**: DVC works with Git to track large data files through content-addressable storage that includes S3, GCS, and local storage options. This is currently one of the most common tools for version controlling large datasets and artifacts.
- **git-annex**: Similar to DVC, git-annex also tracks large files with a different storage model. It is a good option for researchers who have an existing shared file system.
- **OCI Artifact Registries (GitHub Container Registry, Cloud Provider Registries, etc.)**: This allows versioning trace archives along with a containerized simulation environment, maintaining the reproducibility of the pipeline.

If these methods seem too complicated or not feasible due to other factors, at a minimum, version-control your collection scripts and metadata files, check the integrity of the traces using SHA-256 checksums when transferring, and maintain a version-controlled list of all traces and where they are stored.

With trace organization and management covered, let's examine a couple of issues that influence trace fidelity and applicability.

5.7 Trace Fidelity Limitations

There are two common factors that affect the accuracy and applicability of traces in certain scenarios, namely, the user-kernel gap and wrong-path execution. In this section, we will briefly discuss each, take a look at when they matter, and outline some tools to measure the exposure.

5.7.1 The User-Kernel Gap

Frameworks like Pin run in user space and have no visibility when the application makes a system call and execution transfers to the kernel. The kernel may execute thousands or millions of instructions that change microarchitectural states, but the trace will come out as if two adjacent user-space instructions executed without any gap. This can cause the simulation to overestimate metrics such as cache hit rates and branch prediction accuracy for workloads where syscalls are dominant. To be certain whether this matters for your study, you can measure the exposure with perf, as shown in Listing 5-10.

Listing 5-10. Measuring Kernel Time Exposure

```
perf stat -e instructions:u,instructions:k ./application args

# Example output:
#   85,234,567,890   instructions:u    (user space)
#    1,456,789,012   instructions:k    (kernel space)
#
# Kernel fraction: 1.46B / (85.23B + 1.46B) = 1.7%
```

If the kernel fraction is in the low single digits, the impact on simulation accuracy is likely negligible. However, once it reaches double digits, the trace is likely missing enough instructions to impact the results. You should consider using Intel PT or gem5 in full-system mode in this case.

5.7.2 Missing Wrong-Path Execution

Modern out-of-order processors speculatively execute instructions before branches get resolved. If the prediction turns out to be incorrect, the instructions executed on the wrong path can alter microarchitectural states and consume resources in the pipeline, memory, and buses. Since traces only record committed instructions, downstream simulations may end up not faithfully representing the execution. You can decide if this matters for your studies by looking at the branch misprediction rate as shown in Listing 5-11.

Listing 5-11. Measuring Branch Misprediction Rate

```
perf stat -e instructions:u,branch-misses:u ./application args
```

MPKI (mispredictions per kilo-instruction) can be computed as branch_misses X 1000 / instruction_count. A branch MPKI under 5 indicates that the wrong-path fraction is likely not significant and trace-driven simulation is reliable. Above 10 MPKI, the omitted wrong-path traffic is likely significant enough that trace-driven results should be treated cautiously.

Modeling Perspective: These two factors influence fidelity independently. To be absolutely certain, you must assess both when evaluating the suitability of trace-driven simulation for your study.

With an understanding of the mechanics and limitations of trace collection, let us now conclude the chapter with a summary of the key takeaways.

5.8 Summary

This chapter presented the trace-collection phase of the simulation pipeline. The major takeaways are the following:

First, trace collection can be done with three fundamentally different approaches, namely, DBI tracing (Pin/DynamoRIO), hardware tracing (Intel PT/ARM CoreSight), and execution-driven simulation (gem5 full system). Each comes with trade-offs in data richness, perturbation, and fidelity, and the right method depends on your study requirements.

Second, trace quality depends on the collection parameters used, particularly the skip count and the trace length.

Third, early validation methods such as sanity checks, instruction mix analysis, and hardware counter comparisons are essential for ensuring high-quality, reliable use of traces in studies.

Fourth, for trace-driven simulations, fidelity is limited by two important factors: the user-kernel gap and missing wrong-path execution. You should determine your exposure using perf to evaluate suitability and identify any needed remedies for reliability and representativeness.

Fifth, systematic organization is essential to support reproducibility in research. Establishing naming conventions, properly storing metadata files, creating version-controlled manifest files, and utilizing modern artifact management tools are effective ways to achieve this.

In the next chapter we will walk through an effective sampling methodology that enables selecting representative portions of execution to capture the behavior of applications, making simulations efficient and accurate "enough."

Review Questions

1. What information does an instruction trace capture? What information is lost, and how does it affect the validity of downstream simulation?

2. Compare and contrast the primary methods of tracing discussed in the chapter. Describe scenarios where each of these is most appropriate.

3. What is the importance of the skip parameter during trace collection?

4. Describe the validation checks you would perform after capturing a trace. Why is validation necessary at this stage?

5. You are investigating the cache behavior of a database engine, which spends 20% of the time in the kernel and has a branch misprediction rate of 8 MPKI. Which collection technique do you think is most appropriate and why? What fidelity concerns would still exist?

Exercises

Exercise 1: Run the instruction mix script from Listing 5-6 on the following from the companion repository: stream_access.champsimtrace.xz and random_access.champsimtrace.xz (located in ch05-trace-collection/traces/).

To read xz-compressed traces directly, replace open(...) with lzma.open(...) (you will need to import lzma). Compare the fraction of branch and load instructions. Which trace indicates higher memory intensity? Does this match your expectation given the workload names?

Exercise 2: Decompress the three trace files in ch05-trace-collection/traces/ and compare their sizes. All three contain 30 million instructions, yet their compressed sizes vary widely. Reason about the possible cause, relating the compression ratio to the instruction and address patterns of each workload.

Further Reading

Intel Processor Trace documentation from the Intel Software Developer Manual, Volume 3.

Intel Pin User Guide, `https://www.intel.com/content/www/us/en/developer/articles/tool/pin-a-dynamic-binary-instrumentation-tool.html`.

C.-K. Luk et al., "Pin: Building Customized Program Analysis Tools with Dynamic Instrumentation," Proceedings of the 2005 ACM SIGPLAN Conference on Programming Language Design and Implementation (PLDI), 2005. Foundational paper introducing Intel Pin.

D. L. Bruening, "Efficient, Transparent, and Comprehensive Runtime Code Manipulation," Ph.D. dissertation, MIT, 2004. Foundational work underlying DynamoRIO and runtime binary instrumentation.

A. Jaleel, R. S. Cohn, C.-K. Luk, and B. Jacob, "CMP$im: A Pin-Based On-The-Fly Multi-Core Cache Simulator," Proceedings of the Fourth Annual Workshop on Modeling, Benchmarking and Simulation (MoBS), 2008. Early example of using Pin to drive cache simulation.

M. Yourst, "PTLsim: A Cycle Accurate Full System x86-64 Microarchitectural Simulator," Proceedings of the IEEE International Symposium on Performance Analysis of Systems and Software (ISPASS), 2007. Example of a detailed execution-driven x86-64 simulator.

CHAPTER 6

Sampling and Simulation Efficiency

The previous chapter explored various aspects of trace collection, and we worked through basic examples with manageable instruction counts. In the real world, typical workloads execute billions or trillions of instructions, which is impractical to simulate because simulations run orders of magnitude slower than native execution.

In this chapter, we will cover techniques for capturing representative portions of workload execution, such as traces, to achieve simulation turnaround times of hours rather than weeks or months, while providing meaningful results.

First, we will take a look at the reasons naïve approaches fail to address the problem. Then we will go over a standard methodology called SimPoint for systematic sample selection. Following this, we will discuss warm-up strategies that ensure simulation fidelity while using sampled traces. Finally, we will walk through the complete sampling workflow that ties these techniques together and look at some common pitfalls to avoid.

Prerequisites

This chapter assumes you are familiar with

- Trace collection concepts from Chapter 5
- Basic probability and statistics

A. Pareek, *Performance Modeling of Computer Systems*, Maker Innovations Series,
https://doi.org/10.1007/979-8-8688-2476-0_6

6.1 Why Sampling Matters

As we discussed in Chapter 5, different simulation approaches balance speed against modeling detail. At the fastest end, functional simulators process millions of instructions per second but do not model any timing. As you increase modeling detail, trace-driven simulators such as ChampSim, which model cache hierarchies and memory systems, typically execute a few hundred thousand instructions per second. With more detailed timing, simulators get slower by another order of magnitude or even more.

Workloads, on the other hand, execute hundreds of billions or trillions of instructions, and at the rates mentioned above, even trace-driven simulation can take days. Adding detailed timing can stretch this to weeks or even months.

This combination forces a choice between reduced simulation detail (sacrificing accuracy) or fewer instructions simulated (sacrificing representativeness). Sampling makes long-running workload studies practical without losing useful architectural fidelity.

6.1.1 Application Behavior

Many real-world applications pass through distinct phases during execution. Some examples are listed below:

Initialization: Loading data, allocating structures, one-time setup.

Warm-Up: Structures such as caches and branch predictors transitioning from cold to steady state. This natural warm-up is at the application level and different from the simulation technique we will cover in Section 6.3 despite sharing the name.

Steady-State Execution: The application's representative behavior, once warmed up.

Cleanup: Saving results, closing files, deallocating memory.

In most cases, you would focus on steady-state behavior for simulation, with some warm-up. Any other region captured in traces may misrepresent the application and yield less meaningful results.

6.1.2 Phase Behavior in Steady-State

Even during the steady-state region of the workload, distinct, recurring, finer-grained behavioral phases exist. For example, a sorting algorithm behaves differently during partitioning and merging, and a database query exhibits different behavior during index lookup than during data retrieval.

To illustrate this concept, the companion repository includes a visualization script and a multi-phase trace constructed by stitching together segments from two workloads with different memory behavior. You can run it as shown in Listing 6-1.

Listing 6-1. Phase Behavior in a Trace

```
python3 ch06-sampling/scripts/visualize_phases.py \
      ch06-sampling/traces/multi_phase.champsimtrace.xz \
      --output multi_phase_phases.png
```

The script generates a plot (Figure 6-1) that shows the memory intensity (the fraction of instructions accessing memory) across sequential instruction windows. The plot shows clear phase transitions between low and high memory access behavior.

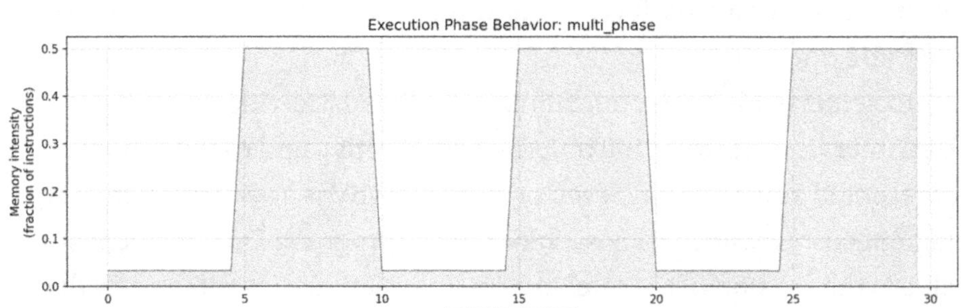

Figure 6-1. *Phase Behavior in a Trace*

Phase recurrence opens up the opportunity to use statistical sampling methods and reduce the information needed to capture the behavior of a workload with fidelity. The core idea is that if a behavioral pattern repeats during execution, we can simulate it once and scale the result by how many times it occurs in the full execution. The next section covers a methodology to achieve this.

6.2 The SimPoint Methodology

Originally developed by Sherwood, Perelman, Hamerly, and Calder at UC San Diego, SimPoint is a commonly used methodology for identifying representative simulation points within a workload. In this section, we will explore the core concepts and walk through practical applications.

6.2.1 Basic Block Vectors

The key insight on which SimPoint relies is that program behavior can be largely characterized by the basic block execution mix of its run. A basic block is a contiguous sequence of instructions with no branches except at the end. In other words, it is a straight-line instruction sequence with one entry and one exit.

To achieve this characterization, a workload is divided into fixed-sized intervals (typically 100 million instructions), and each interval is represented as a basic block vector (BBV). A BBV is a vector where each element corresponds to a basic block in the program. Each element's value is the fraction of the total interval instructions contributed by that specific basic block, normalized by total instructions in the interval. Mathematically it comes out to be the number of times the basic block executes in the interval, multiplied by the number of instructions in it, and divided by the instruction count of the interval.

Similarity in BBV indicates that the intervals execute similar code paths. This, in turn, means that they will likely exhibit similar performance behavior.

Note that heavy data-dependent behavior can break the assumption that the program behavior is driven by the code path; if your workload is strongly data-dependent, BBV similarity may be less representative of workload execution behavior. Listing 6-2 provides a simple example to illustrate BBVs.

Listing 6-2. Basic Block Vector Example

```
Program has 4 basic blocks: A, B, C, D
Interval 1 (100M instructions):
Block A: 2 instructions, 5M executions
Block B: 10 instructions, 4M executions
Block C: 5 instructions, 9M executions
Block D: 1 instruction, 5M executions
BBV_1 = [0.10, 0.40, 0.45, 0.05]
Interval 2 (100M instructions):
Block A: 2 instructions 6M executions
Block B: 10 instructions 3M executions
Block C: 5 instructions 10M executions
Block D: 1 instruction, 8M executions
BBV_2 = [0.12, 0.30, 0.5, 0.08]
BBV_1 and BBV_2 are similar -> similar behavior
```

6.2.2 Clustering and Representative Intervals

Representing each interval as a basic block vector enables us to use statistical operations to understand similarities and differences between intervals. To achieve this, SimPoint uses a well-known technique, k-means clustering, to group similar intervals and identify representative samples to simulate.

While we are not going to cover the process in a detailed manner, the high-level steps involved in clustering are listed below:

1. Collecting BBVs for all intervals from workload execution.
2. Applying dimensionality reduction with random projection to keep clustering computationally manageable.
3. Running k-means clustering for various values of k and selecting a suitable k using the Bayesian Information Criterion (which involves choosing the fewest clusters that reach a high percentage of the observed BIC score range).
4. Choosing one representative interval from each cluster.
5. Using the cluster's share of total intervals to assign weights to the corresponding simulation point.

Carrying out these steps results in a small set of simulation points that represent the entire execution, and makes it possible to run studies and iterate in a manageable time.

6.2.3 SimPoint in the Workflow

SimPoint sits between trace collection and simulation. You need two dependencies to use it: a BBV collector that profiles the application, and the SimPoint tool itself to cluster the BBVs.

For BBV collection, you can use Valgrind's exp-bbv tool. It is widely used with SimPoint and can be built from the source (`https://valgrind.org/`). It is also available through most Linux package managers (e.g., apt install valgrind on Debian/Ubuntu or conda install -c conda-forge valgrind for conda-based environments).

For clustering you can get the SimPoint source from GitHub (github.com/hanhwi/SimPoint) and build it as shown in Listing 6-3. We install SimPoint in the $HOME/simpoint directory and refer to it using the SIMPOINT_ROOT environment variable.

Listing 6-3. Building SimPoint

```
git clone https://github.com/hanhwi/SimPoint.git $HOME/simpoint
cd $HOME/simpoint
make
export SIMPOINT_ROOT=$HOME/simpoint
```

This will generate the binary at $SIMPOINT_ROOT/bin/simpoint.

Using these two tools, we can collect BBVs and cluster them with SimPoint as shown in Listing 6-4 below, with expected outputs. The companion repository provides a pre-built binary (ch06-sampling/examples/phase_test) to serve as an example workload for BBV collection and clustering.

Listing 6-4. SimPoint Pipeline

```
# Step 1: Collect BBVs using Valgrind's exp-bbv tool
valgrind --tool=exp-bbv \
    --bb-out-file=phase_test.bb \
    --interval-size=1000000 \
    ch06-sampling/examples/phase_test

# Valgrind output (among other messages):
#   Total intervals: 48 (Interval Size 1000000)
#   Total instructions: 48400614

# Step 2: Run SimPoint clustering
$SIMPOINT_ROOT/bin/simpoint \
    -loadFVFile phase_test.bb -maxK 30 \
```

```
    -saveSimpoints phase_test.simpoints \
    -saveSimpointWeights phase_test.weights

# SimPoint selects the best clustering: k = 3
#
# phase_test.simpoints:
#   19 0
#    1 1
#   15 2
#
# phase_test.weights:
#   0.666667 0
#   0.083333 1
#   0.250000 2
```

The listing shows the output files dumped by SimPoint. In the phase_test.simpoints file, each line contains an interval number (left) and a cluster label (right). In the phase_test.weights file, each line contains the weight (Section 6.2.5) and the cluster label corresponding to the other file. You can use your own applications instead of phase_test as needed.

Disclaimer: Exact results from SimPoint may vary slightly across tool versions and random initializations within the tools. This includes the selected intervals and their weights. The workflow remains the same and can be applied to varied use cases. The reference outputs used in the listings in the chapter were generated with Valgrind 3.26.0 and Pin 4.2. Furthermore, SimPoint commands were run with -seedkm 4 -seedproj 4 to make clustering reproducible. These flags fix the random initialization seeds within the tools.

If your output differs, compare the workflow and output structure rather than expecting the exact same intervals. **The interval IDs used in this chapter assume the SimPoint output from Listing 6-4.**

The information in these files is useful for the next step where we collect traces for the selected intervals. Table 6-1 summarizes the key parameters used in the workflow. The next section covers how to collect traces for desired intervals.

Table 6-1. *Key Sampling Pipeline Parameters*

Parameter	Tool	Typical Value	Effect
`--interval-size`	Valgrind exp-bbv	100000000	Instructions per interval. Controls granularity of phase detection. Listing 6-4 uses 1M as an illustrative example.
`-maxK`	SimPoint	30	Maximum clusters to search
`-coveragePct`	SimPoint	0.95-1.0	Fraction of execution the selected points must cover
`-numInitSeeds`	SimPoint	5-100	Random initializations per k value. Higher values improve clustering stability

6.2.4 From SimPoint to Traces

As we saw in the last section, SimPoint produces a list of the representative intervals to capture. This information can be used to collect traces for simulation. Commonly used tracers allow you to control the skip count and the trace length. For large workloads with hundreds of billions of instructions, this is essential for efficient storage management. However, for the example workload used (phase_test), the number of instructions is small enough that tracing the entire execution is simpler and practical.

This also allows additional flexibility to work with exercises later. Following the tracing workflow covered in Chapter 5, Listing 6-5 shows how to collect and compress traces for ChampSim. Note that instruction totals reported by different tools may differ slightly as the counting methods are not identical.

Listing 6-5. Collecting a Full Trace

```
$PIN_ROOT/pin \
    -t $CHAMPSIM_ROOT/tracer/pin/obj-intel64/champsim_
    tracer.so \
    -o phase_test.champsimtrace \
    -- ch06-sampling/examples/phase_test

# Example Output: phase_test.champsimtrace (48,400,309
instructions, ~2.9 GB)

xz -9 phase_test.champsimtrace
# Example Compressed Size: phase_test.champsimtrace.xz
(~1.8 MB)
```

To simulate a specific interval, you need to supply the starting point and the interval length to the simulator, along with the trace. The interval start instruction is simply the interval index multiplied by the fixed-size interval length you specified during the BBV creation process (Table 6-1). In our example, for an interval size of 1,000,000, the intervals selected by SimPoint, i.e., 19, 1, and 15, start at instructions 19,000,000, 1,000,000, and 15,000,000, respectively. Listing 6-6 shows an example using interval 19 from Listing 6-4. Since ChampSim does not take a separate interval starting point as an argument, --warmup-instructions is combined to advance through the trace from the beginning up to the measurement point. Section 6.3 covers warm-up in detail.

Listing 6-6. SimPoint Interval Simulation

```
# Reference example using SimPoint-selected interval 19
# Skip: 19 x 1,000,000 = 19,000,000 instructions
# Warmup: 500,000 additional instructions (Section 6.3)
# Simulate: 1,000,000 instructions (one interval)
# Combining warm-up and skip for ChampSim specific flag
# Total warm-up = 19500000

$CHAMPSIM_ROOT/bin/champsim \
    --warmup-instructions 19500000 \
    --simulation-instructions 1000000 \
    phase_test.champsimtrace.xz
# Output: IPC = 2.50
```

Since each interval produces its own metrics on simulation, it is important to aggregate these properly.

6.2.5 Weighted Results

We saw a weight file in the SimPoint output in Section 6.2.3, alongside the simulation points. Each weight represents the fraction of total execution covered by the cluster represented by that simulation point. Weights help in making sure that phases influence the overall result in proportion to the execution time that they represent. Listing 6-7 shows how to compute weighted aggregate IPC using the values measured for the reference intervals in this chapter. We will look at the general aggregation formula and then apply a SimPoint-specific simplification.

Listing 6-7. Weighted Aggregate IPC

```
# Simulation results and weights:
# Interval 19 : IPC = 2.50  (CPI = 0.40), weight = 0.667
# Interval 1  : IPC = 0.70  (CPI = 1.43), weight = 0.083
```

```
# Interval 15 : IPC = 0.12  (CPI = 8.33), weight = 0.250

# Rates such as IPC cannot be averaged directly. The general
# rule is to aggregate the underlying quantities and divide:
#
#   IPC = sum(w_i * instructions_i) / sum(w_i * cycles_i)
#
# Since all SimPoint intervals have the same instruction count
# (1M here), the instruction terms factor out and the
# formula simplifies to a weighted arithmetic mean of CPI.
# It is then inverted to get the IPC.
# When such simplification is not possible, use the
# general formula directly.

CPI = (0.40 x 0.667) + (1.43 x 0.083) + (8.33 x 0.250)
    = 0.267 + 0.119 + 2.083
    = 2.469

IPC = 1 / 2.469 ~= 0.405
```

Some other rate metrics, such as miss rates, bandwidth utilization, and branch misprediction rates, can be computed in a similar way. Additive quantities such as total cycles, energy, or total instructions can be computed with direct weighted summation.

6.2.6 Other Sampling Approaches

Though this book primarily covers SimPoint, other alternatives exist and may be suitable in certain scenarios.

Simpler options, such as random sampling, where we select intervals uniformly at random relying on the law of large numbers for convergence, and systematic sampling, where we select periodic intervals, are suitable when you need easier implementation. These do not explicitly account for phase awareness and can under-represent important regions of the workload.

A more comprehensive, but fundamentally different, approach is SMARTS (Sampling Microarchitecture Simulation). Introduced by Wunderlich et al., it inverts SimPoint's philosophy. Instead of relying on finding and simulating a few long representative intervals, SMARTS simulates a large number of short measurements of a few thousand instructions spread across the full execution of the workload. For this to work, the simulator needs to support the ability to run in fast functional mode between measurement windows (while keeping the microarchitectural state realistic). When a measurement window arrives, a detailed simulation is run, metrics are recorded, and at the end, the mode switches back to fast execution.

This pattern of interleaving fast and detailed simulation makes it more suitable to execution-driven simulators. For more details, you can read the SMARTS paper listed in the Further Reading section.

Modeling Perspective: When conducting comparative analysis, you should check whether the improvements are consistent across simulation points instead of being driven by a very small number of outliers. For example, if one point shows a 40% speedup while the rest are negligible, the weighted average may be misleading. In such cases, reporting the per-point breakdown would make the results more transparent and trustworthy.

As we have seen, SimPoint (and similar approaches) tells us which intervals to simulate. Since our goal is to sample and simulate isolated intervals from workloads while preserving fidelity, we also need to ensure the microarchitectural state at the start of these intervals reflects what occurs in the actual workload run to some degree. The next section explains how to achieve this.

6.3 Warm-Up Strategies

Consider simulating an interval starting from the 50 billionth instruction. In a real execution, all the preceding 50 billion instructions would have influenced the microarchitectural state of the machine. You cannot analytically deduce how the state has been shaped over time. In the extreme case, if you start the simulation fresh at that instruction, the initial cache misses, prefetcher, and branch predictor behavior will not reflect the real execution.

This problem, if left unchecked, will bias results and undermine the advantages of using SimPoint to trim the number of simulated instructions.

This section covers strategies for properly initializing the microarchitectural state at the start of a simulation point (referred to as warm-up), along with guidelines to choose among them.

6.3.1 Functional Warming

Since we are not interested in collecting metrics before the selected interval starts, we can execute the preceding instructions functionally without timing simulation. This works because the primary goal is to populate caches and structures and to train branch predictors and prefetchers without the overhead of tracking latencies, dependencies, or scheduling.

ChampSim achieves this with the --warmup-instructions flag. When you input --warmup-instructions 19500000 (Listing 6-6), ChampSim reads the trace from the beginning until the 19.5 millionth instruction in fast warmup mode, where it populates caches and trains predictors with zero-latency pipeline shortcuts.

6.3.2 Checkpointing

Checkpointing is an alternative to functional simulation. You can save the microarchitectural state at specific points corresponding to the intervals of interest and restore it just before simulating those intervals.

The trade-off here is that saving checkpoints requires a full execution, with the state saving mechanism invoked at desired points. It needs extra storage to save these states as well, which increases proportional to the information being saved.

In this book, we will use functional warm-up as the go-to methodology when needed. The next section covers some guidelines to help with it.

6.3.3 Warming Length Guidelines

It is hard to quantify exactly the amount of warming-up needed, and the effort may not be warranted, given that sampling itself approximates the actual workload execution. A heuristic for verifying whether warming is sufficient is to run the same simulation with twice the warming length. If the results change significantly, it wasn't set right, and you need to add more warming until it stabilizes. A more rigorous approach is plotting metrics such as cache miss rate vs. warmup length and identifying the region where the curve flattens.

Table 6-2 provides rough guidance to be used as a starting point. Specific numbers should be confirmed using the methodology (or heuristic) we discussed above. Since all structures warm up simultaneously, you should choose the length corresponding to the largest structure of your configuration.

Table 6-2. *Recommended Warming Lengths (Heuristic)*

Structure	Typical Size	Recommended Warming
L1 cache	32–64 KB	1–10M instructions
L2 cache	512 KB to 2 MB	10–50M instructions
Last-level cache	2–32 MB	50–200M instructions
Branch predictor	Varies	10–50M instructions

With phase detection, representative selection, trace collection, and warm-up in place, let us cover some common pitfalls that may undermine sampling workflows.

6.4 Common Pitfalls

Several problems can creep in during sampling workflows and quietly produce unreliable results, leading to wasted efforts. Therefore, recognizing these common pitfalls and knowing the symptoms early on is immensely important. The most common issues are listed below.

6.4.1 Insufficient Warming

If you observe severely low hit rates (or high miss rates), the measurement interval may be starting cold, with insufficient warm-up. Check the techniques covered in Section 6.3.3 to recalibrate if needed.

6.4.2 Short Intervals

If the selected interval length isn't long enough to capture or exhibit stable behavior, clustering can become noisy. This would result in SimPoint creating too many clusters. You should start with 100M long intervals and check whether SimPoint selects a k close to your -maxK parameter. If it does, try increasing the interval length. Interval length selection is a balancing act depending on what you want to model. Shorter intervals can help capture finer phase changes, whereas longer ones usually produce stable clustering.

6.4.3 Ignoring Low-Weight Points

Despite having low weight, a simulation point can still be representative of rare phases with an outsized impact. For example, a short LLC thrashing phase may account for most of the off-chip bandwidth needed by the workload. Not considering this point would be to ignore the stressful phases of the workload. You should not discard simulation points because of low weights.

6.4.4 Unweighted Averaging

Using a simple mean is misrepresentative of the underlying workload, as weights indicate the relative impact of phases on performance. See Section 6.2.5 for details.

Avoiding these pitfalls and following the workflow covered in this chapter helps produce high-quality, reliable results that faithfully represent workload behavior.

6.5 Summary

This chapter covered the sampling stage of the simulation pipeline. Starting with collecting BBVs, it covered clustering with SimPoint, tracing with Pin, simulating with ChampSim, and finally, calculating weighted aggregate results. The key takeaways are:

First, sampling is vital and cannot be emphasized enough. Full simulation of multi-billion-instruction workloads is practically impossible within a reasonable amount of time.

Second, we covered SimPoint, a method for systematically identifying representative simulation points. It reduces the sample space by characterizing execution intervals with BBVs and clustering similar intervals.

Third, proper warm-up is extremely important to ensure the validity of sample-based simulation. We discussed two methods, namely functional warming and checkpointing to achieve this.

Fourth, to properly represent a workload, results from individual simulation points must be aggregated with respective SimPoint weights. Additionally, you must check that the results are not driven by outliers and consistently represent the scope of the study.

The next chapter will address the final stage of Part II; it will cover what common simulation metrics mean, how to know if their values are reasonable, and how to compare results across configurations.

Review Questions

1. Why is it not advisable to simulate only the beginning of a workload? What are the common, distinct behavioral phases applications exhibit, and how can this approach capture or miss those?

2. Elaborate on the concept of basic block vectors. How is the similarity in BBVs representative of similar execution behavior?

3. In a hypothetical scenario, you observe that increasing the warm-up from 50M to 100M instructions changes the cache miss rate from 15% to 12%. How can this be interpreted, and what should be the next course of action?

Exercises

Exercise 1: Using the full phase_test trace from Section 6.2.4, simulate the three SimPoint intervals (19, 1, and 15). Compare the IPC values across the three intervals and calculate the weighted IPC using the method shown in Section 6.2.5.

Exercise 2: Pick an interval that SimPoint did not select. Simulate it with ChampSim and compare the resulting IPC to the IPC of the nearest SimPoint representative (closest interval index). How close are the values? What can you infer from this about the quality of SimPoint's clustering?

Exercise 3: Re-run the SimPoint pipeline from Section 6.2.3 on the phase_test binary, using a different interval size (--interval-size=N instead of 1000000). How does this change the number of intervals? Compare the resulting clusters and their weights to the original run. Simulate the newly selected intervals, and compute the weighted IPC. What can you infer about the sensitivity of SimPoint results to the interval size?

Further Reading

T. Sherwood, E. Perelman, G. Hamerly, and B. Calder, "Automatically Characterizing Large Scale Program Behavior," Proceedings of the 10th International Conference on Architectural Support for Programming Languages and Operating Systems (ASPLOS), 2002. The original SimPoint paper.

E. Perelman, G. Hamerly, and B. Calder, "Picking Statistically Valid and Early Simulation Points," Proceedings of the 12th International Conference on Parallel Architectures and Compilation Techniques (PACT), 2003. Extends SimPoint with improved clustering and the BIC-based selection process.

R. E. Wunderlich, T. F. Wenisch, B. Falsafi, and J. C. Hoe, "SMARTS: Accelerating Microarchitecture Simulation via Rigorous Statistical Sampling," Proceedings of the 30th Annual International Symposium on Computer Architecture (ISCA), 2003. An alternative sampling methodology (SMARTS).

SimPoint tool and documentation, `https://cseweb.ucsd.edu/~calder/simpoint/`.

CHAPTER 7

Understanding Simulation Output

The previous two chapters of Part II covered methodologies for producing simulation results that included collecting reliable traces and selecting representative simulation points. In this chapter, we will look at how to proceed once we have simulation results.

Generally, simulator runs (like ChampSim in this case) generate multiple numbers corresponding to architectural states (or derivations from them), including IPC, cache miss rates, branch misprediction counts, and DRAM row buffer stats. It is important to learn how to connect those to architectural conclusions.

Note that the scope of this chapter is bounded on purpose. We will not focus on explaining why the microarchitecture behaves in a particular way, as that is suited to subsequent chapters, where we will have proper foundations to cover it. The charter here is to give you enough to read and reason about the output. Specifically, to know what each field means, whether the value is reasonable, and what it suggests about the workload. We will also briefly cover proper ways to report comparative analysis from different simulations and some sanity checks to make sure the results are valid. Though we will use ChampSim as the example simulator, the concepts transfer to other simulators as well.

A. Pareek, *Performance Modeling of Computer Systems*, Maker Innovations Series,
https://doi.org/10.1007/979-8-8688-2476-0_7

Prerequisites

This chapter assumes you are familiar with

- ChampSim simulation basics and the trace-driven pipeline (Chapters 5 and 6)
- Basic cache and prefetcher-related concepts
- Sampling and weighted averaging from Chapter 6

7.1 Structure of ChampSim Output

Let's take a look at the general structure of the output. ChampSim writes simulation results to standard output by default. Depending on your needs, you can redirect it to a per-trace results file or other files that suit your specific needs.

7.1.1 The Output Report

The output from ChampSim consists of five major sections, printed in order. An annotated example is shown in Listing 7-1.

Listing 7-1. ChampSim Output Structure

```
# -- Section 1: Startup banner --

*** ChampSim Multicore Out-of-Order Simulator ***
Warmup Instructions: 50000000
Simulation Instructions: 100000000
Number of CPUs: 1
Page size: 4096
```

```
# -- Section 2: Heartbeat progress --

Heartbeat CPU 0 instructions: 10000001 cycles: 9050000
heartbeat IPC: 1.105 cumulative IPC: 1.105 (Simulation time: 00
hr 00 min 42 sec)
Heartbeat CPU 0 instructions: 20000003 cycles: 18210000
heartbeat IPC: 1.092 cumulative IPC: 1.098 (Simulation time: 00
hr 01 min 23 sec)

# Printed every 10M instructions during warmup and simulation.
# heartbeat IPC: covers only the most recent 10M-instruction
interval.
# cumulative IPC: covers all instructions from the start of the
current phase.
# Simulation time: wall-clock elapsed time from simulation start.

# -- Section 3: Phase boundaries --

Warmup finished CPU 0 instructions: 50000001 cycles: 45230000
cumulative IPC: 1.106 (Simulation time: 00 hr 03 min 30 sec)
Warmup complete CPU 0 instructions: 50000001 cycles: 45230000
cumulative IPC: 1.106 (Simulation time: 00 hr 03 min 30 sec)

# All prior heartbeats belong to the warmup phase.
# Microarchitectural state is now populated and measurement
starts here.

Simulation finished CPU 0 instructions: 100000000 cycles:
106450000 cumulative IPC: 0.9394 (Simulation time: 00 hr
15 min 12 sec)
Simulation complete CPU 0 instructions: 100000000 cycles:
106450000 cumulative IPC: 0.9394 (Simulation time: 00 hr
15 min 12 sec)

ChampSim completed all CPUs
```

```
# -- Section 4: Region of Interest statistics --

=== Simulation ===
CPU 0 runs traces/example.champsimtrace.xz
Region of Interest Statistics

CPU 0 cumulative IPC: 0.9394 instructions: 100000000 cycles:
106450000
CPU 0 Branch Prediction Accuracy: 97.42% MPKI: 3.245 Average
ROB Occupancy at Mispredict: 48.2
Branch type MPKI
BRANCH_DIRECT_JUMP: 0.0001
BRANCH_INDIRECT: 0.003
BRANCH_CONDITIONAL: 3.049
BRANCH_DIRECT_CALL: 0.183
BRANCH_INDIRECT_CALL: 0.006
BRANCH_RETURN: 0.004

cpu0->cpu0_ITLB TOTAL ACCESS: 12500000 HIT: 12499980 MISS: 20
MSHR_MERGE: 0
cpu0->cpu0_ITLB PREFETCH REQUESTED: 0 ISSUED: 0 USEFUL: 0
USELESS: 0
cpu0->cpu0_ITLB AVERAGE MISS LATENCY: 19.05 cycles
cpu0->cpu0_DTLB TOTAL ACCESS: 38000000 HIT: 37850000 MISS:
150000 MSHR_MERGE: 95000
cpu0->cpu0_DTLB PREFETCH REQUESTED: 0 ISSUED: 0 USEFUL: 0
USELESS: 0
cpu0->cpu0_DTLB AVERAGE MISS LATENCY: 24.31 cycles
cpu0->cpu0_L1I TOTAL ACCESS: 12499980 HIT: 12499600 MISS: 380
MSHR_MERGE: 0
cpu0->cpu0_L1I PREFETCH REQUESTED: 0 ISSUED: 0 USEFUL: 0
USELESS: 0
cpu0->cpu0_L1I AVERAGE MISS LATENCY: 168.2 cycles
```

```
cpu0->cpu0_L1D TOTAL ACCESS: 38000000 HIT: 35000000 MISS:
3000000 MSHR_MERGE: 0
cpu0->cpu0_L1D PREFETCH REQUESTED: 0 ISSUED: 0 USEFUL: 0
USELESS: 0
cpu0->cpu0_L1D AVERAGE MISS LATENCY: 38.51 cycles
cpu0->cpu0_L2C TOTAL ACCESS: 3000380 HIT: 2500000 MISS: 500380
MSHR_MERGE: 0
cpu0->cpu0_L2C PREFETCH REQUESTED: 0 ISSUED: 0 USEFUL: 0
USELESS: 0
cpu0->cpu0_L2C AVERAGE MISS LATENCY: 152.3 cycles
cpu0->LLC TOTAL ACCESS: 500380 HIT: 350266 MISS: 150114 MSHR_
MERGE: 0
cpu0->LLC PREFETCH REQUESTED: 0 ISSUED: 0 USEFUL: 0 USELESS: 0
cpu0->LLC AVERAGE MISS LATENCY: 179.4 cycles

# -- Section 5: DRAM statistics --

DRAM Statistics

Channel 0 RQ ROW_BUFFER_HIT: 80000
ROW_BUFFER_MISS: 70000
AVG DBUS CONGESTED CYCLE: 2.814
Channel 0 WQ ROW_BUFFER_HIT: 20000
ROW_BUFFER_MISS: 10000
FULL: 0
Channel 0 REFRESHES ISSUED: 1842
```

An important marker to watch for is the warm-up boundary. Metrics printed after that reflect the correct statistics for a warmed-up microarchitectural state. As an example, launching ChampSim with --warmup-instructions 50000000 and --simulation-instructions 100000000 should produce the “Warmup finished” and “Warmup complete” messages near the 50M instruction mark. Simulation of the relevant instructions will start from there, and once completed, detailed results appear under the Region of Interest Statistics header. These numbers correspond to the activity during warmed-up simulation and are valid for analysis. For brevity, only partial information is shown for each cache level.

You can monitor the general progress of the simulation with the heartbeat values printed periodically. These show the number of instructions and cycles simulated during each heartbeat interval along with the IPC calculated from these. Additionally, it shows the cumulative IPC, which is the total instructions divided by the cycles taken up to that point, and the wall clock time elapsed from the start. You can use these for sanity checks against bugs or to check the overall phase behavior of the workload.

7.1.2 Output and the Simulation Pipeline

In Chapter 6, we saw how SimPoint produces multiple simulation points, each representing a set number of instructions (e.g., 100M), as a proxy for a full workload. The output structure applies the same way to each point. To report workload-level metrics such as IPC, calculate the weighted mean across all points (or files, if results are stored separately), as discussed earlier. Interpretations in this chapter apply at the per-point level.

Now that we have understood the general output structure, let's work through the important metric families, starting with throughput.

7.2 Throughput Metrics

Throughput metrics capture how efficiently instructions execute through the microarchitecture. Usually, these are headline numbers from a study because they convey the overall performance impact through a single quantity.

7.2.1 Instructions Per Cycle (IPC)

IPC is the standard primary metric for many simulation studies. It is independent of clock frequency and directly reflects how effectively the memory hierarchy and branch predictor are serving the execution core.

The IPC ceiling for a given configuration is determined by the width of the narrowest pipeline stage. It lets you gauge how close the pipeline is to peak efficiency for a given workload. A workload severely below this ceiling is stall-bound (recall the compute-memory balance discussed in Chapter 2). Statistics from units such as the branch predictor and cache can reveal more information on the stalls.

Table 7-1 provides some rough guidelines for interpreting IPC values. These are more for illustrative purposes, and you should rely on your experience, intuition, and workload-specific behavior for real analysis.

Table 7-1. *IPC Reference Ranges (Four-Wide Configuration)*

IPC Range	Interpretation	Likely Bottleneck	Typical Workload Class
3.0–4.0	Near peak throughput; the core is rarely stalled	None dominant; compute-bound	Dense linear algebra, SIMD-heavy loops
2.0–3.0	Good utilization with moderate stalls	L1/L2 misses or branch mispredictions	Efficient integer or FP-dominant compute
1.0–2.0	Significant stalls; memory or branch pressure	L2 or LLC misses	Mixed memory and compute
0.5–1.0	Heavy stalls; memory-bound behavior	LLC misses; DRAM latency	Pointer-chasing, irregular graphs
< 0.5	Extreme stalls; dominated by DRAM latency	LLC MPKI > 10; high DRAM traffic	Large working set, database scans

7.2.2 CPI and the Stall Budget

Sometimes, the inverse of IPC, cycles per instruction (CPI), is more intuitive for stall analysis. Stall contributions are additive to some extent. For example, in principle, total CPI is approximately the base CPI plus stalls from memory misses, branch mispredictions, and other delays if relevant.

This framing offers a useful mental model when low IPC is observed, prompting you to ask which stall component is dominant and directing you toward additional helpful statistics, such as cache and branch prediction metrics. For the scope of the current chapter, this decomposition should be used as a reasoning guide, and detailed microarchitectural analysis will be covered in subsequent chapters focused on CPU modeling.

Since component statistics help us move beyond IPC as the singular performance indicator and verify that overall performance changes are consistent with individual components, let's turn to them in the following sections.

7.3 Cache Metrics

ChampSim outputs separate statistics for each level of the cache subsystem. Let's look at the important metrics and how to read them across levels.

7.3.1 Cache Statistics

The simulation output reports detailed cache statistics for each level. Listing 7-2 shows the full output block for the LLC from Listing 7-1.

Listing 7-2. LLC Cache Statistics

```
cpu0->LLC TOTAL        ACCESS:     500380 HIT:
350266 MISS:     150114 MSHR_MERGE:          0
cpu0->LLC LOAD         ACCESS:        ... HIT:          ...
MISS:        ... MSHR_MERGE:        ...
cpu0->LLC RFO          ACCESS:        ... HIT:          ...
MISS:        ... MSHR_MERGE:        ...
cpu0->LLC PREFETCH     ACCESS:        ... HIT:          ...
MISS:        ... MSHR_MERGE:        ...
cpu0->LLC WRITE        ACCESS:        ... HIT:          ...
MISS:        ... MSHR_MERGE:        ...
cpu0->LLC TRANSLATION  ACCESS:        ... HIT:          ...
MISS:        ... MSHR_MERGE:        ...
cpu0->LLC PREFETCH REQUESTED:     0 ISSUED:
0 USEFUL:     0 USELESS:     0
cpu0->LLC AVERAGE MISS LATENCY: 179.4 cycles
```

The TOTAL line summarizes all access types. ACCESS is the total number of requests to that level, HIT is the count satisfied, and MISS is the number of cache lookups that failed at the cache level. ACCESS equals HIT + MISS. The per-type lines below break this down by access type: LOAD (demand reads), RFO (read-for-ownership), PREFETCH, WRITE (writebacks from upper levels), and TRANSLATION (page table walks).

From the TOTAL fields, we can derive two useful metrics. Hit rate is the fraction of accesses satisfied at a given level, computed as HIT / ACCESS. In the example, 350,266 / 500,380 = 70%. MPKI (misses per kilo instructions) captures the total miss burden per instruction, computed as (MISS / INSTRUCTIONS) * 1000. MPKI folds together the miss rate and the workload's memory access frequency, making it a better indicator of performance impact. For example, a 50% miss rate matters little if the workload rarely accesses memory.

For general guidance, Table 7-2 provides reference MPKI ranges for the LLC. You should only treat them as examples and not strict decision guidelines for your experiments.

Table 7-2. *LLC MPKI Reference Ranges*

LLC MPKI	Characterization	DRAM Traffic Impact	Example Workload Class
< 1	LLC largely absorbs the working set	Low, DRAM is rarely accessed	Compute-bound workloads with moderate working sets
1 -- 5	Significant but manageable LLC pressure	Moderate DRAM traffic	Mixed workloads, some irregular access
5 -- 15	LLC misses are a primary bottleneck	High DRAM traffic; bandwidth may constrain IPC	Large graph workloads, some databases
> 15	LLC cannot contain the working set	DRAM-bound; IPC dominated by latency	Large streaming or pointer-chasing workloads

Beyond hits and misses, the output includes two other fields. MSHR_MERGE (or MISS_MERGE depending on the ChampSim version) counts how many requests to the same cache line were combined with an already-outstanding miss, avoiding redundant accesses to the next level. A high merge count relative to misses indicates repeated accesses to the same lines while they are still being serviced. AVERAGE MISS LATENCY is the average number of cycles from issuing a demand miss to receiving its data, reflecting the combined cost of queuing, lower-level lookups, and DRAM access.

7.3.2 Cross-Level Cache Analysis

By reading cache stats hierarchically, you can see the propagation of the miss stream through access counts at each level. Listing 7-3 shows an example.

Listing 7-3. Cache Hierarchy Miss Propagation

```
Cache TOTAL lines from Listing 7-1:
cpu0->cpu0_L1D  TOTAL ACCESS: 38,000,000 MISS: 3,000,000  ->
MPKI: 30.0
cpu0->cpu0_L2C  TOTAL ACCESS: 3,000,380  MISS: 500,380    ->
MPKI: 5.0
cpu0->LLC       TOTAL ACCESS: 500,380    MISS: 150,114    ->
MPKI: 1.5
L2C ACCESS ~= L1D MISS + L1I MISS (3,000,380 ~ 3,000,000 + 380)
Every L1 miss reaches L2C. Expected.
L2C absorbs 83% of what L1D missed:
(3,000,000 - 500,380) / 3,000,000 ~ 0.833
LLC ACCESS ~= L2C MISS (500,380 ~ 500,380)
Almost every L2C miss reaches LLC. Expected.
LLC absorbs 70% of what L2C missed:
(500,380 - 150,114) / 500,380 = 0.700
150,114 misses reach DRAM per 100M instructions (LLC MPKI 1.5)
```

Per-level MPKI values are indicative of where the application's working set resides. A high L1 cache MPKI paired with a low L2 cache MPKI suggests that the L1 cache is under capacity or conflict pressure, while the L2 is sufficient for the working set. Similarly, a high MPKI at LLC indicates that the working set exceeds on-chip capacity entirely.

7.3.3 Prefetcher Statistics

ChampSim prints prefetch statistics for every cache level in the hierarchy. When prefetching is disabled for a level, the values are all zeroes. Listing 7-4 shows each field using the LLC prefetch line as an example.

Listing 7-4. Prefetcher Statistics

```
cpu0->LLC PREFETCH REQUESTED: 200000 ISSUED: 195000 USEFUL:
117000 USELESS: 78000
```

The output contains four fields. REQUESTED is the number of prefetches generated by the prefetch logic. ISSUED is the number accepted into the prefetch queue. If ISSUED is less than REQUESTED, it indicates that some prefetches were dropped due to lack of space in the queue. USEFUL is the number of prefetched lines accessed by a demand request, and conversely, USELESS counts the number of lines prefetched but evicted without being used.

Beyond the printed stats, prefetcher behavior is commonly characterized by accuracy and coverage. Both are important in understanding the impact of prefetching on performance.

Accuracy is the fraction of all the prefetches issued that served demand. It can be calculated as USEFUL/ISSUED. In Listing 7-4, it is 117,000 / 195,000 = 60%. You may also see it calculated as USEFUL/(USEFUL+USELESS). In the method shown here, we account for pending in-flight and resident prefetches at simulation end. The two formulas typically produce similar values, and we will use USEFUL / ISSUED throughout for consistency.

Coverage denotes the fraction of misses eliminated by prefetching. However, to know the baseline, or the total number of misses without prefetching, you would need to run a simulation with the prefetcher turned off. Once you have the cache misses from both runs, it can be calculated as (baseline MISS - prefetch MISS) / baseline MISS.

High coverage with low accuracy indicates excessive unused prefetching, whereas low coverage and high accuracy point to the prefetcher being too conservative. We will apply these metrics to real experiments in Chapter 9.

After covering cache- and prefetcher-related statistics, let's turn to another output section that helps characterize where execution cycles go, i.e., the branch predictor.

7.4 Branch Predictor Metrics

ChampSim reports branch statistics in a separate block. The statistics reported can be used to assess whether branch behavior is a significant contributor to the observed performance. The branch output block from Listing 7-1 is reproduced in Listing 7-5 with annotations.

Listing 7-5. Branch Prediction Statistics

```
CPU 0 Branch Prediction Accuracy: 97.42% MPKI: 3.245 Average
ROB Occupancy at
  Mispredict: 48.2
  Branch type MPKI
  BRANCH_DIRECT_JUMP: 0.0001
  BRANCH_INDIRECT: 0.003
  BRANCH_CONDITIONAL: 3.049
  BRANCH_DIRECT_CALL: 0.183
  BRANCH_INDIRECT_CALL: 0.006
  BRANCH_RETURN: 0.004
```

The summary line outputs three metrics. Accuracy is the fraction of branches correctly predicted, and MPKI is the total mispredictions per thousand instructions (across all branch types). The third metric, average Re-order Buffer (ROB) Occupancy at Mispredict, is the average number of instructions in the ROB at the time of mispredict detection. It indicates the average utilization level of the CPU pipeline at the time of misprediction. In other words, a higher value indicates a higher misprediction penalty, as more in-flight instructions must be drained or squashed before resuming.

Similar to their cache equivalents, branch MPKI is generally the more actionable metric, as accuracy alone can be misleading due to not accounting for branch frequency. A workload with very few branches can have low accuracy yet low MPKI.

The output also shows a per-type breakdown to identify which category is responsible for the performance impact you observe. It can be used to reason more deeply about workload patterns. For example, high indirect-branch misprediction rates usually indicate a workload that is heavy on polymorphic dispatch or computed jumps, which are common in interpreters and virtual machines.

Some reference ranges for branch MPKI are provided in Table 7-3 as examples. Again, these should be considered for high-level guidance, and your expectations should be validated with your specific workload and configuration.

Table 7-3. *Branch MPKI Reference Ranges*

Branch MPKI	Characterization	Implication for Analysis
< 1.0	Branch prediction is rarely limiting	Unlikely to be primary bottleneck. Focus analysis on other metrics.
1.0–5.0	Moderate misprediction pressure	Contributes to the stall budget alongside memory. Worth noting in the report.
5.0–10.0	Branch prediction is a significant bottleneck	Warrants dedicated analysis.
> 10.0	Highly irregular control flow	Branch behavior likely dominates IPC. Verify workload selection aligns with study goals.

The metrics covered so far help understand the on-chip behavior but do not offer direct visibility into a workload's interaction with DRAM. The next section covers metrics that capture the off-chip behavior.

7.5 DRAM Metrics

After missing in LLC, memory requests are forwarded to DRAM. Hence, understanding these metrics complements your understanding of the memory access patterns of your workload and their interactions with the microarchitecture in your simulation studies. Listing 7-6 shows the DRAM section output from Listing 7-1.

Listing 7-6. DRAM Statistics

```
Channel 0 RQ ROW_BUFFER_HIT: 80000
ROW_BUFFER_MISS: 70000
AVG DBUS CONGESTED CYCLE: 2.814
```

```
Channel 0 WQ ROW_BUFFER_HIT: 20000
ROW_BUFFER_MISS: 10000
FULL: 0
Channel 0 REFRESHES ISSUED: 1842
```

Statistics are reported per channel, and row buffer hits and misses are tracked separately for the read and write queues (RQ and WQ, respectively). Row buffer hit rate measures the frequency of accesses hitting an already open DRAM row. It is calculated as (ROW_BUFFER_HIT) / (ROW_BUFFER_HIT + ROW_BUFFER_MISS). For the example shown, it is 53% for the RQ. A high hit rate indicates sequential or strided access patterns, whereas a low hit rate indicates pointer chasing or large random working sets. This characterization helps assess the application's access locality and working set size.

AVG DBUS CONGESTED CYCLE shows the average wait time when a request finds the data bus occupied. Higher values indicate that requests are frequently queuing behind each other.

WQ FULL is the number of times an incoming write could not be enqueued because of no space in the write queue. In other words, it denotes write-queue pressure.

REFRESHES ISSUED is the number of DRAM refreshes executed during the simulation.

We will cover more focused DRAM analysis in Chapter 10, such as timing parameters, row buffer management policies, and memory controller scheduling. At this stage, it is sufficient to understand that these statistics primarily verify whether the workload's access patterns are DRAM-friendly.

Now that we have covered some individual metrics in isolation, we have a sense of component-level impact on performance. The next logical step is to view them comparatively across configurations and workloads to answer architectural questions.

7.6 Comparative Analysis

Most of the time, you would be evaluating architectural features in terms of their performance impact, directionally and quantitatively. This will inevitably take the form of a comparative analysis with and without the features on hand. Let's look at how to do it rigorously.

7.6.1 Normalized Speedup

Normalized speedup is usually the standard way to express performance comparison. It is computed by dividing (or "normalizing") the IPC of the configuration under study by the IPC of the baseline configuration. An example is shown in Listing 7-7.

Listing 7-7. Normalized Speedup Calculation

```
Baseline (LRU replacement): IPC = 0.847
New configuration (SHiP policy): IPC = 0.912
speedup = IPC_new / IPC_baseline = 0.912 / 0.847 = 1.077
This means new policy is 7.7% faster than baseline.
Report as: "SHIP achieves a 7.7% IPC improvement over LRU"
or: "a speedup of 1.077 X over LRU"
```

You should make sure to explicitly name the baseline, as claiming an X% improvement is insufficient without specifying over which configuration. Note that this method assumes both configurations execute the same number of instructions. If the technique under study changes the instruction count, for example through compiler optimizations, you should compare cycles or wall-clock time instead.

7.6.2 Geometric Mean for Multi-workload Studies

As we covered in previous chapters on workload selection, you would usually run and publish the normalized speedup across a suite of benchmarks. For properly aggregating speedup numbers from multiple workloads, geometric mean (GM) is the preferred method.

Mathematically, normalized speedups average properly under GM. It is scale-invariant and more resilient to outlier effects (where the aggregate gets biased in one direction due to a small number of outliers). An example is shown in Listing 7-8.

Listing 7-8. Geometric vs. Arithmetic Mean

```
Three workloads, speedups over LRU baseline:
mcf: 1.22
gcc: 1.04
omnetpp: 1.08
Arithmetic mean: (1.22 + 1.04 + 1.08) / 3 = 1.113 (11.3%)
Geometric mean: (1.22 * 1.04 * 1.08)^(1/3) = 1.111 (11.1%)
For balanced speedups, the difference is minor.
With an outlier (e.g., one workload at 2.5X), the
arithmetic mean
overstates the typical benefit while the geometric mean
is affected less.
```

7.6.3 General Guidelines for Reporting Results

Alongside reporting whether the technique under study wins or loses on average, a well-structured comparative analysis should also report which workloads gain or lose performance, with metrics to support the hypothesis and the result. Table 7-4 provides general guidelines for achieving this. The exact metrics to report depend on the type of study, but the bottom line is to provide comprehensive visibility into the results and not just a few top-level numbers.

Table 7-4. *Reporting Checklist for Comparative Studies*

Element	Single-Workload Study	Multi-Workload Study	Notes
Primary metric	IPC	Geometric mean speedup	Always communicate the baseline
Supporting metrics	LLC MPKI, branch MPKI	Per-workload breakdown	Include regressions, not just improvements
Metrics targeting the feature under study	Example for Prefetcher: Coverage and accuracy	Per-workload breakdown	Report all metrics relevant to the feature being studied
Regression disclosure	Highlight speedup < 1.0	Report worst-case regression	Omitting regressions is a common error

As we approach the end of the chapter, the next section outlines some sanity checks that help us validate the study and its conclusions quickly and avoid flawed decisions based on inconsistent data.

7.7 Sanity Checks

The ability to draw correct conclusions from a simulation study involving multiple workloads and complex features depends on deliberate verification. While it is impossible to analytically examine every micro-level detail from the numbers, let's go over a few checks relevant to the scope of the chapter.While it is impossible to analytically examine every micro-level detail from the numbers, let's go over a few checks relevant to the scope of the chapter.

7.7.1 Internal Consistency Checks

These checks are usually obvious and purely mathematical. They essentially mean you must make sure the numbers in the output are self-consistent. Table 7-5 provides some important checks as guidance.

Table 7-5. *Internal Consistency Checks*

Check	Rule
IPC bounds	0 < IPC <= fetch_width. IPC of zero means no instructions retired. IPC above the minimum intended pipeline width may indicate a configuration error.
Hit + Miss = Access	HIT + MISS must roughly match ACCESS at each cache level. Any major mismatches should be supported by simulator reporting conventions or genuine pipeline intricacies.
Cache access chain	L2C ACCESS should approximately equal L1D MISS + L1I MISS (ignoring write-backs) when no L2 prefetcher is enabled. With prefetching, L2C ACCESS will be larger due to prefetch-generated requests.
Prefetch identity	USEFUL + USELESS <= ISSUED. REQUESTED >= ISSUED.
Instruction count	Finished instructions should match the simulation-instructions flag.

If any of these checks fail, you should check if the output format has a nuance you have not accounted for or if coding your feature into the simulator has altered something unintentionally. Checking the simulator documentation against your version also helps in eliminating any wrong assumptions.

7.7.2 Cross-Metric Plausibility Checks

To verify further, we can go to the second layer beyond the individual numbers and check if the relationship between the metrics is sensible. Table 7-6 lists some such patterns and their usual causes.

Table 7-6. *Cross-Metric Plausibility Checks*

Observation	Why It Is Implausible	Some Likely Causes
High LLC MPKI but high IPC	LLC misses stall the ROB, so high MPKI and high IPC rarely coexist.	MPKI is misread (demand vs. total including prefetch), or high memory-level parallelism (MLP) hides latency.
Prefetch coverage near 100% but no IPC improvement	If prefetches eliminate demand misses, IPC should rise.	Prefetches arrive too late, or pollution offsets the benefit.
LLC miss rate improved, but IPC unchanged	Fewer LLC misses should reduce stalls.	Workload is not LLC-bound, and the bottleneck is elsewhere (branch pressure or L1/L2).
Identical IPC for very different cache sizes	A 2X cache size change usually moves MPKI.	Wrong configuration file was loaded, or the working set does not stress the cache at either size, if that is the intention.
Speedup > 2.0 from a minor policy change	Policy changes rarely produce such large gains.	The baseline is misconfigured, or the comparison is not as intended.

You must investigate such patterns before attempting to explain them logically. This could involve ensuring the configuration file is correct, that the simulation is fully completed, that the heartbeat IPC progression isn't anomalous, and so on. Explanations using genuine architectural phenomena should be reserved for later, after making sure there are indeed no other issues.

7.7.3 Reference Data Comparison

For widely used benchmarks, it is relatively easy to find published results in the architecture literature to use as a cross-check. For example, IPC for a known workload on a standard ChampSim configuration should not deviate substantially from published values. While we do not expect exact matches, large deviations should prompt you to examine your trace collection and simulation parameters carefully before proceeding.

For proprietary or novel workloads where no reference exists, you can use hardware counter data, such as IPC, cache miss rates, etc., from perf stat to form some expectations about their behavior.

A good rule of thumb is that the relative ordering of the workloads and their qualitative characteristics, such as boundedness (compute or memory) and working set size expectations, should be consistent.

Modeling Perspective: The goal of sanity checking is to make sure the results are defensible and consistent. Publishing an IPC of 2.1 for a workload that commonly appears at around 0.8 should have enough supporting evidence to counter possible questions. Without any explanation of discrepancies, it is difficult to form a convincing story about the conclusions.

7.8 Summary

This chapter presented how to read and evaluate simulation results to draw conclusions about workload behavior. The key takeaways are listed below.

First, ChampSim's output is organized into clear, modular sections. The warm-up boundary is clearly indicated in the results, and you should only use post-warm-up statistics for any analysis.

Second, while IPC is a great way to communicate the overall impact with a single number, you can also use the inverse, or CPI, to form a mental model for attributing stall cycles to branches, cache misses, or other sources.

Third, cache statistics report hits, misses, and accesses, and these can be used to derive hit rate and MPKI. MPKI captures the per-instruction impact of cache effectiveness, making it more suitable in certain scenarios. Analyzing these metrics hierarchically conveys more information than looking at individual levels in isolation. For example, tracing misses from L1 to the last level can help estimate the working set size.

Fourth, accuracy and coverage together characterize the effectiveness of prefetching. High coverage with low accuracy suggests excessive prefetching, while the opposite suggests that it is conservative.

Fifth, branch MPKI can be used to assess whether mispredictions contribute meaningfully to stalls.

Sixth, DRAM row buffer statistics are useful in revealing access locality beyond the LLC. For example, a low row buffer hit rate can point to scattered access patterns.

Seventh, normalized speedups and geometric means are effective metrics for reporting comparative analysis results. You must include regressions and other supporting metrics in your report to make a convincing case.

Eighth, sanity-checking is an essential step in any study. You should verify internal consistency, cross-metric plausibility, and, if possible, compare against reference data to avoid publishing results based on erroneous or corrupted code or traces.

Having established how to read simulation output and infer relevant details from it, let's move to hands-on simulation practice. The next chapter establishes conceptual foundations of the memory system (cache, prefetcher, and DRAM), and subsequent chapters will follow this up with guided simulation work.

Review Questions

1. A ChampSim result shows cumulative IPC = 0.46 for a four-wide configuration with the LLC MPKI of 18.2. What conclusion can you draw about the workload's bottleneck? What other metrics in the output can help examine or confirm the hypothesis you made?
2. For two cache replacement policies across four workloads, the speedups over the LRU baseline are 1.35, 1.04, 0.98, and 1.05. What is the geometric mean speedup? What would the lowest value (0.98) direct you to investigate and report?
3. Imagine a SimPoint study on a 4-wide CPU configuration that outputs an IPC of 3.9 for one simulation point, while 0.7-1.5 for all other points. Does this trigger any sanity checks? Would you consider the 3.9 number valid under any conditions?

4. Suppose you come across a study that claims that the newly developed prefetcher "achieves an 85% row buffer hit rate." Is this a prefetcher or a DRAM metric? What does the claim convey about the prefetcher's effect on access patterns?

Exercises

Exercise 1: Consider the following results of a study conducted with ChampSim using two configurations and three workloads:

Workload	Baseline IPC	New Config IPC
mcf	0.42	0.51
gcc	1.85	1.82
lbm	0.68	0.74

Calculate the normalized speedup for each workload and then compute the geometric and arithmetic mean speedups. Explain your observations about the difference in the values obtained. Do you see any regressions? Analyze your results using guidelines from Table 7-4.

Exercise 2: You come across the following simulation output from a ChampSim run. Apply the cross-metric plausibility checks from Table 7-6 on the data and identify if you need to investigate any implausible observations.

IPC: 2.8

L1D MPKI: 1.2

L2C MPKI: 0.4

LLC MPKI: 22.5

Branch MPKI: 0.8

LLC AVERAGE MISS LATENCY: 185.3 cycles

Further Reading

ChampSim project, source code, and documentation, `https://github.com/ChampSim/ChampSim`.

J. L. Hennessy, D. A. Patterson, and C. Kozyrakis, Computer Architecture: A Quantitative Approach, 7th Edition, Morgan Kaufmann, 2025. General reference for the concepts used throughout this chapter.

A. Jaleel, K. B. Theobald, S. C. Steely Jr., and J. Emer, "High Performance Cache Replacement Using Re-Reference Interval Prediction (RRIP)," Proceedings of the 37th Annual International Symposium on Computer Architecture (ISCA), 2010. A representative example of cache simulation in published research.

PART III

Memory System Modeling

CHAPTER 8

Memory System Architecture

This chapter covers the architectural foundation necessary to understand the systems you will model in Chapters 9 and 10.

Staying with the common theme of the book, we will take the modeler's perspective and not rederive or extensively cover the theory found in architecture textbooks. You are encouraged to follow external resources to dive deeper into the topics touched upon in the chapter.

The chapter is organized around four major components of the memory system, namely cache hierarchy, DRAM, memory controllers, and address translation. For each component, we will cover the architectural mechanisms, the parameters that govern behavior, and the modeling considerations to guide the simulation work in later chapters.

8.1 Cache Architecture

Caches are small, fast storage structures that keep copies of frequently accessed data closer to the execution core and reduce memory access time. It is important to understand cache organization because the parameters defining it, such as capacity, associativity, etc., are control knobs that configure simulation tools and act as the levers enabling architectural exploration. In this section, we will cover the main relevant concepts.

A. Pareek, *Performance Modeling of Computer Systems*, Maker Innovations Series,
https://doi.org/10.1007/979-8-8688-2476-0_8

8.1.1 Set-Associative Organization

Modern caches use a set-associative organization. The storage is divided into sets that contain multiple ways for data to reside. For a memory request, the cache uses a portion of the address to identify which set might contain the data, then searches all the ways within that set for a match on the tag. A cache with an associativity of n-way allows n blocks with the same index to coexist in a set. The two extreme end cases for associative caches are direct-mapped caches (associativity of 1) and fully associative caches (the whole cache is a single set).

The primary parameters that define the organization are capacity (C), block size (B), and associativity (A). Once decided, the number of sets can be computed as S = C / (B x A). As an example, a 32 KB cache with 64-byte blocks and 8-way associativity contains 32,768 / (64 x 8) = 64 sets. With a 48-bit physical address, the lowest 6 bits identify the byte within the 64-byte block, the next 6 bits (the index) select one of the 64 sets, and the remaining 36 bits define the tag that distinguishes between multiple memory blocks residing in the set. Figure 8-1 illustrates how this process works.

```
Example: 32 KB cache, 64-byte blocks, 8-way associativity, 48-bit address

Address
+----------------------+----------+-----------+
|    Tag (36 bits)     | Index(6) | Offset(6) |
+----------------------+----------+-----------+
            |                |
            |                +-----------------> select 1 of 64 sets
            |
            +----------------------------------> compare tag against all 8 ways

Selected set
+-------+-----------+------------+
| Way 0 | StoredTag | Data block |
| Way 1 | StoredTag | Data block |
| Way 2 | StoredTag | Data block |
| Way 3 | StoredTag | Data block |
|  ...  |    ...    |    ...     |
| Way 7 | StoredTag | Data block |  <- tag match -> cache hit
+-------+-----------+------------+
```

Figure 8-1. *Cache Access Flow in a Set-Associative Cache*

Conflict arises when more than n blocks map to the same set in an n-way set-associative cache, necessitating the removal of some to make space. While it may seem tempting to keep the associativity as high as possible to avoid this, higher associativity comes with increased access latency as more ways must be searched to find the right block to read or evict. Commonly, L1 caches use 4- to 12-way associativity to minimize latency, while last-level caches use 8- to 16-way or more because the longer baseline access latency makes the extra cost less critical.

Table 8-1 shows representative parameters for a typical cache hierarchy drawn from modern high-performance processors.

Table 8-1. *Representative Cache Hierarchy Parameters*

Level	Size	Associativity	Block Size	Latency	Shared/Private
L1-I	32–64 KB	4- to 8-way	64 B	~4–5 cycles	Private per core
L1-D	32–64 KB	4- to 12-way	64 B	~4–5 cycles	Private per core
L2	256 KB to 2 MB	4- to 16-way	64 B	~10–15 cycles	Private per core
L3/LLC	8–64 MB	8- to 16-way	64 B	~30–60 cycles	Shared across cores

A Note on VIPT Addressing: As you may be aware, modern L1 caches use virtually indexed, physically tagged (VIPT) addressing to reduce lookup latency. For simulation purposes, this detail is typically abstracted away unless address translation is being studied. Hence, VIPT mechanics are not covered in this chapter.

8.1.2 Cache Miss Classification

Cache misses are classified into three types, namely compulsory, capacity, and conflict, based on the underlying cause. Commonly referred to as the "Three Cs," this categorization helps guide optimization strategies or identify issues with the system being studied.

Compulsory (cold) misses occur during the first access of a block. Since the data has never been fetched, these are unavoidable except with prefetching.

Capacity misses occur when the working set size exceeds the cache capacity. These exist even if the cache is made fully associative, i.e., the organization is not the cause.

Conflict misses arise when more blocks map to the same set than the number of ways per set. As a result, evictions occur even if unused capacity remains elsewhere in the cache.

For your performance studies, distinguishing among the types of misses can guide you toward the right optimization. With high compulsory miss rates, improvement in prefetching (Section 8.1.4) may help. Similarly, high capacity miss rates call for larger caches or software-level improvements to improve locality. High conflict misses, on the other hand, indicate that higher associativity or alternate indexing schemes may be the best direction to pursue. Simulators can help you track and classify misses with proper experimentation, providing a clearer picture of the path forward.

8.1.3 Replacement Policies

Replacement policies serve as the decision mechanism for finding and evicting the "least useful" cache block in case of a cache miss (when the set is full). Since it is not possible to keep an unlimited amount of data in a set, we have to resort to the next best alternative: evicting the least impactful data. The policy used for achieving this significantly affects the hit rate, especially when the workload is near capacity. We will briefly discuss some commonly used policies.

LRU (least recently used) assumes that blocks that have not been accessed for the longest time are the least useful. In other words, it evicts blocks that are the least temporally local. Perfectly achieving this (True-LRU) can become prohibitive due to the need to track the complete ordering of all ways, which increases access latency and storage requirements (relative to the cache size) to keep all the ordering bits. Hence, practical solutions, such as pseudo-LRU (pLRU) approximations, exist to address this. A common example is the tree-based pLRU.

Last level caches see access streams already filtered by upper levels. This weakens the recency signals, and hence, in such cases, prediction-based approaches can perform better than LRU variants. RRIP (re-reference interval prediction) is a commonly used prediction methodology. It keeps a small counter to predict when a line will be reused. The line with the most distant predicted reuse is chosen for eviction.

While it may seem counterintuitive, selecting an eviction candidate at random also performs surprisingly well in large, highly associative caches, depending on the workload mix. In such scenarios, the cost of evicting a suboptimal line is not as detrimental as one would expect. Since it represents a simple non-predictive solution, it is often useful as a baseline for relevant simulation studies.

When evaluating replacement policies, you should make sure that the workload suite exercises diverse access patterns to avoid biased results and surprises later.

8.1.4 Prefetching

In addition to replacement policies, caches can use prefetching to reduce miss penalties. A prefetcher monitors the access stream and attempts to predict which cache lines will be needed next, fetching them before the processor requests them. When accurate, prefetching hides memory latency by overlapping data transfer with computation. When inaccurate, it wastes bandwidth and can evict useful data (cache pollution). The tension between coverage and accuracy (Section 7.3.3) is central to the design and evaluation of prefetchers.

Prefetcher design is motivated by the patterns they target. The simplest form is the next-line prefetcher, which fetches the cache line immediately following the one just accessed. This works well for strictly sequential access patterns but fails for more complex ones. A stride prefetcher tracks the difference in addresses between consecutive accesses from the same instruction and prefetches along that delta once a consistent stride is detected. This handles some slightly more complex patterns such as array traversals with fixed steps. It is an active research area, and many complex designs exist catering to varied spatial and temporal access patterns of memory accesses.

Prefetched requests consume shared resources such as MSHRs (miss status holding registers) as they traverse through the memory hierarchy. When prefetch traffic is high, these can get saturated and end up stalling demand requests or the prefetcher itself. Hence, unbalanced aggressiveness can undermine the intended benefits from prefetching.

8.1.5 Write Policies

While reads are usually more latency critical as the processor waits for data, writes are somewhat flexible and can be buffered and committed later. However, write policies matter as much as read policies for correctness and overall performance. Hence, caches need to handle writes well. There are a few choices to achieve this with different tradeoffs.

The write-back policy defers writes to the next cache level until eviction. This reduces write traffic downstream but necessitates tracking modified lines for coherence and correctness.

A write-through policy involves propagating writes immediately to the next level, which could go all the way to memory depending on the design. This simplifies handling dirty state at the cache level but increases the bandwidth pressure.

For handling write misses, there is an additional choice between two policies. With the write-allocate policy, the block is fetched into the cache before writing. The write-no-allocate policy, in contrast, sends writes directly to the next level, and usually all the way to memory depending on the design.

8.1.6 Inclusion Policies

Inclusion policies define how levels in the cache hierarchy interact. In an inclusive cache, any line in a cache level closer to the processor must also exist in every level farther from it. For example, in a strictly inclusive cache, each line in L1 exists in L2 and LLC. Evicting a line from LLC involves back-invalidating corresponding lines in L1 and L2. While this simplifies tracking needed to maintain coherence and allows progressive eviction in the event of replacement, it wastes capacity on duplicate data.

An exclusive cache hierarchy provides an alternative by keeping each line at exactly one level. This increases the capacity but comes at the cost of complicating coherence.

Since both of these policies are somewhat at extremes of design points, many modern processors use relaxed hybrid policies, often called non-inclusive/non-exclusive (NINE), and the exact behavior varies by microarchitecture.

While caches are extremely effective at absorbing most memory accesses, the misses that get through must be serviced by main memory (DRAM). Next, let's look at how DRAM is organized and why the requests that reach it have variable latency depending on access patterns.

8.2 DRAM Architecture

Main memory, or DRAM, has fundamentally different organization and timing constraints than caches due to the different underlying technology. For modeling and interpreting memory-intensive workloads effectively, it is essential to understand the architecture to a sufficient level.

8.2.1 DRAM Organization

At the highest abstraction level, a channel is an independent path to the memory, with its own data bus and command interface. For example, if a system has two channels, two independent paths to memory exist. Individual channels can service different requests concurrently, subject to controller and system-level constraints, and provide substantial bandwidth improvement.

Each channel consists of one or more ranks. A rank is a group of DRAM chips working together to provide a set width (e.g., 64 bits) of data per transfer. Ranks on the same channel share the data bus, so only one rank can transfer data at a time. However, operations can be overlapped to hide latency; for example, you can issue commands to one rank while another is transferring.

Each rank contains multiple banks (e.g., 16 in DDR4 and 32 in DDR5). Banks are essential for exploiting benefits from parallelism. Each bank can operate independently; for example, one can be transferring data while another is activating a row, and a third is precharging. The memory controller (Section 8.3) exploits this by interleaving and keeping multiple operations in flight.

Typically, banks are organized into bank groups within a rank, and accessing banks back-to-back in different groups within a rank is faster than accessing them within the same group.

At the most fine-grained level, each bank is a two-dimensional array of rows and columns. To access any data, you must first activate (open) the row, which loads its contents into the row buffer (essentially the bank's sense amplifiers). Once a row is open, individual columns can be read and written to quickly. Note that only one row can be open for a bank at a time, and accessing another row requires first closing (precharging) the current one. Figure 8-2 shows the DRAM hierarchy and the structure of a single bank.

```
DRAM hierarchy                    Inside one bank
--------------                    ---------------

Channel                           +----------------------+
  |                               |  Row / Column Array  |
  +-- Rank                        | -------------------- |
        |                         |  Row 0               |
        +-- Bank Group 0          |  Row 1               |
        |     +-- Bank 0          |  Row 2  <- active    |
        |     +-- Bank 1          |  Row 3               |
        |                         |  ...                 |
        +-- Bank Group 1          +----------------------+
              +-- Bank 2                     |
              +-- Bank 3                     v
                                    +----------------------+
                                    | Row Buffer / Sense   |
                                    | Amplifiers           |
                                    +----------------------+
                                               |
                                               v
                                     read or write columns
```

Figure 8-2. *DRAM organization and bank structure*

8.2.2 Timing Parameters

DRAM operations must adhere to strict timing constraints that the memory controller must account for. Table 8-2 shows a representative example of numbers from a DDR4 specification. You must ensure you use the correct timing constraints for your version when simulating workloads.

Table 8-2. *Example DDR4 Timing Values*

Parameter	Name	Value	Significance
tCL (sometimes tCAS)	CAS Latency	22 cycles (13.75 ns)	Column read latency once the row is open
tRCD	RAS to CAS Delay	22 cycles (13.75 ns)	Row activation latency
tRP	Row Precharge	22 cycles (13.75 ns)	Time to close an open row
tRAS	Row Active Time	52 cycles (32.5 ns)	The minimum duration the row must stay open
tFAW	Four Activate Window	32 cycles (20 ns)	Limits activation rate across banks
tRFC	Refresh Cycle	350 ns	Duration of refresh operation

Three scenarios are possible when a request arrives at a bank. First, the requested row is open already, or there is a row buffer hit. Second, no row is open, but the bank is precharged, or there is a row buffer miss. And finally, third, when a different row is open, that must be closed first, referred to as a row buffer conflict.

These scenarios primarily determine the access latency. For example, a row buffer hit only needs tCL cycles, while a row buffer miss needs tRCD + tCL cycles. Similarly, a row buffer conflict requires tRP + tRCD + tCL cycles, corresponding to the three sequential operations of precharge, activate, and column access, respectively. These are first-order estimates, and other factors such as controller queuing, bank group timing, and refresh interference also influence the latency.

These first-order access-dependent latencies matter for detailed DRAM modeling but also add unnecessary complexity if the study doesn't need an extensive treatment of memory behavior.

8.2.3 Refresh Overhead

Due to capacitor leakage, DRAM cells need periodic refresh to maintain data integrity. During refresh, the affected banks are unavailable for access. This creates refresh overhead, consuming a portion of the available bandwidth. This overhead has grown to consume a non-trivial fraction of available bandwidth over time, and newer technologies offer some mechanisms to mitigate this (such as same-bank refresh). For short simulations, refresh effects may be negligible, but you must account for refresh interference on long-running or real-time workloads.

Modeling Perspective: Common DRAM simulators like DRAMsim3 and Ramulator offer the ability to model refresh in detail. If your study involves sustained memory-intensive operation, make sure that refresh is modeled, else you may overestimate the achievable bandwidth.

So far, we have covered how DRAM is organized and how accesses are serviced. Next, let's look at how the memory controller orchestrates these requests, which bridges the cache hierarchy to main memory.

8.3 Memory Controller

The memory controller acts as an interface between processor requests and DRAM operations. It carries out operations such as mapping physical addresses to DRAM locations, enforcing timing constraints, and scheduling commands to optimize performance. Since its behavior can significantly influence achieved bandwidth and latency, it is important to understand it well enough to model it accurately for memory-intensive studies.

8.3.1 Address Mapping

The memory controller is responsible for mapping physical addresses to channel, rank, bank, row, and column. A common approach is to use the low address bits for columns, the middle bits for bank and channel fields, and the high bits for row mapping. This approach aims to spread consecutive cache lines across banks and channels and to maximize parallelism for sequential access patterns. Note that the mapping is applied at cache-line granularity. The byte-offset bits within a cache line are stripped first so that a single cache line maps to one DRAM location.

Many alternative mapping schemes exist, catering to specific scenarios. For example, XOR-hash-based mappings that reduce bank conflicts for strided patterns or row-interleaved mappings that maximize row buffer locality for streaming patterns at the cost of reduced parallelism.

Dedicated DRAM simulators typically allow you to configure the mapping scheme, enabling you to experiment and tune it to the dominant patterns within the scope of your study.

8.3.2 Scheduling Policies

The memory controller is also responsible for tracking pending requests and selecting which to service next. This scheduling can substantially affect bandwidth utilization and latency distribution. Two simple and common policies are listed below.

FCFS (first-come first-served) picks requests in arrival order, as the name suggests. It is simple and fair but ignores opportunities for optimization.

FR-FCFS (first-ready FCFS) prioritizes requests that can be serviced immediately (Section 8.3.3), for example, selecting requests with row buffer hits first and then the rest in FCFS order. A sustained stream of hits can cause starvation with this policy and must be taken care of.

Many more sophisticated policies exist, such as write batching, critical awareness, and others that aim to ensure fairness along certain criteria.

8.3.3 Row Buffer Management

The final functionality of the memory controller we will cover is managing when to close the row buffer, which involves tradeoffs between hit rate and conflict penalty.

With an open-page policy, the row buffer is left loaded after each access. This incurs only column-access latency if the subsequent access hits the same row. If not, the three operations take place sequentially. With a close-page policy, as the alternative, pre-charge happens immediately after each access completes, which means that activation and column access latencies are incurred regardless of the address.

If your workload has good row locality, open-page is preferable; if not, close-page will perform better. It is also possible to implement adaptive policies that monitor hit rates per bank and dynamically switch strategies.

All the topics we covered so far, including cache indexing, DRAM addressing, and controller scheduling, operate on physical addresses. The applications themselves, however, work with virtual addresses. The next section covers how this address translation works and when and where it matters for modeling.

8.4 Address Translation and TLBs

Address translation is the mechanism that bridges virtual addresses used by applications to physical addresses that the structures and policies we covered so far operate on. It can incur enough overhead to impact performance for certain workloads. This section covers basic details to enable you to understand when it matters for modeling decisions.

A virtual address consists of two parts: the virtual page number (upper bits) and the page offset (lower bits). Translation essentially involves replacing the virtual page number with the corresponding physical page number, keeping the offset unchanged.

Page tables are special data structures designed to store these mappings. Instead of linearly allocating space for all possible virtual pages, which is prohibitively expensive, modern processors use multi-level page tables. This saves space by allocating translation entries only as needed (to a certain extent) but increases lookup latency. This is because a complete translation now requires walking through multiple levels of tables to find the physical page number. To overcome this issue and provide fast translations for frequently accessed pages, specialized translation caches called TLB (Translation Lookaside Buffer) are added.

Similar to caches, modern processors implement multi-level TLB hierarchies. The commonly used organization consists of a small, fast L1 TLB (often split into instruction and data) backed by a larger unified L2 TLB. Representative microarchitectures typically include 64–128 entries for L1 DTLB and 1,024–2,048 entries for L2 TLB.

For 4 KB pages, a 1,024-entry TLB will only cover 4 MB of address space. Hence, workloads with larger footprints will still experience TLB misses. As modern server-level and memory-intensive workloads grow, larger page sizes are getting increasingly common. Often referred to as "huge pages," they dramatically extend TLB coverage with 2 MB (and sometimes up to 1 GB) per page. As an example, a 1,024-entry TLB with 2 MB pages covers 2 GB, which can dramatically reduce TLB misses for many such workloads.

Modeling Perspective: Your workload's memory footprint relative to TLB coverage can be used as a first-pass heuristic in deciding whether you need to model translation effects. If the footprint fits comfortably within TLB reach, TLB modeling will add complexity without changing results meaningfully. If the footprint exceeds coverage, it may provide important insights that a physical-address-only simulation would miss. Page size, access locality, and page-walk cost also influence this choice.

8.5 Summary

This chapter covered the architectural concepts necessary for modeling memory systems. The key takeaways are listed below:

First, cache behavior and performance are influenced by multiple factors. These include organization parameters (capacity, associativity, block size), miss type (compulsory, capacity, or conflict), replacement policy, prefetching, write handling, and inclusion policy. Each entails distinct performance tradeoffs.

Second, DRAM access latency is dependent on access patterns. Row buffer locality and bank-level parallelism affect performance, and the memory controller's scheduling leverages them to improve throughput.

Third, address translation can add non-trivial overhead when the memory footprint exceeds TLB coverage.

Fourth, modeling details should match the scope of the research question. While cache replacement studies need accurate cache modeling and can treat DRAM simply, memory scheduling studies need detailed modeling of DRAM timing.

With the important concepts covered, the rest of Part III puts them into practice and takes you from knowledge to real simulation work.

Review Questions

1. A 64 KB, 4-way set-associative cache has 64-byte blocks. How many sets does it contain? For a 48-bit physical address, how many bits are used for the tag, index, and offset fields?

2. What is the difference between capacity and conflict misses? What architectural change addresses each of these?

3. How does FR-FCFS scheduling improve DRAM bandwidth utilization compared to simple FCFS? What is the potential drawback when using it?

4. For a 1,024-entry TLB using 4 KB pages, what is the maximum memory footprint that can be covered without TLB misses? How does this change if the page size is increased to 2 MB?

Further Reading

J. L. Hennessy, D. A. Patterson, and C. Kozyrakis, "Computer Architecture: A Quantitative Approach," 7th Edition, Morgan Kaufmann. General reference for cache design, memory hierarchy fundamentals, page tables, TLBs, and huge page support.

A. Jaleel et al., "High Performance Cache Replacement Using Re-Reference Interval Prediction (RRIP)," ISCA 2010. Introduced the RRIP family of scan-resistant replacement policies.

The Cache Replacement Championship (CRC) proceedings. Document state-of-the-art replacement policies.

B. Jacob, S. Ng, and D. Wang, Memory Systems: Cache, DRAM, Disk, Morgan Kaufmann, 2008. Provides good coverage of DRAM organization and timing.

K. K. Chang et al., "Understanding Latency Variation in Modern DRAM Chips," SIGMETRICS 2016. Characterizes DRAM timing behavior across multiple vendors.

S. Rixner et al., "Memory Access Scheduling," ISCA 2000. Introduced FR-FCFS scheduling.

CHAPTER 9

Cache and Prefetcher Simulation

This chapter explains how to put the concepts from Chapter 8 into practice. You will inspect and modify cache and prefetcher mechanisms and run focused experiments on ChampSim using intentionally designed workloads. Furthermore, you will use simulation results to draw architectural conclusions for each experiment.

Each experiment follows a consistent workflow:

- Predict the effects of an architectural change.
- Implement this change by making a directed modification to the code or config.
- Run one or two workloads that are sensitive to the change.
- Check relevant metrics in the output.
- Reason about the observed changes versus the hypothesis we started with.

By the end of the chapter, you will learn the experimental rigor and analysis methodology to apply to your own studies. The focus should be on the directional changes observed in the experiments, not on replicating the

A. Pareek, *Performance Modeling of Computer Systems*, Maker Innovations Series,
https://doi.org/10.1007/979-8-8688-2476-0_9

printed values as exact targets. While ChampSim is used as the simulator of choice here, the concepts apply universally across the trace-driven simulator landscape.

Prerequisites

This chapter assumes you are familiar with:

- Running ChampSim, as illustrated in Chapter 6
- Simulation output interpretation from Chapter 7
- Cache architecture, replacement policies, and prefetching concepts from Chapter 8
- Basic modern C++ programming

A Note on ChampSim Version: The code listings and interfaces used in this chapter are based on ChampSim at commit 06de8d3 (November 17, 2025). For brevity, only the core logic is shown, and the file path is listed. If your ChampSim version differs, the exact code and its location may change, but the concepts and methodology remain the same.

9.1 Simulator Configuration

Before we begin experimentation, let's explore the default cache organization in ChampSim and how to change the configuration.

9.1.1 Cache Hierarchy Organization

By default, ChampSim models a commonly used configuration consisting of a three-level CPU cache hierarchy with separate instruction and data L1 caches, a private L2 cache, and a shared last-level cache (LLC).

Each level is defined by its capacity, associativity, block size, and access latency. In ChampSim, the capacity is inferred through the combination of sets, ways, and global block_size. Chapter 8 covered how these parameters interact with each other. Table 9-1 shows a representative configuration from the current ChampSim defaults.

Table 9-1. *Example Cache Configuration from ChampSim*

Level	Sets	Ways	Size	Block Size	Latency	Scope
L1-I	64	8	32 KB	64 B	4 cycles	Private
L1-D	64	12	48 KB	64 B	5 cycles	Private
L2C	1024	8	512 KB	64 B	10 cycles	Private
LLC	2048	16	2 MB	64 B	20 cycles	Shared (if multi-core)

9.1.2 Modifying Parameters

ChampSim uses a JSON file to define its configuration and a script to apply it to the build. A fully specified config file for the default configuration is supplied at $CHAMPSIM_ROOT/champsim_config.json.

To modify a subset of parameters, you can use a configuration file containing only the relevant fields. The remaining fields are filled by ChampSim's internal default configuration logic. Listing 9-1 shows examples of changing some specific fields.

Listing 9-1. Example Cache Configuration Overrides

```
#Double L2 capacity from 512 KB to 1 MB
{
  "L2C": {
    "sets": 2048,
    "ways": 8
  }
```

```
}

#Switch the LLC replacement policy:
{
  "LLC": {
    "replacement": "srrip"
  }
}

#Enable a next-line prefetcher at L2:
{
  "L2C": {
    "prefetcher": "next_line"
  }
}
```

Once you have a configuration file ready, you can build using the command shown in Listing 9-2.

Listing 9-2. Basic ChampSim Configuration and Build Flow

```
cd $CHAMPSIM_ROOT
./config.sh my_config.json
make -j$(nproc)
```

To avoid misleading simulation results, it is recommended to verify the intended cache level and the cache geometry in the configuration you use before running the corresponding simulation.

The next section describes the workloads chosen for the workflow in this chapter, along with the architectural reasons behind their selection.

9.2 Experimental Design

Before running any experiments, you should clearly formulate what to run, what to measure, and how to sequence the simulation runs. Let's take a look at the workloads, metrics, and the general experimental process.

9.2.1 Workload Selection

While you will study a wide variety of complex workloads in the real world, for this chapter, two workloads are chosen for their sensitivity to the mechanism under study (Chapter 3). We have kept the workload set small to keep the experiments focused and deliberate. Table 9-2 lists the workload and the intention behind using each.

Table 9-2. *Custom Workloads for Cache Modeling*

Workload	Access Pattern	Working Set	Purpose	Notes
stream	Two interleaved sequential regions	4 MB scan (>LLC) + 768 KB reuse	Exposes scan resistance and shows why coarse prefetch filters can fail on structured streams	Interleaved unit-stride streams
random	Random access	8 MB (>LLC)	Exposes pathological locality and poor prefetch choices	No useful sequence

Despite its name, the stream workload is not one global next-line stream. It consists of two unit-stride streams, one large enough to pressure the LLC and another small enough to remain in the cache.

9.2.2 Key Metrics

The simulator output fields relevant to the studies in this chapter are listed below:

- CPU 0 cumulative IPC.
- The LLC TOTAL line showing HIT and MISS counts.
- The L2C PREFETCH line showing REQUESTED, ISSUED, USEFUL, and USELESS counts.

For a more comprehensive description of each, refer to Chapter 7.

Additionally, these metrics can be used to derive LLC MPKI as LLC_misses / (simulated_instructions / 1000) and prefetch accuracy as USEFUL / ISSUED.

9.2.3 Experimental Process

An effective understanding of the experimental motive and results comes from proper methodology. You should start with one workload intended to expose the mechanism you are studying and one contrasting workload to test the limits or the no-change case. To that effect, we will use stream as the structured case and random as the contrast. This keeps the cause-and-effect immediately visible and enables you to broaden to other traces later.

9.2.4 Companion Repository Setup

For the experiments in this chapter, the relevant configuration and trace files are located in the companion repository at ch09-cache-pref-sim under configs/ and traces/. Complete modified files for all code changes are located at ch09-cache-pref-sim/listing-files. You should also set the CHAPTER_DIR environment variable to point to the chapter's directory in the companion repository:

```
export CHAPTER_DIR=/path/to/ch09-cache-pref-sim
```

Let's now get our hands dirty and experiment with cache policies next.

9.3 Cache Replacement Policies

As you are familiar with from Chapter 8, replacement policies decide which line to evict when the cache is full. This section illustrates the general replacement policy interface in ChampSim, how the LRU and SRRIP policies are implemented using it, and then walks you through an experiment comparing them.

9.3.1 Replacement Policy Interface

ChampSim exposes a fixed interface to implement custom replacement policies as shown in Listing 9-3. The key functions of the interface are:

- find_victim(): Chooses which way should be evicted when a fill needs space.
- update_replacement_state(): Updates metadata when a tag check completes.
- replacement_cache_fill(): Initializes metadata when a new line is filled.

Listing 9-3. ChampSim Replacement Policy Interface

```
#include "cache.h"
#include "modules.h"

class my_policy : public champsim::modules::replacement {
public:
  explicit my_policy(CACHE* cache);
```

```
  long find_victim(uint32_t triggering_cpu, uint64_t instr_id,
  long set,
    const champsim::cache_block* current_set,
    champsim::address ip, champsim::address full_addr,
    access_type type);

  void update_replacement_state(uint32_t triggering_cpu, long
  set, long way,
    champsim::address full_addr,
    champsim::address ip,
    champsim::address victim_addr,
    access_type type, uint8_t hit);

  void replacement_cache_fill(uint32_t triggering_cpu, long
  set, long way,
    champsim::address full_addr,
    champsim::address ip,
    champsim::address victim_addr,
    access_type type);
};
```

Understanding the interface is necessary to understand policy implementations. Let's look at how LRU and SRRIP are implemented next.

9.3.2 LRU

LRU policy evicts the line that has remained untouched the longest. ChampSim implements this by tracking a cycle stamp (as a timestamp) per cache line. A hit refreshes this stamp, a new install replaces it with the current cycle, and during victim selection, the line with the smallest value is chosen. The LRU policy serves as a strong baseline because its behavior is intuitive. Listing 9-4 shows the core logic of the LRU replacement policy. The code follows the LRU policy description in Chapter 8.

Listing 9-4. LRU Core Logic (from $CHAMPSIM_ROOT/replacement/lru/lru.cc)

```
long lru::find_victim(uint32_t triggering_cpu, uint64_t instr_
id, long set,
  const champsim::cache_block* current_set,
  champsim::address ip, champsim::address full_addr,
  access_type type)
{
  auto begin = std::next(std::begin(last_used_cycles), set *
  NUM_WAY);
  auto end = std::next(begin, NUM_WAY);
  auto victim = std::min_element(begin, end);
  return std::distance(begin, victim);
}

void lru::replacement_cache_fill(uint32_t triggering_cpu, long
set, long way,
  champsim::address full_addr,
  champsim::address ip,
  champsim::address victim_addr,
  access_type type)
{
  last_used_cycles.at((std::size_t)(set * NUM_WAY + way)) =
  cycle++;
}

void lru::update_replacement_state(uint32_t triggering_cpu,
long set,
  long way, champsim::address full_addr,
  champsim::address ip,
  champsim::address victim_addr,
  access_type type, uint8_t hit)
```

```
{
  if (hit && access_type{type} != access_type::WRITE)
    last_used_cycles.at((std::size_t)(set * NUM_WAY + way)) =
    cycle++;
}
```

9.3.3 SRRIP

ChampSim implements the static version of RRIP, or SRRIP. Briefly, from Chapter 8, the mechanics of this policy involve setting RRPV to 0 on hits and a high value at the time of a new line installation. During eviction, the line with the highest RRPV is chosen for replacement. Listing 9-5 shows the core logic of the SRRIP implementation using the same interface functions, implemented differently from LRU.

Listing 9-5. SRRIP Core Logic (from $CHAMPSIM_ROOT/replacement/srrip/srrip.cc)

```
long srrip::find_victim(uint32_t triggering_cpu, uint64_t
instr_id, long set,
  const champsim::cache_block* current_set,
  champsim::address ip, champsim::address full_addr,
  access_type type)
{
  return sets.at(static_cast<std::size_t>(set)).victim();
}

void srrip::update_replacement_state(uint32_t triggering_cpu,
long set,
  long way, champsim::address full_addr,
  champsim::address ip,
  champsim::address victim_addr,
  access_type type, uint8_t hit)
```

```
{
  sets.at(static_cast<std::size_t>(set)).update(way, hit);
}

long srrip_set_helper::victim()
{
  auto victim = std::max_element(std::begin(rrpv_values),
    std::end(rrpv_values));
  std::transform(std::cbegin(rrpv_values), std::cend(rrpv_
  values),
    std::begin(rrpv_values),
    [diff = maxRRPV - *victim](auto x) { return x + diff; });
  return std::distance(std::begin(rrpv_values), victim);
}

void srrip_set_helper::update(long way, bool hit)
{
  get_rrpv(way) = hit ? 0 : (maxRRPV - 1);
}
```

Now that we understand the internals of both policies, let's proceed to the experiment.

The Experiment

This experiment evaluates SRRIP against LRU replacement on stream and random workloads. Before running and evaluating the results, you should reason about which workload(s) would benefit from this change. Recall from Chapter 8 that SRRIP is designed to improve scan resistance of the cache.

Many simulators come prepackaged with common replacement policies, and as we just saw, ChampSim offers both LRU and SRRIP pre-built. Hence, the experiment only requires switching the replacement policy in the configuration. Listing 9-6a illustrates how to build both the configs.

Listing 9-6a. LRU vs. SRRIP Build

```
# Configuration file ($CHAPTER_DIR/configs/ch9_baseline_
lru.json):
{
  "executable_name": "ch9_baseline_lru"
}

# Configuration file ($CHAPTER_DIR/configs/ch9_srrip.json):
{
  "executable_name": "ch9_srrip",
  "LLC": {
    "replacement": "srrip"
  }
}

# Build:
cd $CHAMPSIM_ROOT
./config.sh $CHAPTER_DIR/configs/ch9_baseline_lru.json
make -j$(nproc)

./config.sh $CHAPTER_DIR/configs/ch9_srrip.json
make -j$(nproc)
```

Once we have the corresponding builds, we can run each simulation as shown in Listing 9-6b.

Listing 9-6b. LRU vs. SRRIP Run

```
# Run stream and random with LRU:
cd $CHAPTER_DIR
$CHAMPSIM_ROOT/bin/ch9_baseline_lru --warmup-instructions
1000000 \
  --simulation-instructions 2000000 \
  traces/stream.champsimtrace.xz > results/stream_lru.txt

$CHAMPSIM_ROOT/bin/ch9_baseline_lru --warmup-instructions
1000000 \
  --simulation-instructions 2000000 \
  traces/random.champsimtrace.xz > results/random_lru.txt

# Run stream and random with SRRIP:
$CHAMPSIM_ROOT/bin/ch9_srrip --warmup-instructions 1000000 \
  --simulation-instructions 2000000 \
  traces/stream.champsimtrace.xz > results/stream_srrip.txt

$CHAMPSIM_ROOT/bin/ch9_srrip --warmup-instructions 1000000 \
  --simulation-instructions 2000000 \
  traces/random.champsimtrace.xz > results/random_srrip.txt
```

After the runs complete, check the metrics “CPU 0 cumulative IPC” and “LLC TOTAL MISS count” for all four runs and verify if the results match your expectations. Does the streaming workload expose the effectiveness of scan resistance more than randomness?

Results and Explanation

As you may have expected, SRRIP helps substantially on stream, with a 1.16x IPC speedup and a 23% reduction in MPKI. This is because it effectively prevents the large sequential region accesses, which keep applying scan pressure, from evicting the smaller interleaved reuse region data. At random, the effect is negligible (1.01x IPC) because irregular access patterns have no useful recency information to preserve. Table 9-3 shows metrics and normalized speedups from reference runs.

Table 9-3. *LRU vs. SRRIP Reference Values*

Workload	Policy	IPC (approx.)	IPC Speedup	LLC MPKI (approx.)	MPKI Reduction
stream	LRU (baseline)	~0.64	-	~30.0	-
stream	SRRIP	~0.74	1.16x	~23.0	23%
random	LRU (baseline)	~0.43	-	~74.9	-
random	SRRIP	~0.43	1.01x	~73.7	2%

The first experiment demonstrates the pattern we will use throughout. It involves predicting the performance effect from a single controlled architectural change, implementing it, running both workloads with it, and explaining the results. Recall from Chapter 3 that these illustrative conclusions should be evaluated across a broader representative workload suite before being generalized.

Now that we have applied this workflow on replacement policies, let's turn to prefetching and experiment with the simplest variant: the next-line prefetcher.

9.4 Prefetchers

Prefetchers aim to reduce access latency by fetching data before it is accessed by the core (Chapter 8). Let's see how ChampSim implements this functionality.

9.4.1 Prefetcher Interface

Similar to replacement policies, ChampSim provides an interface to enable and implement prefetching policies. The main functions in this interface are

- prefetcher_cache_operate(): Called at tag-check. The prefetching decision is made here.
- prefetcher_cache_fill(): Called when a miss is filled.
- prefetcher_cycle_operate(): Optional per-cycle hook for asynchronous behavior.

Additionally, prefetch_line() is called to issue a prefetch. Listing 9-7 shows the main prefetcher interface.

Listing 9-7. Prefetcher Interface

```
#include "address.h"
#include "modules.h"

struct my_prefetcher : public champsim::modules::prefetcher {
  using prefetcher::prefetcher;

  uint32_t prefetcher_cache_operate(champsim::address addr,
    champsim::address ip,
    uint8_t cache_hit,
    bool useful_prefetch,
    access_type type,
    uint32_t metadata_in);

  uint32_t prefetcher_cache_fill(champsim::address addr, long
  set, long way,
    uint8_t prefetch,
    champsim::address evicted_addr,
```

```
    uint32_t metadata_in);

  void prefetcher_cycle_operate();
};
```

Let's look at how a next-line prefetcher is implemented using this interface.

9.4.2 Next-Line Prefetcher

The next-line prefetcher operates on a simple algorithm: when the cache accesses line A, prefetch line A + 1. Listing 9-8 shows how ChampSim implements it.

Listing 9-8. Next-Line Prefetcher Implementation (from $CHAMPSIM_ROOT/prefetcher/next_line/next_line.cc)

```
uint32_t next_line::prefetcher_cache_
operate(champsim::address addr,
  champsim::address ip,
  uint8_t cache_hit,
  bool useful_prefetch,
  access_type type,
  uint32_t metadata_in)
{
  champsim::block_number pf_addr{addr};
  prefetch_line(champsim::address{pf_addr + 1}, true,
  metadata_in);
  return metadata_in;
}
```

There is no state or filtering; the decision is a single line call with the address incremented by 1 (the next line). Let's try to change the code and intentionally break the algorithm in the next experiment.

The Experiment

The intention behind this experiment is to evaluate the effects of intentionally wrong data access prediction. To implement this, we will replace next-line with a deterministic pseudo-random wrong-distance prefetcher. Before you run and analyze, consider your expectations for the resulting IPC, cache misses, and useful prefetches. To add this modification to the code, change the lines in prefetcher/next_line/next_line.cc as shown in Listing 9-9.

Listing 9-9. Pseudo-Random Wrong-Distance Modification (in $CHAMPSIM_ROOT/prefetcher/next_line/next_line.cc)

```
// Change:
champsim::block_number pf_addr{addr};
prefetch_line(champsim::address{pf_addr + 1}, true,
metadata_in);

// To:
champsim::block_number cl_addr{addr};
uint64_t seed = cl_addr.to<uint64_t>();
seed ^= (seed << 13);
seed ^= (seed >> 7);
seed ^= (seed << 17);
auto offset = 32 + static_cast<champsim::block_
number::difference_type>(seed % 64);
prefetch_line(champsim::address{cl_addr + offset}, true,
metadata_in);
```

For the next steps, Listing 9-10 shows the configuration and commands to run the experiment on the stream and random workloads.

Listing 9-10. Next-Line Prefetcher Build and Run

```
# Configuration file ($CHAPTER_DIR/configs/ch9_nextline.json):
{
  "executable_name": "ch9_nextline",
  "L2C": {
    "prefetcher": "next_line"
  }
}

# Build with default next-line (forward):
cd $CHAMPSIM_ROOT
./config.sh $CHAPTER_DIR/configs/ch9_nextline.json
make -j$(nproc)

# Run stream and random with forward prefetch:
cd $CHAPTER_DIR
$CHAMPSIM_ROOT/bin/ch9_nextline --warmup-instructions 1000000 \
  --simulation-instructions 2000000 \
  traces/stream.champsimtrace.xz > results/stream_
  nextline_fwd.txt

$CHAMPSIM_ROOT/bin/ch9_nextline --warmup-instructions 1000000 \
  --simulation-instructions 2000000 \
  traces/random.champsimtrace.xz > results/random_
  nextline_fwd.txt

# After changing prefetcher/next_line/next_line.cc to the
pseudo-random variant, rebuild and run:
cd $CHAMPSIM_ROOT
./config.sh $CHAPTER_DIR/configs/ch9_nextline.json
make -j$(nproc)

cd $CHAPTER_DIR
```

```
$CHAMPSIM_ROOT/bin/ch9_nextline --warmup-instructions 1000000 \
  --simulation-instructions 2000000 \
  traces/stream.champsimtrace.xz > results/stream_nextline_
  pseudorand.txt

$CHAMPSIM_ROOT/bin/ch9_nextline --warmup-instructions 1000000 \
  --simulation-instructions 2000000 \
  traces/random.champsimtrace.xz > results/random_nextline_
  pseudorand.txt
```

After the runs, check the relevant metrics: IPC, L2C - PREFETCH REQUESTED, ISSUED, USEFUL, and USELESS counts, for all runs.

Results and Explanation

The pseudo-random prefetcher performs much worse on stream (0.77x IPC vs. the +1 line) because it fetches lines far ahead, with no correlation to the streaming pattern.

At random, the change in IPC is negligible because next-line is essentially a randomly selected pattern for an access stream that is random by design. However, if you compare the performance of random against the no-prefetcher baseline from Table 9-3, both the forward and pseudo-random configurations perform worse (0.79x and 0.81x IPC, respectively). With over 170,000 useless prefetches resulting in cache pollution, the metrics clearly show that the prefetching algorithm's effectiveness is highly workload-dependent. Table 9-4 shows the reference metrics and normalized comparisons.

Table 9-4. Next-Line Prefetcher Reference Values

Workload	Config	IPC (approx.)	vs. Forward	vs. No-Pref (Tbl 9-3)	USEFUL	USELESS
stream	Forward	~0.74	-	1.16x	96,462	1,561
stream	Pseudo-random	~0.57	0.77x	0.89x	2,972	14,190
random	Forward	~0.34	-	0.79x	6,048	181,433
random	Pseudo-random	~0.35	1.03x	0.81x	491	170,133

With an experiment involving a minor code change run and analyzed, let's proceed further and work on a deeper code change using the same next-line prefetcher.

9.4.3 Adding a Simple Filter to the Next-Line Prefetcher

The stock next-line prefetcher, while being effective, lacks any selectivity whatsoever. It blindly issues the next address without checking whether there is, in fact, a repeating pattern in our access stream. Adding selectivity sounds like a good idea in theory, and in fact, many state-of-the-art prefetchers have such confidence counters. Let's see the effect of adding it to the next-line prefetcher.

The Experiment

This experiment adds two pieces of state to the next-line prefetcher: the last accessed cache line and the last observed stride. Further, it issues a next-line prefetch only after observing two consecutive accesses with a unit stride (+1). Before you run and analyze the output, note down your expectations and reasoning so you can compare them later. Listings 9-11a and 9-11b show the code changes needed.

Listing 9-11a. Add State in $CHAMPSIM_ROOT/prefetcher/next_line/next_line.h

```
#include <optional>
std::optional<champsim::block_number> last_cl_addr;
champsim::block_number::difference_type last_stride = 0;
```

Listing 9-11b. Update Logic in $CHAMPSIM_ROOT/prefetcher/next_line/next_line.cc

```
champsim::block_number cl_addr{addr};
if (last_cl_addr.has_value()) {
  auto stride = champsim::offset(*last_cl_addr, cl_addr);
  if (stride == 1 && stride == last_stride)
    prefetch_line(champsim::address{cl_addr + 1}, true,
    metadata_in);
  last_stride = stride;
}
last_cl_addr = cl_addr;
```

You can use the same next-line configuration file from Listing 9-10. Listing 9-12 shows the full flow of commands for this experiment.

Listing 9-12. Filtered Next-Line Build and Run

```
# Build the original next-line prefetcher:
cd $CHAMPSIM_ROOT
./config.sh $CHAPTER_DIR/configs/ch9_nextline.json
make -j$(nproc)
```

```
# Run stream and random with the original next-line prefetcher:
cd $CHAPTER_DIR
$CHAMPSIM_ROOT/bin/ch9_nextline --warmup-instructions 1000000 \
  --simulation-instructions 2000000 \
  traces/stream.champsimtrace.xz > results/stream_
  nextline_fwd.txt

$CHAMPSIM_ROOT/bin/ch9_nextline --warmup-instructions 1000000 \
  --simulation-instructions 2000000 \
  traces/random.champsimtrace.xz > results/random_
  nextline_fwd.txt

# After adding the filter in prefetcher/next_line/next_line.h
and prefetcher/next_line/next_line.cc, rebuild:
cd $CHAMPSIM_ROOT
./config.sh $CHAPTER_DIR/configs/ch9_nextline.json
make -j$(nproc)

# Rerun stream and random with the filtered prefetcher:
cd $CHAPTER_DIR
$CHAMPSIM_ROOT/bin/ch9_nextline --warmup-instructions 1000000 \
  --simulation-instructions 2000000 \
  traces/stream.champsimtrace.xz > results/stream_nextline_
  filtered.txt

$CHAMPSIM_ROOT/bin/ch9_nextline --warmup-instructions 1000000 \
  --simulation-instructions 2000000 \
  traces/random.champsimtrace.xz > results/random_nextline_
  filtered.txt
```

Once the runs complete, note down the IPC and the L2C PREFETCH REQUESTED, ISSUED, USEFUL, and USELESS counts.

Results and Explanation

Randomly, the filter helps (1.26x vs. forward) because it shuts down useless next-line prefetches for an access pattern with no inherent sequence. If you compare the results against the no-prefetcher baseline from Table 9-3, random recovers the loss incurred by adding the next-line prefetcher (1x IPC). This confirms that, for this access pattern, not using this prefetcher is the best choice.

On stream, filtering shows the opposite impact (0.88x IPC versus +1 line). Its access pattern consists of two interleaved sequences that break the confirmation requirement of a steady stride (while each sequence still maintains it individually). Relevant metrics from the reference run are shown in Table 9-5.

Table 9-5. *Filtered Next-Line Reference Values*

Workload	Config	IPC (approx.)	vs. Forward	vs. No-Pref (Tbl 9-3)	USEFUL	USELESS
stream	Forward	~0.74	-	1.16x	96,462	1,561
stream	Filtered	~0.65	0.88x	1.02x	1,266	0
random	Forward	~0.34	-	0.79x	6,048	181,433
random	Filtered	~0.43	1.26x	1.00x	0	0

Now that you have worked on three real simulation experiments with increasing complexity applied to cache and prefetcher implementations in ChampSim, let's summarize what we have covered.

9.5 Summary

This chapter connected the concepts covered in Chapter 8 to three focused simulation experiments. While we used ChampSim due to its simplicity and focus on cache and prefetchers, the techniques are applicable across a broad range of similar simulators.

The first experiment focused on configuration-level changes and compared LRU and SRRIP replacement policies.

The second experiment walked you through a small coding exercise to change the behavior of the built-in next-line prefetcher. It demonstrated how prefetching can actively degrade performance on workloads that don't adhere to the patterns it's designed to handle.

The third experiment increased the complexity of code modification to enable more functionality for the same prefetcher. It demonstrated how confirmation can mitigate performance loss caused by workload and prefetcher mismatches.

All the experiments used two directed workloads, purposefully designed with streaming and random memory accesses. This enabled us to view the impact of the same architectural change on two completely different patterns.

The next chapter applies the same methodology to DRAM and walks you through conducting experiments with relevant architectural features.

Review Questions

1. How differently do stream and random workloads amplify the difference between LRU and SRRIP? Can you explain the difference?

2. Why does random improve on the filtered next-line experiment, and why does the stream get worse?

3. Recall and explain the general methodology that leads to a successful experiment and analysis workflow. What metrics would you use to report the results, and why?

Exercises

Exercise 1: Extend the SRRIP study with one or more workloads using traces from ch09-cache-pref-sim/traces. Run the baseline LRU and SRRIP and compare the results with stream and random using the same metrics. Given the trace name and the results you see, can you infer the access patterns of the trace you used?

Exercise 2: Can you recover stream's performance with the filtered next-line prefetcher? Starting from the filtered next-line experiment (Section 9.4.3), instead of saving a global last stride and last cache line, use per-instruction pointer values. Run it with stream and random and compare it against the original next-line and the filtered next-line you developed in the chapter. Explain whether the stream recovers with this extension and why.

CHAPTER 10

DRAM Simulation

This chapter continues the hands-on workflow you conducted in Chapter 9 and applies it to main memory (or DRAM). Using relevant concepts from Chapter 8, you will inspect, configure, and modify the DRAM subsystem and run experiments with intentionally designed workloads.

Each experiment follows the same steps you carried out in Chapter 9:

- Predict the effects of an architectural change.
- Implement this change by making a directed modification to the code or config.
- Run one or two workloads that are sensitive to the change.
- Check relevant metrics in the output.
- Reason about the observed changes versus the hypothesis we started with.

By the end of the chapter, you will have an understanding of how DRAM timing and row buffer management affect performance and how to design experiments and use appropriate workloads to isolate these effects. As before, the focus should be on the observed directional changes, not on replicating the printed values as exact targets.

A. Pareek, *Performance Modeling of Computer Systems*, Maker Innovations Series,
https://doi.org/10.1007/979-8-8688-2476-0_10

Prerequisites

This chapter assumes you are familiar with:

- Installing and running ChampSim, as illustrated in Chapters 5 and 6
- Cache simulation experiments from Chapter 9
- DRAM architecture, timing parameters, and memory controller concepts from Chapter 8
- Simulation output interpretation, specifically DRAM statistics, from Chapter 7
- Basic modern C++ programming

A Note on ChampSim Version: The code listings and interfaces used in this chapter are based on ChampSim at commit 06de8d3 (November 17, 2025). For brevity, only the core logic is shown, and the file path is listed. If your ChampSim version differs, the exact code and its location may change, but the concepts and methodology remain the same.

10.1 Simulator Configuration

Let's first explore how DRAM is modeled in ChampSim and how to change the relevant parameters.

10.1.1 DRAM Organization

By default, ChampSim models a single-channel DDR configuration, and the default parameters are listed in Table 10-1.

Table 10-1. *Default DRAM Configuration in ChampSim*

Parameter	Value	Description
Channels	1	Independent memory paths
Ranks	1	Ranks per channel
Bank Groups	8	Bank groups per rank
Banks	4	Banks per bank group
Rows	65,536	Rows per bank
Columns	1,024	Columns per bank
Channel Width	8 bytes	Data bus width
tCAS	24 cycles	Column access latency
tRCD	24 cycles	Row activation latency
tRP	24 cycles	Row precharge latency
tRAS	52 cycles	Minimum row active time
Data Rate	3200 MT/s	Transfers per second

In Chapter 8, we saw that access latency depends on the row buffer state and that the timing parameters listed in Table 10-1 largely define it. To recap briefly, a row buffer hit incurs a latency of tCAS cycles, a miss with the bank precharged (clean miss) incurs tRCD + tCAS cycles, and a conflict (when a different row is open) incurs tRP + tRCD + tCAS cycles. With the default values shown, these come out to be 24, 48, and 72 cycles, respectively. Note that these cycles are measured by DRAM's own clock, which is configured separately from the CPU's and runs at its own rate. A latency expressed in DRAM cycles maps to a proportional number of CPU cycles, and the conversion is set by the ratio of the two clock rates.

10.1.2 Modifying Parameters

You can configure DRAM parameters using JSON configuration files, as we covered in Chapter 9. The section name is "physical_memory," and Listing 10-1 shows examples of modifying specific DRAM parameters.

Listing 10-1. Example DRAM Configuration Overrides

```
# Tighten DRAM timing (faster memory):
{
  "physical_memory": {
    "tCAS": 12,
    "tRCD": 12,
    "tRP": 12
  }
}

# Add a second channel:
{
  "physical_memory": {
    "channels": 2
  }
}
```

With the right config file, the build workflow is the same as before, as shown in Listing 10-2.

Listing 10-2. Basic Build and Run Flow

```
cd $CHAMPSIM_ROOT
./config.sh $CHAPTER_DIR/configs/<config_file>.json
make -j$(nproc)
```

10.2 Experimental Design

This section covers the workload, relevant metrics, and the general experimental process suitable for DRAM experimentation.

10.2.1 Workload Selection

The workloads developed for cache and prefetcher exploration in Chapter 9 can be used here with a slight modification. The stream workload we used earlier has two streams, and one of those contains a reuse region that fits in the LLC. This is primarily to test scan resistance and is not particularly useful from the DRAM perspective. To make it more relevant to main memory analysis, the stream workload for this chapter is a single streaming access over a large array that exceeds the LLC capacity, making it fully DRAM-exposed.

The workloads we will use are listed below:

- **stream**: Sequential accesses exhibit high row buffer locality as they frequently target the same DRAM row.
- **random**: Scattered accesses exhibit poor row locality. Most accesses target different rows and result in row buffer misses and conflicts.

The intentionally contrasting behavior makes these effective in illuminating the effects of DRAM-level mechanisms.

A Note on Virtual Memory Randomization: To ensure the workloads produce their intended access patterns, we have disabled virtual memory randomization in the configurations used for the experiments of this chapter.

10.2.2 Key Metrics

The DRAM-specific output fields relevant to this chapter are listed below:

- CPU 0 cumulative IPC.
- Channel RQ ROW_BUFFER_HIT and ROW_BUFFER_MISS counts.
- Channel WQ ROW_BUFFER_HIT and ROW_BUFFER_MISS counts.
- AVG DBUS CONGESTED CYCLE.

You can compute the row buffer hit rate for both RQ (Read Queue) and WQ (Write Queue) as ROW_BUFFER_HIT/(ROW_BUFFER_HIT + ROW_BUFFER_MISS). Chapter 7 contains a more detailed description of these fields.

10.2.3 Experimental Process

We will follow the same methodology as before to keep cause and effect clearly visible.

You will start with an experiment with only configuration-level changes, then proceed to experiments with progressively more code modifications in $CHAMPSIM_ROOT/src/dram_controller.cc.

10.2.4 Companion Repository Setup

You can locate the relevant configuration files, traces, and modified source files for this chapter in the companion repository at ch10-dram-sim/. The CHAPTER_DIR environment variable should point to this directory:

```
export CHAPTER_DIR=/path/to/ch10-dram-sim
```

With the setup in place, let's work through the first experiment, following the trend in Chapter 9.

10.3 DRAM Timing

Timing knobs offer a direct way to evaluate the effect of access latency on DRAM performance. By now, you understand how tCAS, tRCD, and tRP affect access latency depending on the access pattern. In this experiment, we will examine how changing these affects performance. Table 10-2 shows the values we will use for each step.

Table 10-2. *Access Latency by Row Buffer State*

Scenario	Default (24/24/24)	Tight (12/12/12)	Loose (48/48/48)
Row buffer hit (tCAS)	24 cycles	12 cycles	48 cycles
Row buffer miss (tRCD + tCAS)	48 cycles	24 cycles	96 cycles
Row buffer conflict (tRP + tRCD + tCAS)	72 cycles	36 cycles	144 cycles

10.3.1 The Experiment

This experiment compares three timing configurations: default, tight (halved), and loose (doubled). Before viewing results, consider how the workloads' access patterns amplify or suppress effects. Listing 10-3 shows configuration files and commands.

Listing 10-3. DRAM Timing Build and Run

```
# Configuration file ($CHAPTER_DIR/configs/ch10_baseline.json):
{
  "executable_name": "ch10_baseline"
}
```

```
# Configuration file ($CHAPTER_DIR/configs/ch10_tight_timing.json):
{
  "executable_name": "ch10_tight_timing",
  "physical_memory": {
    "tCAS": 12,
    "tRCD": 12,
    "tRP": 12
  }
}

# Configuration file ($CHAPTER_DIR/configs/ch10_loose_timing.json):
{
  "executable_name": "ch10_loose_timing",
  "physical_memory": {
    "tCAS": 48,
    "tRCD": 48,
    "tRP": 48
  }
}

# Build all three:
cd $CHAMPSIM_ROOT
./config.sh $CHAPTER_DIR/configs/ch10_baseline.json
make -j$(nproc)

./config.sh $CHAPTER_DIR/configs/ch10_tight_timing.json
make -j$(nproc)

./config.sh $CHAPTER_DIR/configs/ch10_loose_timing.json
make -j$(nproc)

# Run all six combinations:
cd $CHAPTER_DIR
$CHAMPSIM_ROOT/bin/ch10_baseline --warmup-instructions 1000000 \
```

```
  --simulation-instructions 2000000 \
  traces/stream.champsimtrace.xz > results/stream_baseline.txt

$CHAMPSIM_ROOT/bin/ch10_baseline --warmup-instructions 1000000 \
  --simulation-instructions 2000000 \
  traces/random.champsimtrace.xz > results/random_baseline.txt

$CHAMPSIM_ROOT/bin/ch10_tight_timing --warmup-instructions
1000000 \
  --simulation-instructions 2000000 \
  traces/stream.champsimtrace.xz > results/stream_tight.txt

$CHAMPSIM_ROOT/bin/ch10_tight_timing --warmup-instructions
1000000 \
  --simulation-instructions 2000000 \
  traces/random.champsimtrace.xz > results/random_tight.txt

$CHAMPSIM_ROOT/bin/ch10_loose_timing --warmup-instructions
1000000 \
  --simulation-instructions 2000000 \
  traces/stream.champsimtrace.xz > results/stream_loose.txt

$CHAMPSIM_ROOT/bin/ch10_loose_timing --warmup-instructions
1000000 \
  --simulation-instructions 2000000 \
  traces/random.champsimtrace.xz > results/random_loose.txt
```

Once complete, check the IPC values and the DRAM row buffer statistics for all runs.

10.3.2 Results and Explanation

The results show the expected directional changes. Tightening DRAM timing improves IPC for both workloads, and vice versa. Table 10-3 shows the results.

Table 10-3. *Timing Experiment Results*

Workload	Baseline IPC	Tight IPC	IPC Speedup	Loose IPC	IPC Speedup	Baseline RQ Hit Rate	Tight RQ Hit Rate	Loose RQ Hit Rate
stream	~0.83	~0.86	1.04x	~0.62	0.75x	95.2%	95.4%	94.1%
random	~0.43	~0.7	1.64x	~0.24	0.56x	1.4%	1.5%	1.3%

You should note that the row-buffer hit rate remains relatively stable across configurations. This means that the performance difference is due to timing changes, not the access pattern.

The effect of the difference in access patterns shows up in the relative performance gain between stream and random. For both configs, random experiences a higher change in either direction than stream (e.g., 1.64x vs. 1.04x IPC for the tighter config). This is because random has a nearly zero row-buffer hit rate and incurs the full timing cost for almost all accesses. This sensitizes it more to the timing changes.

Now that we have understood the impact of timing parameters on each workload, we can shift our attention to another critical factor in DRAM performance: row buffer management policies.

10.4 Row Buffer Management

In this experiment, you will explore the effects of row buffer policy on the performance of stream and random workloads.

By default, ChampSim keeps the row buffer open after a request is serviced (open-page policy). The row buffer state is tracked per-bank through the open_row field in the BANK_REQUEST structure. Listing 10-4 shows the relevant functions: service_packet() and finish_dbus_request().

Listing 10-4. Row Buffer Management in ChampSim (from $CHAMPSIM_ROOT/src/dram_controller.cc)

```
// In service_packet():
bool row_buffer_hit = (bank_request[op_idx].open_row.
has_value()
                             && *(bank_request[op_idx].open_row) ==
                             op_row);
```

```
auto row_charge_delay = champsim::chrono::clock::duration{
  bank_request[op_idx].open_row.has_value() ? tRP + tRCD :
  tRCD};

bank_request[op_idx] = {true,  row_buffer_hit,        false,
                        false, std::optional{op_row},
                        current_time + tCAS + (row_buffer_hit
                          ? champsim::chrono::clock::duration{}
                          : row_charge_delay),
                        pkt};

// In finish_dbus_request():
// The row stays open -- open_row is NOT reset after the
request completes.
active_request->valid = false;
active_request->pkt->reset();
active_request = std::end(bank_request);
```

There are two important observations you can make in the code:

- The finish_dbus_request() marks the bank as no longer valid but does not reset open_row. This means that it remains open for the next access to be checked for a hit.
- The latency is appropriately calculated for all three cases we looked at earlier. The code uses row_buffer_hit, row_charge_delay, and has_value() to apply the right timing at the final step. This means that though the statistics counter ROW_BUFFER_MISS lumps clean and conflict misses together, the code internally applies the correct latency values.

10.4.1 The Experiment

We can implement a close-page policy by adding a single line in finish_dbus_request() that resets the open_row after each completed request. Before running it, decide which workload should benefit from keeping rows open and which one from closing them aggressively. Listing 10-5 shows the modification needed for implementation.

Listing 10-5. Close-Page Modification (in $CHAMPSIM_ROOT/src/dram_controller.cc)

```
// In finish_dbus_request(), after "active_request->valid =
false;", add:
active_request->open_row.reset();
```

This change ensures that the row buffer is closed after each request completes. You should check Listing 10-4 to see how this change will affect the timing of access. With this change incorporated, you can build and run the simulations as shown in Listing 10-6.

Listing 10-6. Row Buffer Policy Build and Run

```
# Build with default open-page policy:
cd $CHAMPSIM_ROOT
./config.sh $CHAPTER_DIR/configs/ch10_baseline.json
make -j$(nproc)

# Run stream and random with open-page:
cd $CHAPTER_DIR
$CHAMPSIM_ROOT/bin/ch10_baseline --warmup-instructions
1000000 \
  --simulation-instructions 2000000 \
  traces/stream.champsimtrace.xz > results/stream_openpage.txt
```

```
$CHAMPSIM_ROOT/bin/ch10_baseline --warmup-instructions 1000000 \
  --simulation-instructions 2000000 \
  traces/random.champsimtrace.xz > results/random_openpage.txt

# After adding the close-page line in finish_dbus_request(),
rebuild and run:
cd $CHAMPSIM_ROOT
./config.sh $CHAPTER_DIR/configs/ch10_baseline.json
make -j$(nproc)

cd $CHAPTER_DIR
$CHAMPSIM_ROOT/bin/ch10_baseline --warmup-instructions
1000000 \
  --simulation-instructions 2000000 \
  traces/stream.champsimtrace.xz > results/stream_closepage.txt

$CHAMPSIM_ROOT/bin/ch10_baseline --warmup-instructions
1000000 \
  --simulation-instructions 2000000 \
  traces/random.champsimtrace.xz > results/random_closepage.txt
```

After the experiment, observe and compare IPC and row buffer statistics. Do you think the row-buffer hit-rates make sense?

10.4.2 Results and Explanation

There is a clear contrast in the workloads. They move in the opposite direction.

Table 10-4. *Row Buffer Policy Results*

Workload	Open-Page IPC	Close-Page IPC	IPC Speedup	Open-Page RQ Hit Rate	Close-Page RQ Hit Rate	Open-Page DBUS	Close-Page DBUS
stream	~0.83	~0.65	0.79x	95.2%	0.0%	2.998	2.878
random	~0.43	~0.57	1.34x	1.4%	0.0%	2.913	2.925

stream drops to 0.79x IPC with the close-page policy. With the open-page policy, it has a high row buffer hit rate (95.2%). Collapsing the row buffer hits forces every access to incur tRCD + tCAS (48 cycles). This effectively doubles the latency for 95% of accesses.

random, on the other hand, improves by 1.34x with this change. The reason is clear if you look at the row buffer hit rates. With the open-page policy, random has a low hit rate of 1.4%, or a miss rate of 98.6%. Most of those misses are conflicts, as the access pattern is completely random. Turning all accesses to clean misses reduces the access latency and saves the extra tRP incurred earlier. This results in a substantial gain given the high miss-rate.

You should cross-compare these results with the previous experiment and try to reason how timing changes compare with row-buffer management for each workload.

The result illustrates how the effectiveness of row-buffer policy depends on the corresponding access patterns, as we covered in Chapter 8. Let's explore how an adaptive approach can help in picking the best of both worlds in the next experiment.

10.5 Adaptive Row Buffer Management

The simple open or close row policy deliberately favors one type of access pattern. Open row policy benefits from consecutive hits, while the other is tuned for handling consecutive conflicts effectively. An adaptive policy that closes a row only when a conflict occurs may offer a solution.

For implementation, recall from Listing 10-4 that service_packet() checks open_row.has_value() to determine if it is a clean miss or a conflict. Though this information is used to derive latency values, it doesn't persist beyond that point. You will record this value and decide whether to close the row or keep it open after each access.

10.5.1 The Experiment

You need two small code changes to implement this policy. First, add a tracking field to the BANK_REQUEST structure, as shown in Listing 10-7. This is to enable tracking one additional piece of state: whether the current access was a row conflict.

Listing 10-7. Adding Conflict Tracking (in $CHAMPSIM_ROOT/inc/dram_controller.h)

```
// In the BANK_REQUEST struct, add row_conflict after row_
buffer_hit:
// Original:
bool valid = false, row_buffer_hit = false, need_refresh =
false, under_refresh = false;

// Modified:
bool valid = false, row_buffer_hit = false, row_conflict =
false, need_refresh = false, under_refresh = false;
```

Next, you need to detect conflicts in service_packet() and pass it on to bank_request initialization as shown in Listing 10-8.

Listing 10-8. Detecting Conflicts (in $CHAMPSIM_ROOT/src/dram_controller.cc, in service_packet())

```
// After the existing row_buffer_hit line, add:
bool row_conflict = (!row_buffer_hit && bank_request[op_idx].
open_row.has_value());

// And update the aggregate initialization to include row_
conflict:
// Original:
bank_request[op_idx] = {true,  row_buffer_hit,        false,
                        false, std::optional{op_row}, ...};

// Modified:
bank_request[op_idx] = {true,  row_buffer_hit,        row_
conflict,
                        false, false, std::optional
                        {op_row}, ...};
```

As the next step, you need to add the conditional closure in finish_dbus_request() as shown in Listing 10-9.

Listing 10-9. Close-On-Conflict (in $CHAMPSIM_ROOT/src/dram_controller.cc, in finish_dbus_request())

```
// After "active_request->valid = false;", add:
if (active_request->row_conflict) {
  active_request->open_row.reset();
}
```

Once done, you are ready to build and run, as shown in Listing 10-10. Before running, reason about how each workload should respond to this change given its well-defined access pattern.

Listing 10-10. Adaptive Policy Build and Run

```
# First, run the open-page baseline (reuse from Section 10.4 if
available):
cd $CHAMPSIM_ROOT
./config.sh $CHAPTER_DIR/configs/ch10_baseline.json
make -j$(nproc)

cd $CHAPTER_DIR
$CHAMPSIM_ROOT/bin/ch10_baseline --warmup-instructions
1000000 \
  --simulation-instructions 2000000 \
  traces/stream.champsimtrace.xz > results/stream_openpage.txt

$CHAMPSIM_ROOT/bin/ch10_baseline --warmup-instructions
1000000 \
  --simulation-instructions 2000000 \
  traces/random.champsimtrace.xz > results/random_openpage.txt

# After applying the three modifications (Listings 10-7, 10-8,
10-9), rebuild and run:
cd $CHAMPSIM_ROOT
./config.sh $CHAPTER_DIR/configs/ch10_baseline.json
make -j$(nproc)

cd $CHAPTER_DIR
$CHAMPSIM_ROOT/bin/ch10_baseline --warmup-instructions
1000000 \
  --simulation-instructions 2000000 \
  traces/stream.champsimtrace.xz > results/stream_
  closeonconflict.txt

$CHAMPSIM_ROOT/bin/ch10_baseline --warmup-instructions
1000000 \
```

```
--simulation-instructions 2000000 \
traces/random.champsimtrace.xz > results/random_
closeonconflict.txt
```

After the runs, compare IPC and row buffer statistics across all three policies. Use data from Section 10.4 for open-page and close-page performance numbers.

10.5.2 Results and Explanation

Table 10-5. Three-Way Row Buffer Policy Comparison

Policy	Stream IPC	IPC Speedup	Stream RQ Hit Rate	Random IPC	IPC Speedup	Random RQ Hit Rate
Open-Page	~0.83	-	95.2%	~0.43	-	1.4%
Close-Page	~0.65	0.79x	0.0%	~0.57	1.34x	0.0%
Close-on-Conflict	~0.82	0.99x	93.8%	~0.48	1.13x	0.7%

As we intended, the close-on-conflict policy offers a good tradeoff between the strict close-page and open-page policies.

For the stream, you can see the performance is almost identical to the open page. Since this hybrid policy only closes the row on a conflict, most of the original row buffer hits are preserved. There is a slight penalty when a small number of conflicts occur, but the access stream is mostly sequential and returns to the hit-dominated regime quickly.

This policy also performs better than open page for random, achieving a 1.13x IPC speedup. It does not match close-page fully because it introduces a one-access hysteresis. A conflict triggers closure, which benefits subsequent accesses, but the opened row will conflict again due to the random access pattern. Hence, it saves tRP on every other access.

The three policies we explored in this chapter form a spectrum. Open page is optimal for sequential access, while close-page favors patterns with low row-locality. The close-on-conflict provides a middle ground that avoids the worst-case behavior on each extreme. Let's recap what we learned in this chapter.

10.6 Summary

This chapter applied the concepts from Chapter 8 through three increasingly complex simulation experiments. We used the same random workload from the last chapter but modified the stream workload for better alignment with DRAM experimentation.

The first experiment explored the sensitivity of the chosen workloads to DRAM timing through the parameters exposed by ChampSim. The results indicated that random is more sensitive than stream because it cannot exploit the timing benefits of row-buffer hits.

The second experiment changed ChampSim's default row-buffer management policy to close-page through a simple code change. The results moved the workloads in the opposite direction, illustrating that policy effectiveness depends on access patterns.

The third experiment built on the previous and implemented an adaptive policy. It handled the worst case for both open page and close page, offering a middle ground.

With the memory system exploration and experimentation complete, let's move to Part IV, where we shift to CPU core modeling and hands-on simulations.

Review Questions

1. Explain why random exhibits higher sensitivity to DRAM timing changes than stream. Which of the three timing parameters has the highest impact on its performance?

2. Consider a sequence of four accesses to the same bank under the close-on-conflict policy that target different rows. Walk through the row-buffer state and latency at each step. Do you see any patterns?

3. Explain the reason behind the close-page policy degrading the performance for stream while doing the opposite for random. What does it tell you about choosing a row buffer policy in practice?

Exercises

Exercise 1: Run a variant of the timing experiment where you only change tCAS and leave others at their default values. Compare the results with the original timing experiment. Which workload experiences the most change from changing tCAS, and why?

Exercise 2: Implement another adaptive policy that tracks row buffer hit rate per bank over a window of recent accesses and only close the row if the hit rate drops below a chosen threshold. Run it with the two workloads and compare against the results from the other policies that we explored in the chapter.

PART IV

CPU Core Modeling

CHAPTER 11

CPU Core Architecture

After exploring the memory subsystem, its architectural foundation, and performing hands-on experiments in Part III, we now turn to CPU core architecture. This chapter covers the essential architectural concepts you need to understand the systems modeled in Chapters 12 and 13.

Staying with the book's common theme, the chapter takes the modeler's perspective and does not aim to rederive or extensively cover the theory found in architecture textbooks. You are encouraged to consult external resources to go deeper into the chapter's topics.

The chapter follows the lifecycle of an instruction as it moves through the processor. First, pipeline fundamentals are covered as the foundation. Following that, we cover the pipeline in two parts: front-end and back-end. The former supplies instructions to the latter for execution. We will then walk through the core-memory interface as the complementary view of some topics covered in Chapter 8, from the core side. Finally, the chapter will extend the scope to multicore execution and cover important concepts relevant to performance and simulation.

Let's start with the first concept, i.e., pipelining.

A. Pareek, *Performance Modeling of Computer Systems*, Maker Innovations Series,
https://doi.org/10.1007/979-8-8688-2476-0_11

11.1 Pipeline Fundamentals

Pipelining allows a processor to overlap the execution of multiple instructions, achieving higher throughput than sequential execution. Parameters defining pipeline organization are usually the first-level levers available in common simulators for architectural exploration and set the ceiling that other mechanisms in this chapter work against. In this section, we will understand the basic execution model and an important tradeoff that comes with pipelined architecture.

11.1.1 Pipeline Organization

A pipelined processor divides instruction execution into a series of stages. Commonly, at a high level, these are fetch, decode, rename, dispatch, execute, and retire. By dividing execution this way, different instructions can occupy each of these stages simultaneously, rather than waiting for one instruction to complete end-to-end. This enables a higher aggregate throughput, even though each stage processes one instruction at a time. Figure 11-1 shows a simple pipeline.

```
                Front End                                       Back End
         +----------------------+      +---------------------------------------------------------------------------+
         |                      |      |                                                                           |
PC ------> [ Fetch ] --> [ Decode ] --> [ Rename ] --> [ Dispatch ] --> [ Schedule ] --> [ Execute ] --> [ Retire ]
             |              |             |              |                |                |               |
           L1-I          ISA instr      Map Table      Allocate:        Wait for         ALU, FP,        Dequeue
           BTB              |           Free List      - ROB entry      operands         SIMD,           from ROB
           I-TLB            v                          - RS entry       + free unit      Load/Store      head
                         micro-ops                     - LQ/SQ entry                                     (in-order)
```

Figure 11-1. *Pipeline Stages and Front-End/Back-End Split*

A pipeline is commonly defined by its width (W) and depth (D). Width determines how many instructions advance through a stage in a cycle (sometimes the most bottlenecked stage). Depth counts the number of stages from fetch to retire. In an ideal, simple case, a pipeline with width W retires W instructions per cycle in steady state. IPC equals the pipeline width under ideal conditions, i.e., no front-end stalls, perfect branch prediction, no cache misses, sufficient back-end resources, and enough independent instructions to fill the pipeline.

In reality, workloads fall short of this ceiling. Three main issue categories affect throughput. Data hazards occur when instructions reference the same register and create dependencies that constrain execution order. Control hazards arise from branches that redirect the instruction stream, causing the pipeline to discard in-flight work. Structural hazards occur when multiple instructions compete for shared hardware resources, such as a functional unit, buffer, or port.

Developing architectural mechanisms to manage these problems is the core of CPU architecture research and simulation. These mechanisms have evolved over time, making the pipeline far more complex than the simple stages like fetch, decode, etc. Table 11-1 shows representative parameters from a modern CPU pipeline as an example. The subsequent sections cover the important ones.

Table 11-1. *Representative CPU Pipeline Parameters*

Parameter	Typical Value	Description
Pipeline Width	4–8	Instructions fetched/decoded/dispatched per cycle (sometimes just the most bottlenecked stage)
Pipeline Depth	15–25 stages	Number of stages from fetch to retire
ROB Entries	256–512	Maximum in-flight instructions
Physical Int Registers	180–384	Physical integer register file size
Physical FP Registers	160–384	Physical floating-point register file size

(*continued*)

Table 11-1. *(continued)*

Parameter	Typical Value	Description
Reservation Station Entries	92–160	Entries in the scheduler
Fetch Buffer	16–32 entries	Buffer between fetch and decode
Branch Predictor	TAGE-like	Direction predictor type
BTB Entries	4096–8192	Branch target buffer size
RAS Entries	32–64	Return address stack depth
Load Queue Entries	72–128	Outstanding loads tracked
Store Queue Entries	56–72	Outstanding stores tracked
L1-I MSHRs	4–8	Outstanding instruction cache misses
L1-D MSHRs	10–16	Outstanding data cache misses

11.1.2 Depth and Frequency Tradeoff

Increasing pipeline length breaks each stage into smaller work units. This enables higher clock frequencies because each stage completes more quickly. Although this may seem straightforward, it has the trade-off of progressively higher costs for pipeline disruptions.

The most familiar example is the branch misprediction penalty. When a branch is mispredicted, the processor must flush every instruction fetched and executed along the wrong path. The amount of work that must be discarded increases with depth, so a 26-stage pipeline may lose nearly twice as much work as a 13-stage pipeline. This can also occur with exceptions, memory-ordering flushes, etc.

At this level of detail, pipeline stages fall into two categories: front-end and back-end. The front-end supplies instructions to the back-end for execution and committing. The exact terms for front-end, middle-machine, and back-end vary in the literature and industry, but the underlying stages remain the same. Let's follow the order of an instruction entering the processor pipeline and discuss the front-end in the next section.

11.2 Front End

The front-end consists of the fetch and decode stages. Due to the challenges of branch prediction and instruction cache behavior, fetch is more complex than the two. The role of the front-end, particularly the fetch stage, is critical because the inability to keep up with the back-end's throughput results in unused execution capacity. Modern state-of-the-art processors have complex pipelines within the front-end for this purpose, and we will cover the essential relevant concepts in this section.

11.2.1 Fetch and Decode

The fetch stage retrieves instructions from the L1 instruction cache (L1-I) using the address in the Program Counter (PC). This process is similar to the data cache access covered in Chapter 8. For a typical L1-I cache with 32KB capacity, 64-byte lines, and 8-way associativity, the number of sets is 64. The low 6 bits of the PC identify the byte within the line. The next 6 bits select the set. The remaining bits match the tags and select the correct line from the set. Because the program operates with virtual addresses, the fetch unit contains an instruction TLB (I-TLB) to cache virtual-to-physical address translations. The I-cache also has its own MSHRs and a mechanism to fill missing data from the L2 cache, LLC, and DRAM. Higher-level caches (L2 and LLC) and main memory are shared with the data side.

The fetch unit typically does not consume the entire cache line at once. It accesses a fetch-width number of instructions per cycle and uses the remainder later. If a branch occurs within the fetched instructions, some may be discarded based on signals from the branch predictor.

The decode stage translates ISA-level instructions into internal representations of the operations they encode (micro-ops). This is relatively more straightforward for RISC architectures such as ARM or RISC-V. Since the format is consistent across the base ISA, the extraction can be done in parallel in a single cycle. CISC ISAs, such as x86, introduce additional complexity by using variable-length instructions that need to be properly parsed and split into internal micro-ops. This can take multiple cycles depending on the design.

Modern processors sometimes introduce optimizations to improve decode throughput. For example, they internally fuse micro-ops to support downstream optimizations. Some architectures cache recently decoded micro-op sequences and bypass the decoder when executing the same code again. Careful tuning and sizing of these elements is needed to balance complexity and performance.

Modeling Perspective: The decode stage can usually be abstracted as a fixed-width pipeline stage, unless specific mechanisms similar to those outlined above are to be studied. In most simulation scenarios, decode width can be matched to the fetch width for a reasonable simplification.

11.2.2 Branch Prediction

Branches constitute a significant portion of dynamic instructions in a typical workload. Without predicting the outcome of a branch, the fetch unit would have to wait until the outcome is fully resolved, usually until the execution unit completes the branch instruction. This can cause significant bubbles every few instructions, especially in deep pipelines.

Branch prediction offers a solution by letting the fetch unit continue speculatively on a predicted path. Once the actual outcome is known, the processor either flushes incorrectly fetched instructions or continues as normal.

A modern branch predictor addresses three key questions for instruction flow. First, it predicts whether conditional branches are taken or not taken. Second, it determines the target to fetch if the branch is taken. Third, it identifies return targets for function calls. Three independent structures manage these tasks alongside cache access. In modern designs, the branch prediction machinery may run many instructions ahead, depending on accuracy, to boost throughput. Let's take a brief look at these three structures.

Direction Prediction: At the most basic level, direction prediction is achieved by using a dedicated table of small saturating counters indexed by the branch PC. For example, the bimodal predictor uses a 2-bit saturating counter table. Each value denotes a prediction confidence, i.e., strongly taken, weakly taken, weakly not-taken, and strongly not-taken. The value determines the direction the fetch unit takes during a lookup and is incremented or decremented depending on the resolution outcome. If the branch is taken, it is incremented; else, it is decremented. Modern predictors add quite a few signals and algorithmic complexities on top of the base. Some examples are Gshare, TAGE, tournament predictor, and Perceptron (uses weighted sums instead of counter tables).

Branch Target Prediction: This is commonly achieved using a dedicated structure called the Branch Target Buffer (BTB). It is a small cache, indexed by the branch PC, that stores the target addresses of previously seen branches. A BTB hit supplies the fetch target in time for the next fetch cycle, while a miss introduces a bubble as the fetch unit needs to wait for the target resolution a few stages down the pipeline. BTB should be sized appropriately for the branching patterns of the target workloads. Table 11-1 shows the typical sizes in modern processors.

Return Target Prediction: Returns from function calls are data-independent but call-site-dependent. The same return instruction at the end of a function may return to multiple different call sites depending on the program patterns. Since BTBs are not efficient for storing this, a specialized stack-based structure called the Return Address Stack (RAS) is used. Every call instruction pushes the return address to this LIFO structure, and every return instruction pops it. Except for deep recursion, where the call stack exceeds the RAS size, it serves as an efficient, low-overhead mechanism to achieve accurate return target prediction.

As the pipeline gets deeper, the accuracy demands on these structures increase, or else the recovery cost can get prohibitive. For example, consider a workload with 20% branches and a 5% misprediction rate. 1% of instructions trigger a flush, which comes out to 10 flushes per 1000 instructions. In a pipeline with a fetch-to-branch resolution distance of 10 stages, this costs about 100 cycles of bubbles per 1000 instructions, which can be significant.

Branch prediction is an active research area with constant innovation and increasing complexity. The main tenet is to keep the backend from idling or waiting for instructions to achieve a high throughput (IPC). You can follow periodic championship branch prediction contests to stay up-to-date with state-of-the-art mechanisms.

When the front-end successfully delivers instructions, the back-end must execute them as fast as possible. The next section covers some mechanisms that enable this.

11.3 Execution Back End

The central challenge here is to execute as many micro-ops in parallel as possible while maintaining the appearance of sequential execution for correctness. The mechanisms used for this, such as register renaming, reorder buffer, and buffer sizes for tracking simultaneous work, are impactful parameters available in most simulators for conducting modeling studies. This section covers these sequentially.

11.3.1 Execution Models

In-order execution is the simplest way to execute pipelined instructions. It ensures that the next instruction to execute is always the oldest one (when its operands are ready). If the oldest instruction is blocked, all instructions, even if their operands are ready, must wait. This exposes the latency of a single high-latency operation, potentially stalling the entire execution engine.

Out-of-order execution offers a relaxed alternative that allows instructions to execute as soon as their operands are ready, regardless of program order. This enables higher throughput by hiding the latency through instruction-level parallelism (ILP). Note that architectural state is only committed to in program order to maintain correctness. While this approach is highly effective and performant, it is accompanied by a substantial increase in area, complexity, and power consumption. Consequently, high-performance cores optimized for single-thread throughput are usually out-of-order, while energy-constrained cores often stick with the in-order design. Both design points are actively used depending on the application scenario.

11.3.2 Rename and Dispatch

Registers store the data used and generated by instructions and inherently communicate their dependencies. However, because ISAs expose only a limited number of architectural registers, compilers are forced to reuse registers even when no real dependencies exist. These false dependencies, namely write-after-read (WAR) and write-after-write (WAW), can force the back-end to serialize logically parallel work.

Register renaming is a mechanism to eliminate these by mapping each architectural register to a unique physical register from a pool of available registers in the processor's hardware. Table 11-1 shows representative sizes of these register pools in the real world. At the simplest level, the rename stage maintains two structures. The first is a map table that holds one entry per architectural register and contains the physical register to which the corresponding architectural register is mapped. The second is a free list of physical registers that have not been mapped to an architectural register. Upon entering the rename stage, the instruction's source architectural registers are replaced with the corresponding physical registers from the map table, and the destination architectural register is mapped to a new physical register from the free list. This mechanism removes both types of false dependencies, as every write to the same architectural register uses a different physical register, generating new dependency streams for each write.

The size of the physical register file determines how many in-flight instructions can hold unique mappings simultaneously. If the free list is empty, rename stage stalls until a physical register is released through a retiring instruction. Simulation is routinely used to tune the free list size to avoid this type of stall across the target workload set.

After renaming, each instruction passes through a short dispatch step that allocates the back-end resources it needs to continue through the rest of the pipeline. This includes the reorder buffer, an entry in the scheduler, load or store queue entries if it is a memory instruction, and many other structures depending on the specific architecture. It is usually a short, fixed-width stage and not often a bottleneck on its own. Throughput mostly depends on the availability of downstream space.

11.3.3 Reorder Buffer

The Reorder Buffer (ROB) is the essential structure that enables extracting ILP by allowing instructions to complete out of order while still maintaining correctness and the program order of instruction completion (retire or commit). It achieves this by recording every dispatched instruction in program order before any out-of-order work begins. Each entry typically stores the instruction's PC, the physical destination register, and a few status bits and flags denoting completion, speculation, exception, etc. Instructions only retire from this structure in FIFO order when their execution is fully complete.

Besides maintaining the correct externally visible architectural state, it also enables precise exceptions and the bookkeeping needed by rename to maintain the pool of free physical registers. The ROB also defines the instruction window, which is the span of instructions within which the back-end can search for independent work. A larger ROB provides more opportunities for ILP but also increases wasted work in the case of exceptions, flushes, etc.

Modeling Perspective: ROB size is commonly swept in core-level studies. It should be sized in proportion to other back-end structures that track in-flight instructions, such as the physical register file, the scheduler, and load and store queues. Since dispatch stalls when any of these fill up, the smallest structure can become the true binding constraint, making it look like the ROB size doesn't matter above that point. This can lead to misleading conclusions about the true size of the ROB needed when the bottleneck lies elsewhere.

11.3.4 Scheduling and Execution

After the dispatch step, instructions enter the scheduling stage, where they wait in a queue until the source operands are ready and the corresponding functional unit is available. Table 11-1 shows representative sizes of the scheduler queue from real-world designs. The size of this queue limits the number of instructions that can wait concurrently for execution. The exact architecture and algorithm for scheduling vary widely across industry and research architectures. The fundamental process remains the same.

In most modern processors, the functional units are organized behind issue ports, and when an instruction becomes ready to execute, it is issued to the corresponding port to begin execution.

Once the execution begins, the completion latency varies by operation type. Table 11-2 shows representative execution latencies for common operations.

Table 11-2. *Representative Execution Latencies*

Operation	Latency (cycles)	Pipelined?
Integer Add/Sub	1	Yes
Integer Multiply	3	Yes
Integer Divide (32-bit)	10–26	No
Integer Divide (64-bit)	17–44	No
FP Add/Sub	3–5	Yes
FP Multiply	3–5	Yes
FP Divide (single)	10–14	No
FP Divide (double)	10–22	No
FP Fused Multiply-Add	4–5	Yes
SIMD (128-bit) Add	1	Yes
SIMD (256-bit) Add	1	Yes
Load (L1 hit)	4–5	Yes
Store (to store buffer)	1	Yes

You should note that most common arithmetic operations are pipelined themselves, meaning that a new instruction can enter the execution unit each cycle, while the previous ones are still executing (in different internal stages).

When multiple ready instructions compete for the same functional unit in the same cycle, contention arises because only one instruction can be issued to a given port in a given cycle. This creates a throughput bottleneck even when other resources are plentiful. Workloads with high concentrations of a single operation type are particularly susceptible to this. Simulation helps evaluate various combinations of ports, execution units, and scheduling policies.

Modeling Perspective: Scheduler size, port mapping, and operation latencies are first-order parameters in cycle-accurate CPU simulators, and you should carefully match them to the target architecture instead of leaving them at default values. Over-provisioning the scheduler or port mapping can mask real contention effects and produce overly optimistic performance numbers.

11.3.5 Retirement

The retirement stage involves dequeuing instructions from the ROB head in program order once they have completed execution. This essentially commits the instruction to the external world. The width of this stage caps the maximum rate at which instructions leave the pipeline and release the resources for other incoming instructions.

Retirement can become a flow-control bottleneck when the ROB head is waiting on a long-latency instruction. This can eventually lead to dispatch stalling and the pipeline idling.

This issue is a case in point for the importance of memory-level parallelism for out-of-order cores. Overlapping multiple cache misses lets them resolve in parallel and clear potential ROB blocks, which can occur when they are processed serially. The structures that allow MLP reside in the core-memory interface, which is the subject of the next section.

11.4 Core-Memory Interface

Chapter 8 covered the memory subsystem from the storage side. The topics we examined included cache organization, memory controllers, and DRAM operation. This section turns to the complementary core-side structures that generate and manage the memory traffic originating from the program.

11.4.1 Load/Store Queue

Memory instructions have different execution phases than straightforward arithmetic instructions, which perform a computation on their operands. After dispatch, a load waits for the operands, computes its address, issues a cache request, and waits for the data to arrive before being ready to retire. Similarly, in a simple design, a store computes its address and data, holds them until retirement, and then drains the data to the cache in subsequent cycles. The back-end needs to track per-instruction state for the full duration of these operations. The structures where this is commonly done are called the load queue (LQ) and the store queue (SQ), which are sometimes combined into a single load-store queue (LSQ).

Beyond simple bookkeeping, the LSQ also enables optimizations such as store-to-load forwarding, which allows a younger load to read from an address that an older, still-in-flight store has not yet committed to the cache. Depending on the architecture, it may act as a smaller scheduler in its own right and let loads complete out-of-order as they become ready. These optimizations add extra complexity to track memory-order violations and ensure that program correctness is not sacrificed.

11.4.2 MSHRs and Memory-Level Parallelism

Miss status holding register (MSHR) entries are allocated to track outstanding requests when an access misses in the cache. If a subsequent load misses the same line before the previous returns, it merges into an existing entry.

This is commonly referred to as miss-coalescing. Table 11-1 contains representative numbers from real designs. Letting multiple outstanding misses coexist in the pipeline creates opportunity for MLP. Note that other structures, such as the LQ, physical register file, etc., should be sized sufficiently to allow enough parallel load opportunities to reach the MSHRs.

11.4.3 Store Buffer

The store buffer holds committed stores that have retired from the ROB but have not been written to the cache. This decoupling prevents any store from waiting for a free cache-write port before retiring and releasing ROB resources, thereby preventing stalling of retirement during bursty phases of write traffic. Adding a buffer moves the pressure point from retirement stalling to the buffer's capacity. The depth of this buffer thus determines how many retired stores can be in flight at once. For workloads with steady-state store streams interleaved with other work, a shallow buffer should suffice, but for store-heavy bursty workloads, it needs to be sized correctly to handle high-demand phases.

So far, we have explored the processor pipeline and relevant structures from a single-core perspective. Modern processors integrate multiple cores on a single die, introducing shared resources and coherence requirements that create additional performance considerations. The next section walks through key architectural considerations for multiple-core interactions.

11.5 Multicore Execution

With multiple cores running simultaneously, shared-cache contention, coherence traffic, interconnect latency, and synchronization emerge as overheads with significant performance implications. Understanding and modeling them accurately is essential whenever the architecture under study involves more than one active core.

11.5.1 Shared Resources and Contention

In common multicore designs, L1 and L2 caches are private to each core, while the LLC and main memory are shared across all cores. This sharing creates contention effects outlined below.

LLC capacity contention arises when the combined working sets of active cores exceed the cache's capacity. As an example, in a quad-core system with 16 MB LLC, each core running with a 5 MB active working set would not cause any capacity issues, but as soon as they run simultaneously, the total demand of 20 MB exceeds the capacity by 25%. The individual behavior of each core remains the same, but the combination experiences a new pressure point.

Memory bandwidth contention is a similar pressure applied to the DRAM bandwidth. When aggregate memory traffic approaches the memory bandwidth, queuing delays increase across all cores, even though each core, in isolation, remains well below the limit.

Both of these issues can also occur in asymmetric scenarios where some cores run workloads without aggressively using shared resources yet still get unfairly starved by other "neighbors" that place a high demand on those resources. Many real-world architectural optimizations aim to ensure fairness for all cores and protect each against "noisy neighbors."

For studies involving multiple cores and memory-intensive workloads, these effects should be modeled accurately through simulation or reasonable proxies that account for contention.

11.5.2 Cache Coherence

If we turn to the private cache levels per core, another problem emerges in the multicore setting. Each core can hold private copies of the same data in L1 or L2 without the others knowing. This calls for a mechanism to ensure that all cores observe a coherent view of the memory. Without it, one core could read stale data that another has modified but not written to the LLC or the memory. Cache coherence protocols provide a systematic approach to handling these issues.

These protocols fall into two main categories. Snoop-based protocols broadcast coherence messages to all caches and leave it to them to respond or manage their internal data if there is a hit. This method is simple and quick for a small number of cores but scales poorly as the memory bandwidth required to broadcast these operations can become prohibitively expensive at high core counts. As an alternative, directory-based protocols maintain a directory of the caches holding a particular line and the "home" node that manages it. This enables a core to communicate only with the relevant cores, rather than broadcasting to all. While it looks cleaner, it comes with additional storage requirements and lookup latency.

Along with the communication mechanics, these protocols also need to track the state of a cache line to know what operations are permitted to avoid incoherent or uncommunicated updates. The MESI protocol family is the most widely used starting point. Each cache line is assigned one of four states: modified, exclusive, shared, or invalid. A modified state means the line is dirty (written to without others knowing) and exists in only one cache. Exclusive means it is a clean line that exists in only one cache and serves as a precursor to moving it to the M state. Shared means the line is clean, exists in multiple caches, and is safe to read. Finally, Invalid means the line is not usable and must be requested fresh from another core or LLC. In the real world, many other states are used for optimization, such as the MOESI protocol, and to ensure the atomicity of state transitions. Figure 11-2 shows state transitions in the MESI protocol as an example.

```
  +-----------+           local read miss           +-----------+
  |  Invalid  | ----------(no sharers)-----------> | Exclusive |
  |    (I)    |                                    |    (E)    |
  +-----------+                                    +--+-----+--+
       ^                                              |     |
       |                                         other|   local
other core                                        core|   write
writes:                                          reads|  (silent)
invalidate                                            |     |
       |                                 +------------+     |
       |                                 |                  |
       |                                 v                  v
  +--+--------+        writeback + share        +-----------+
  |  Shared   | <------------------------------ | Modified  |
  |    (S)    |                                 |    (M)    |
  +-----+-----+                                 +-----------+
        |               local write                   ^
        +-----------(invalidate others)---------------+
```

Figure 11-2. *MESI Cache Coherence State Transitions*

False sharing is an important and commonly observed side effect of coherence that can degrade performance. When two cores write different variables that happen to reside on the same cache line, each write invalidates the other's copy of the entire line. This triggers coherence misses, unnecessary communication, bandwidth usage, and extra latency. It is usually identifiable in simulation studies as high coherence miss rates on lines where no true data sharing exists. The common solution is to pad or align the data to make independent variables land on separate lines.

11.5.3 On-Chip Interconnect

The on-chip interconnect is the connection infrastructure within a multicore chip that is used to communicate control signals and data to other units of the chip (other cores, LLC slices, DRAM, etc.).

The interconnect topology affects the latency of accessing different components, including LLCs and the private caches of other cores (for coherence). It also dictates how the latency grows under load, which depends on the link bandwidth and routing congestion. For example, depending on the topology, a core that sits close to the LLC slice it needs to access will see a lower access latency than one that is many hops away. This non-uniformity can create performance asymmetries and potential issues that do not exist in isolated single-core runs with the same workloads.

Common topology options form a spectrum. A bus is at the simplest end, where all units share a single broadcast medium. While it provides low latency at a small scale, contention and bottlenecks increase rapidly as the core count grows. A crossbar topology uses a dedicated path between each pair of units, but the area grows quadratically with the number of units. A mesh topology arranges nodes in a grid with each node connected to its immediate neighbors. Communication occurs as messages hop from node to node through the grid between the source and destination nodes. This topology scales well with the number of nodes as the aggregate bandwidth grows proportionally. However, it has higher latencies and greater implementation complexity than the other two.

In the real world, many other topologies exist. Each is tailored to the chip's core count, memory organization, and area and power budget. You are encouraged to follow current research in the area to know more.

11.5.4 Synchronization Cost

At the program level, threads must synchronize accesses to shared data using locks or atomic operations. At the hardware coherence level, this usually translates to acquiring cache lines in the modified state and triggering invalidations for other holders of the data. Contention at this level can cause the line to bounce between caches, creating serialization bottlenecks and bandwidth pollution. Additionally, depending on the locking algorithm, other cores may spin on the lock and generate coherence traffic, worsening the problem as contention grows. These issues will not occur if a single core runs in isolation, even with threads, locking mechanisms, and synchronization enabled.

11.6 Summary

This chapter covered architecture concepts necessary for simulating CPU cores. The key takeaways are:

First, pipelining is a foundational architectural mechanism that allows higher instruction throughput while still executing individual instructions serially. Data, control, and structural hazards limit the achievable throughput. Deeper pipelines enable higher clock frequencies at the cost of increased penalty from pipeline disruptions.

Second, fetch bandwidth, branch prediction accuracy, and instruction cache behavior govern the front-end's ability to supply enough instructions to the back-end to keep it running at full capacity.

Third, out-of-order execution enables the core to extract opportunities to execute instructions in parallel and keep the resources busy. This is enabled through register renaming and dynamic scheduling. The ROB ensures that the retirement occurs in program order for correctness. The size of the ROB influences the instruction window within which independent work can be found.

Fourth, the core-memory interface, which consists of the LQ, SQ, MSHRs, and the store buffer, determines the effectiveness of exploiting memory-level parallelism in the core. These structures must be sized with other back-end buffers, including the ROB, to avoid unintentional hidden bottlenecks.

Fifth, multicore execution introduces shared resource contention, synchronization overhead, and coherence traffic. These must be modeled carefully to accurately estimate their impact on performance. Since these effects are absent in isolated single-core simulations, accurate multicore modeling is essential for such cases.

With the basic concepts covered, the next chapters put them into practice through simulations. Chapter 12 introduces CPU simulation for single-core systems, and Chapter 13 extends it to multicore systems. Since

ChampSim primarily focuses on the memory subsystem and models only a simplistic CPU pipeline, we will use gem5 as the simulator for experiments in these chapters.

Review Questions

1. Why do deeper pipelines require progressively more accurate branch predictors? Think through the effects of misprediction on the execution state and how branch outcomes are resolved after fetching from the predicted path.
2. You conduct a simulation study and find that reducing the number of MSHRs from 16 to 8 decreases the IPC significantly for one workload and barely moves the needle for another. Can you reason why?
3. What is false sharing, and how can it be identified in a simulation?

Further Reading

J. L. Hennessy, D. A. Patterson, and C. Kozyrakis, "Computer Architecture: A Quantitative Approach," 7th Edition, Elsevier. General reference for pipeline design, out-of-order execution, branch prediction, and memory hierarchy fundamentals.

J. E. Smith and A. R. Pleszkun, "Implementing Precise Interrupts in Pipelined Processors," ISCA 1985. Foundational work on the reorder buffer and precise exceptions.

A. Seznec, "TAGE-SC-L Branch Predictors Again," JILP 2016. Describes the TAGE family of branch predictors used in modern high-performance processors.

V. Nagarajan, D. J. Sorin, M. D. Hill, and D. A. Wood, "A Primer on Memory Consistency and Cache Coherence," 2nd Edition, Morgan & Claypool, 2020. Comprehensive treatment of coherence protocols.

T. E. Jeremiassen and S. J. Eggers, "Reducing False Sharing on Shared Memory Multiprocessors through Compile Time Data Transformations," PPOPP 1995. Early work on identifying and mitigating false sharing.

S. Eyerman and L. Eeckhout, "System-Level Performance Metrics for Multiprogram Workloads," IEEE Micro, 2008. Discusses metrics for evaluating multicore performance beyond single-thread IPC.

N. Binkert et al., "The gem5 Simulator," ACM SIGARCH Computer Architecture News, 2011. Describes the gem5 simulation framework used in Chapters 12 and 13.

CHAPTER 12

CPU Simulation

This chapter walks you through hands-on experiments on CPU pipeline behavior using concepts from Chapter 11. ChampSim was well-suited for memory-system studies in Chapters 9 and 10 because the experiments primarily involved working with the cache, the prefetcher, and DRAM behavior, using a simple, unchanged core model.

In this chapter, however, we will work on the pipeline behavior itself and need a simulator with detailed core modeling capabilities. Hence, we will switch to gem5 as the simulator of choice. The workflow will involve configuring gem5, modifying a few pipeline mechanisms, and running focused experiments with intentionally designed workloads.

Each experiment follows the familiar workflow from Chapters 9 and 10, outlined below:

- Predict the effects of an architectural change.
- Implement this change by modifying the code or config.
- Run workloads that are sensitive to the change.
- Check relevant metrics in the output.
- Reason about the changes observed.

By the end of the chapter, you will understand how instruction-window size, execution throughput, and misprediction recovery affect performance in a CPU core. The focus should be on the directional

A. Pareek, *Performance Modeling of Computer Systems*, Maker Innovations Series,
https://doi.org/10.1007/979-8-8688-2476-0_12

changes observed in the experiments, not on replicating the numerical values exactly.

Prerequisites

This chapter assumes you are familiar with:

- CPU core architecture concepts from Chapter 11
- Simulation output interpretation from Chapter 7
- Basic Python and modern C++ programming

A Note on gem5 Version: The code listings and configurations used in this chapter are based on gem5 v25.1.0.0 at commit 7a2b0e4 (December 31, 2025). If your gem5 version differs, the exact code and its location may change, but the concepts and methodology remain the same.

Tool Setup

Since we switched to gem5 as the simulator for this chapter, let's walk through the setup process in Listing 12-1.

Listing 12-1. Installing gem5

```
git clone https://github.com/gem5/gem5.git
cd gem5

# Install the build dependency used here
pip install scons

# Build the X86-optimized binary
scons build/X86/gem5.opt -j$(nproc)

# Set the environment variable for this chapter
export GEM5_ROOT=$PWD
```

The build produces build/X86/gem5.opt, the simulator binary for experiments. Unlike ChampSim, which requires a rebuild for configuration changes, gem5 uses both its simulator binary and a Python configuration script to describe the simulated system. Only source code changes require rebuilding, and simulations involving only configuration modification don't need it.

12.1 Simulator Configuration

Before we begin experimentation, let's first explore the CPU models available in gem5 and how to use configuration scripts. We will then review the default relevant CPU pipeline parameters and finally look at some snippets showing how gem5 models key pipeline stages.

12.1.1 CPU Models

gem5 includes several CPU models with different levels of timing details. Table 12-1 lists the important ones.

Table 12-1. *gem5 CPU Models*

Model	Type	Description
AtomicSimpleCPU	Functional	Executes each instruction in a single cycle. No pipeline timing. Mainly for fast-forwarding.
TimingSimpleCPU	In-order	Models memory timing but uses a simplified single-stage pipeline.
MinorCPU	In-order	Four-stage in-order pipeline with configurable latencies.
O3CPU	Out-of-order	Full out-of-order superscalar pipeline with configurable width, depth, and queue sizes.

Note Since this chapter is focused on studying out-of-order core behavior, we will use gem5's O3CPU in all experiments.

12.1.2 Configuration Script

To configure the system for simulation, gem5 uses a Python script-based description of the instantiation and connections of individual components within the architecture. Listing 12-2 shows the example of the baseline script we will use throughout this chapter.

Listing 12-2. Baseline Configuration Script ($CHAPTER_DIR/configs/ch12_run.py)

```
import argparse, os
import m5
from m5.objects import *
from gem5.components.boards.simple_board import SimpleBoard
from gem5.components.cachehierarchies.classic \
    .private_l1_private_l2_cache_hierarchy import (
    PrivateL1PrivateL2CacheHierarchy,
)
from gem5.components.memory import SingleChannelDDR3_1600
from gem5.components.processors.cpu_types import CPUTypes
from gem5.components.processors.simple_processor import
SimpleProcessor
from gem5.isas import ISA
from gem5.resources.resource import BinaryResource
from gem5.simulate.simulator import Simulator
from gem5.utils.requires import requires

requires(isa_required=ISA.X86)
```

```
parser = argparse.ArgumentParser()
parser.add_argument("--binary", type=str, required=True)
parser.add_argument("--rob-size", type=int, default=192)
args = parser.parse_args()

cache_hierarchy = PrivateL1PrivateL2CacheHierarchy(
    l1d_size="32KiB",
    l1i_size="32KiB",
    l2_size="256KiB",
)

memory = SingleChannelDDR3_1600(size="512MiB")

processor = SimpleProcessor(
    cpu_type=CPUTypes.O3, isa=ISA.X86, num_cores=1,
)

for core in processor.cores:
    core.core.numROBEntries = args.rob_size

board = SimpleBoard(
    clk_freq="3GHz", processor=processor,
    memory=memory, cache_hierarchy=cache_hierarchy,
)

board.set_se_binary_workload(
    BinaryResource(local_path=os.path.abspath(args.binary))
)

simulator = Simulator(board=board)
simulator.run()
```

The script adds a --binary flag to specify the workload and a --rob-size flag to set the ROB size. You can choose any other parameter to be passed as flags, such as cache hierarchy sizes, frequency, and so on, depending on your needs. The chapter hardcodes many options, including CPU type, which remain constant throughout the experiments covered. Note that gem5 here runs in syscall-emulation mode, which allows it to trap and emulate kernel-level system calls without booting a full operating system.

12.1.3 Default CPU Parameters

Since you will only be working with a limited set of flags exposed above, let's take a look at the default settings under the hood so we are aware of the CPU architecture we are modeling and can draw appropriate conclusions during experimental analysis. Table 12-2 lists the main CPU parameters used in this chapter, with their default values.

Table 12-2. *O3CPU Parameters*

gem5 Parameter	Default	Concept
fetchWidth	8	Pipeline width (fetch)
decodeWidth	8	Pipeline width (decode)
dispatchWidth	8	Pipeline width (dispatch)
issueWidth	8	Pipeline width (issue)
commitWidth	8	Pipeline width (retire)
numROBEntries	192	Reorder buffer size
numPhysIntRegs	256	Physical register file
numPhysFloatRegs	256	Physical register file
LQEntries	32	Load queue size
SQEntries	32	Store queue size
branchPred	TournamentBP (via default BranchPredictor)	Branch predictor type

If needed, you can change these parameters by accessing the CPU object directly in the configuration script. As an example, to set the Fetch Width to 4:

```
for core in processor.cores:
    core.core.fetchWidth = 4
```

12.1.4 Pipeline in Code

It is helpful to get an idea of the key control points in the O3 CPU source code. To that end, some important code regions are covered briefly in this section. You are encouraged to explore the codebase in detail to fully understand it.

Listing 12-3 shows the main fetch loop from fetch.cc. It pulls up to fetchWidth instructions per cycle from the I-cache and stops when the fetch queue is full or a predicted-taken branch redirects the stream.

Listing 12-3. Fetch Loop (from $GEM5_ROOT/src/cpu/o3/fetch.cc)

```
// Keep issuing while fetchWidth is available and branch is not
// predicted taken
while (numInst < fetchWidth && fetchQueue[tid].size() <
fetchQueueSize
       && !predictedBranch && !quiesce) {
    ...
    numInst++;
    ...
}
```

Listing 12-4 shows the retirement loop from commit.cc. It similarly retires up to commitWidth instructions per cycle from the head of the ROB and stops when no instruction is ready.

Listing 12-4. Commit Retirement Loop (from $GEM5_ROOT/src/cpu/o3/commit.cc)

```
while (num_committed < commitWidth) {
    ThreadID commit_thread = getCommittingThread();
    if (commit_thread == -1 || !rob->isHeadReady(commit_thread))
        break;

    head_inst = rob->readHeadInst(commit_thread);
    bool commit_success = commitHead(head_inst, num_committed);

    if (commit_success) {
        ++num_committed;
    }
}
```

Listing 12-5 shows the path in commit.cc where branch misprediction is detected. Note that in gem5, issue, execute, and writeback are combined into a single stage called the I/E/W stage. When it signals a squash with a mispredicted instruction, commit enters the ROBSquashing state, and the misprediction counter is incremented.

Listing 12-5. Branch Misprediction Handling (from $GEM5_ROOT/src/cpu/o3/commit.cc)

```
if (fromIEW->squash[tid] &&
    commitStatus[tid] != TrapPending &&
    fromIEW->squashedSeqNum[tid] <= youngestSeqNum[tid]) {
    if (fromIEW->mispredictInst[tid]) {
        // ... squash setup ...
        commitStatus[tid] = ROBSquashing;
        // ... forward squash signal to IEW ...
        if (toIEW->commitInfo[tid].mispredictInst) {
            ++stats.branchMispredicts;
```

```
        }
    }
}
```

Listing 12-6 shows the transition to recovery. Once the ROB finishes squashing, commit transitions back to running, and normal retirement resumes.

Listing 12-6. Squash Recovery Transition (from $GEM5_ROOT/src/cpu/o3/commit.cc)

```
if (commitStatus[tid] == ROBSquashing) {
    if (rob->isDoneSquashing(tid)) {
        commitStatus[tid] = Running;
    } else {
        rob->doSquash(tid);
        toIEW->commitInfo[tid].robSquashing = true;
    }
}
```

The experiments we will conduct modify some of these directly, and the others provide context for understanding pipeline behavior. Let's now take a look at the experimental design for this chapter to get ready for the hands-on work.

12.2 Experimental Design

Before running any experiments, you should clearly formulate what to run, what to measure, and how to sequence the simulation runs. Let's take a look at the workloads, metrics, and the general experimental process.

12.2.1 Workload Selection

Following the trend established in earlier experimental chapters, the workloads used in this chapter are specifically designed to expose core behavior while keeping other effects small and predictable. Table 12-3 lists the workload and the intended use for each.

Table 12-3. *Custom Workloads for CPU Pipeline Modeling*

Workload	Access Pattern	Working Set	Purpose
high_ilp	Eight independent arithmetic chains with very few branches	Register-only hot loop	Exposes the benefit of OoO execution
dep_chain	One long serial arithmetic dependency chain	Register-only hot loop	Exposes the limit of OoO execution when no independent work exists
branch_heavy	Many data-dependent conditional branches over a small array	Fits in L1 cache	Exposes the cost of misprediction and recovery

To summarize, high_ilp is designed to give the core many independent operations to overlap, while dep_chain works as a control with almost no ILP opportunities. branch_heavy keeps the data footprint small but requires frequent branch decisions, making it useful for front-end and recovery experiments.

12.2.2 Key Metrics

The gem5 statistics most useful for analyzing the experiments in this chapter are listed in this section. By default, gem5 writes the full statistics report to the file m5out/stats.txt. To keep your simulation runs organized in the results/ folder, you can use the command line option -d $CHAPTER_DIR/results/<run_name>. This will place the statistics file at $CHAPTER_DIR/results/<run_name>/stats.txt, with strings formatted as shown below.

- board.processor.cores.core.ipc: Instructions per cycle.
- board.processor.cores.core.commitStats0.numInsts: Total committed instructions.
- board.processor.cores.core.numSquashedInsts: Instructions squashed due to speculation failure.
- board.processor.cores.core.fetchStats0.numInsts: Total fetched instructions.
- board.processor.cores.core.fetch.status: Cycles spent in each fetch state.
- board.processor.cores.core.commit.branchMispredicts: Total branch mispredictions.
- simSeconds: Total simulated time.

We will primarily use IPC in the results, as it condenses the overall performance change into a single number. The other metrics, such as squashed-instruction counts, fetched-instruction counts, and branch mispredictions, can help you investigate and correlate the underlying causes during your own runs.

12.2.3 Experimental Process

We will follow the methodology outlined in Chapters 9 and 10 to maintain a clear view of the cause-and-effect relationship. To recap, we will start with one workload intended to expose the mechanism under study and one contrasting workload to test its limits or serve as the no-change case.

12.2.4 Companion Repository Setup

The configuration script, workloads, and modified source files for this chapter are located in the companion repository at ch12-cpu-sim/. The workloads/paths used later in this chapter refer to the supplied binaries in the repository.

Set the environment variables as shown below before running the experiments:

```
export CHAPTER_DIR=/path/to/ch12-cpu-sim
export GEM5_ROOT=/path/to/gem5
```

With the setup in place, let's begin with the first experiment on instruction-window size.

12.3 ROB Size and the Instruction Window

Recall from Chapter 11 that the ROB (Reorder Buffer) defines the instruction window at a given time. A larger window lets the back end look further ahead for independent work and more ILP. This experiment measures the effect of sweeping ROB size from well below the default up to the default value and notes how two ILP-contrasting workloads respond.

Sweeping below the default size (192 entries) also shows where the window stops being the binding resource. Once there is enough lookahead to cover independent work, adding more ROB entries is not of use unless other structures change.

The Experiment

This experiment runs gem5 (with O3CPU) on high_ilp and dep_chain with ROB sizes of 4, 16, 64, and 192 entries, while keeping the other parameters unchanged at default values. Before running, you should predict and reason which workload should benefit more from a larger ROB, given the fact (Section 12.2.1) that high_ilp contains eight independent arithmetic chains while dep_chain contains a single serial one.

Listing 12-7 shows how to run the experiment using a bash for loop. Note that the loop syntax should work in other POSIX-compliant shells, such as zsh. If you use a shell that doesn't support it, each gem5.opt command can be run individually.

Listing 12-7. ROB Size Sweep

```
cd $CHAPTER_DIR

# Sweep ROB size on high_ilp
for ROB in 4 16 64 192; do
    $GEM5_ROOT/build/X86/gem5.opt \
        -d results/high_ilp_rob${ROB} \
        configs/ch12_run.py --rob-size $ROB \
        --binary workloads/high_ilp
done

# Sweep ROB size on dep_chain
for ROB in 4 16 64 192; do
    $GEM5_ROOT/build/X86/gem5.opt \
        -d results/dep_chain_rob${ROB} \
        configs/ch12_run.py --rob-size $ROB \
        --binary workloads/dep_chain
done
```

After the runs complete, compare the IPC metric across the four ROB sizes for each workload. To do so, you can read board.processor.cores.core.ipc from each run directory's stats.txt. Does the workload with more independent work benefit as you predicted?

Results and Explanation

Table 12-4. *ROB Size Sweep Reference Values*

ROB Entries	high_ilp IPC	dep_chain IPC
4	0.52	0.22
16	1.72	0.67
64	5.02	0.80
192	5.02	0.80

For high_ilp, the IPC rises from 0.52 at ROB = 4 to about 5.02 at ROB = 64, almost a 10x gain, and then stays flat. Once the instruction window is large enough to exploit all the ILP available, the ROB no longer limits performance (given that other pipeline structures stay the same), and the gain levels off. The default size of 192 indicates that the ROB is not the limiting resource for this workload at the default configuration.

On dep_chain, IPC rises from 0.22 to about 0.80, about 3.6x, then plateaus at that level. This rise is not a sign of hidden ILP. Even a serial chain needs enough in-flight ROB slots to keep the pipeline fed. A very small ROB starves the back end and holds IPC below the chain's natural ceiling. Once the ROB gets large enough for the pipeline to be continuously occupied (around 64 entries here), IPC reaches the dependency ceiling set by the critical-path latency of each operation, and larger ROBs add no further value.

You may wonder why the default ROB is 192 at all if 64 looks enough for both workloads. This is because the workloads we used are deliberately designed microbenchmarks with no memory stalls or other complexities. Real-world workloads routinely encounter load and store misses and use the larger ROB capacity to issue independent instructions during any stalls. The default size of 192 is tuned for the common case on real workloads.

After a simple parameter sweep, let's peek under the hood with an experiment involving a minimal source code change. In the next section, we will modify the size of the integer arithmetic functional unit pool and examine how execution bandwidth limits the exploitation of ILP.

12.4 Execution Unit Bandwidth

The number of integer ALUs in the functional unit pool directly constrains the number of integer operations that can be executed in the same cycle and thereby influences the ability to make use of the available ILP. This experiment measures the effect of sweeping the IntALU count on the performance of the chapter's workloads.

The Experiment

In gem5, the functional-unit pool is defined in FuncUnitConfig.py. Listing 12-8a shows the default IntALU class. It defines six integer ALU units with a one-cycle operation latency.

Listing 12-8a. Default IntALU Definition (from $GEM5_ROOT/src/cpu/o3/FuncUnitConfig.py)

```
class IntALU(FUDesc):
    opList = [OpDesc(opClass="IntAlu")]
    count = 6
```

To change the number of integer ALUs or the corresponding execution bandwidth, set the count field to the desired value and rebuild.

Listing 12-8b. Reducing IntALU Count (in $GEM5_ROOT/src/cpu/o3/FuncUnitConfig.py)

```
# Original:
count = 6

# Modified (example for 2 ALUs):
count = 2
```

After each change, rebuild gem5. Since it is incremental, it should take a much shorter time than the first compilation:

```
cd $GEM5_ROOT
scons build/X86/gem5.opt -j$(nproc)
```

Run simulations with the high_ilp and dep_chain workloads at each count value (1, 2, 4, 6 as the baseline, 8, and 10). Before running, predict and reason about the performance impact you expect for each workload. The commands to run are shown in Listing 12-8c.

Listing 12-8c. Int ALU Count Sweep Run Commands

```
cd $CHAPTER_DIR

# Example for one rebuilt IntALU setting. Replace the suffix
with the
# current count after each rebuild, then repeat for 1, 2, 4, 6,
8, and 10.
$GEM5_ROOT/build/X86/gem5.opt \
    -d results/high_ilp_alu2 \
    configs/ch12_run.py --binary workloads/high_ilp
```

```
$GEM5_ROOT/build/X86/gem5.opt \
    -d results/dep_chain_alu2 \
    configs/ch12_run.py --binary workloads/dep_chain
```

After all runs are complete, compare IPC across the count settings for each workload (using the respective stats.txt). At what count does the scaling stop? Does it match your prediction?

Results and Explanation

Table 12-5 shows how IPC evolves for both workloads as the number of integer ALUs increases.

Table 12-5. *Int ALU Count Sweep Reference Values*

IntALU Count	high_ilp IPC	dep_chain IPC
1	0.84	0.40
2	1.68	0.80
4	3.35	0.80
6 (default)	5.02	0.80
8	5.30	0.80
10	5.30	0.80

On high_ilp, IPC scales almost linearly with the ALU count up to 6, gains modestly at 8, and then plateaus after that. Each additional ALU lets one more of the eight independent chains execute in parallel until other pipeline constraints, including issue width, start constraining performance.

On dep_chain, IPC is 0.80 for any count of 2 or higher, identical to the baseline (6 ALUs). A serial dependency chain issues one integer operation at a time, and more than one ALU provides no benefit. Note that with an

ALU count of 1, integer arithmetic and other operations share the same unit (branches, for instance). This restricts them by forcing each to take turns, and the resulting contention drops throughput.

This experiment essentially isolates execution bandwidth from window size. The previous experiment showed the limit of ILP regarding how far the core can look, determined by the size of the ROB. This experiment shows how execution rate limits it. In other words, even though there are enough instructions to identify ILP opportunities, the execution rate can still limit performance meaningfully. For dep_chain, however, the serial dependency chain is the primary constraint, regardless of the pipeline depth or width, in most cases.

Before moving further, restore the IntALU count to its default value (6) and rebuild. You can simply use git checkout src/cpu/o3/FuncUnitConfig.py to discard local edits in that file:

```
cd $GEM5_ROOT
git checkout src/cpu/o3/FuncUnitConfig.py
scons build/X86/gem5.opt -j$(nproc)
```

So far, we have covered two sweep-style experimental analyses commonly used in research and industry. Next, let's conduct one that includes more complex code modification to measure the cost of branch misprediction recovery.

12.5 Squash Recovery Delay

As you know by now, deeper pipelines pay a larger penalty when a branch misprediction forces recovery. This experiment simulates that effect by adding a fixed delay after a squash before the commit resumes retirement. The predictor accuracy and the workload remain the same, and we only change the cycles per recovery. This should isolate the penalty due to depth directly.

The Experiment

The source code modifications you need to make involve the retirement loop and the recovery transition after squashing completes (Section 12.1.4). The algorithm adds a countdown to block retirement for a fixed number of cycles after squashing finishes. If the countdown is nonzero, the retirement loop exits immediately, causing the retirement to stall even though the ROB may hold instructions ready to retire. Listings 12-9a to 12-9e show the changes needed to enable this algorithm.

Listing 12-9a. Recovery Delay Parameter (in $GEM5_ROOT/src/cpu/o3/BaseO3CPU.py)

```
# After the existing trapLatency parameter, add:
squashRecoveryDelay = Param.Unsigned(
    0, "Extra stall cycles after squash before commit resumes
(0 = disabled)"
)
```

Listing 12-9b. Commit Recovery State (in $GEM5_ROOT/src/cpu/o3/commit.hh)

```
// In the private section of the Commit class, after "CPU
*cpu;", add:
const unsigned squashRecoveryDelay;
unsigned recoveryCountdown;
```

Listing 12-9c. Commit Constructor Initialization (in $GEM5_ROOT/src/cpu/o3/commit.cc, in Commit::Commit())

```
// In the initializer list, after "cpu(_cpu),", add:
squashRecoveryDelay(params.squashRecoveryDelay),
recoveryCountdown(0),
```

Listing 12-9d. Trigger Recovery Delay (in $GEM5_ROOT/src/cpu/o3/commit.cc, in Commit::tick())

```
// Inside the if (rob->isDoneSquashing(tid)) block, after
// "commitStatus[tid] = Running;", add:
if (squashRecoveryDelay > 0)
    recoveryCountdown = squashRecoveryDelay;
```

Listing 12-9e. Stall During Recovery (in $GEM5_ROOT/src/cpu/o3/commit.cc, in Commit::commitInsts())

```
// At the start of the function, before
// "DPRINTF(Commit, \"Trying to commit instructions in the
ROB.\\n\");", add:
if (recoveryCountdown > 0) {
    recoveryCountdown--;
    return;
}
```

After applying the code changes, rebuild gem5. You also need to add one argument to the configuration script to control the delay from the command line and assign it to the CPU without rebuilding. Listing 12-9f shows the change needed.

Listing 12-9f. Delay Argument (in $CHAPTER_DIR/configs/ch12_run.py)

```
# After the --rob-size argument, add:
parser.add_argument("--squash-delay", type=int, default=0)

# After creating the processor, add:
processor.cores[0].core.squashRecoveryDelay = args.squash_delay
```

For the experiment, we will compare delay = 0 (mechanism disabled) against delay = 25 on branch_heavy and dep_chain workloads. You should reason about the results you expect to observe before running the experiment. Listing 12-9g shows the process to run the full experiment.

Listing 12-9g. Squash Recovery Delay Run Commands

```
cd $CHAPTER_DIR

# branch_heavy: baseline vs. delay = 25
$GEM5_ROOT/build/X86/gem5.opt -d results/branch_heavy_delay0 \
    configs/ch12_run.py --squash-delay 0 \
    --binary workloads/branch_heavy

$GEM5_ROOT/build/X86/gem5.opt -d results/branch_heavy_delay25 \
    configs/ch12_run.py --squash-delay 25 \
    --binary workloads/branch_heavy

# dep_chain: baseline vs. delay = 25
$GEM5_ROOT/build/X86/gem5.opt -d results/dep_chain_delay0 \
    configs/ch12_run.py --squash-delay 0 \
    --binary workloads/dep_chain

$GEM5_ROOT/build/X86/gem5.opt -d results/dep_chain_delay25 \
    configs/ch12_run.py --squash-delay 25 \
    --binary workloads/dep_chain
```

After the runs, compare IPC values between the baseline and delayed case for each workload. Does the branch-heavy workload experience more change?

Results and Explanation

Table 12-6. *Squash Recovery Delay Reference Values*

Workload	Delay	IPC	Change
branch_heavy	0	0.93	-
branch_heavy	25	0.70	0.75x
dep_chain	0	0.80	-
dep_chain	25	0.80	1.00x

As you may have expected for branch_heavy, the IPC drops considerably, from 0.93 to 0.70. By design, the experiment increased the number of cycles lost per misprediction, and the high-misprediction workload directly amplified this into a 25% IPC loss.

On dep_chain, the IPC remains unchanged. Since this workload mispredicts infrequently and is not branch-heavy, a larger penalty for a rare event produces a negligible change in performance. This complements the branch-heavy result directly. The same knob that costs branch_heavy a quarter of its IPC has no effect on dep_chain, because the two workloads trigger the target mechanism at very different rates.

With all three experiments under the belt, let's summarize what we covered in the chapter.

Note Before moving on, revert the gem5 source changes and the two temporary lines in configs/ch12_run.py, then rebuild:

```
cd $GEM5_ROOT
git checkout src/cpu/o3/commit.cc src/cpu/o3/commit.hh \
             src/cpu/o3/BaseO3CPU.py
scons build/X86/gem5.opt -j$(nproc)
```

12.6 Summary

This chapter connected the concepts from Chapter 11 to three focused experiments on the gem5 out-of-order core simulator.

The first experiment swept ROB size across high_ilp and dep_chain workloads and illustrated the effect of instruction window size on the ability to exploit available ILP.

The second experiment swept the number of integer ALUs in the functional-unit pool and showed how execution throughput limits performance even in the presence of high ILP and sufficient instruction window length. Together, the first two experiments showed that window size and execution bandwidth are complementary aspects of back-end throughput.

The third experiment illustrated the effect of adding branch misprediction recovery delay while holding the predictor and the program constant. It highlighted that the same change can yield very different outcomes depending on the frequency of mispredictions, underscoring the importance of including a diverse set of workloads in your performance studies.

Together, the three experiments illustrate the general principle that a single architectural change can help one workload, do nothing for another, and even hurt a third.

The next chapter extends this methodology from a single core to multicore systems, where you will explore the effects of shared resources, coherence traffic, and synchronization overheads that single-core simulations cannot capture.

Review Questions

1. Why do the workloads high_ilp and dep_chain behave differently as ROB size is changed in Section 12.3?

2. Explain the reason high_ilp IPC scales nearly linearly with IntALU count while dep_chain is flat for count >= 2 in Section 12.4. Describe what happens at count = 1 that breaks the pattern for dep_chain.

3. In Experiment 3 (Section 12.5), we didn't touch the branch predictor or the workload. Reason whether the misprediction rate should change due to only adding the extra recovery delay. What does that imply about the sensitivity of each workload to the knob?

Exercises

Exercise 1: Extend Experiment 1 (Section 12.3) by changing another window-related structure, such as the physical integer register count or the issue width. Compare the IPC change against the ROB-only sweep, and reason whether the ROB remains the bottleneck or whether another structure constrains performance first.

Exercise 2: In Experiment 2 (Section 12.4), hold the Int ALU count at the default of 6 and instead sweep issueWidth from 2 to 8. Compare the result against the ALU count sweep from Experiment 2. When does issue width become the binding limit rather than the ALU count? Explain why. Repeat the same with other ALU count values.

CHAPTER 13

Multicore CPU Simulation

The previous chapter restricted experimental analysis to a single core to focus on pipeline mechanics and their effects on performance. Most modern systems run multithreaded workloads across several cores, sharing resources such as caches, memory, and interconnects. Understanding a single core in isolation, while extremely important, provides only part of the picture regarding the impact of architectural decisions on performance.

Hence, this chapter extends the single-core methodology from Chapter 12 to multicore systems. In multicore simulations, we will observe serialization-imposed limits, false sharing, and synchronization overheads that are invisible in single-core simulations, using three focused experiments. We will use gem5's Ruby memory system to aid in this exploration. Each experiment follows the same workflow as before.

By the end of the chapter, you will understand how workload parallelism, data layout, and synchronization patterns influence multicore performance. You will also be able to read coherent traffic statistics and explain how a core-count or layout change affects the memory system. As usual, focus on the directional changes observed in the experiments and not on replicating the exact printed values.

A. Pareek, *Performance Modeling of Computer Systems*, Maker Innovations Series,
https://doi.org/10.1007/979-8-8688-2476-0_13

Prerequisites

This chapter assumes you are familiar with

- Multicore concepts from Chapter 11
- gem5 single-core simulation workflow from Chapter 12
- Basic Python and C programming, including pthreads

A Note on gem5 Version: The code listings and configurations used in this chapter are based on gem5 v25.1.0.0 at commit 7a2b0e4 (December 31, 2025). If your gem5 version differs, the exact code and its location may change, but the concepts and methodology remain the same.

Tool Setup

In this chapter, you will work with gem5's Ruby memory system with the MESI two-level coherence protocol. This is needed because Ruby reports per-controller coherence message statistics that are not available with the classic memory system. Hence, we will compile and use a new binary as outlined in Listing 13-1.

Listing 13-1. Building the Ruby MESI Two-Level Binary

```
cd $GEM5_ROOT

# Build the X86 variant with the MESI two-level Ruby protocol
scons build/X86_MESI_Two_Level/gem5.opt -j$(nproc)
```

The build produces build/X86_MESI_Two_Level/gem5.opt, which we will use for all experiments in this chapter.

13.1 Simulator Configuration

Before we begin experimenting, let's cover some important concepts to lay the foundation. These include the two memory-system implementations that gem5 offers, the specific coherence hierarchy you will use in this chapter, the baseline configuration script, and an important constraint the simulator imposes for multithreaded simulations.

13.1.1 Classic and Ruby Memory Systems

gem5 offers two memory-system implementations, depending on the level of simulation complexity. Chapter 12 used the classic memory system, which provides a fast and easily configurable cache hierarchy. It is insufficient for this chapter, however, as the coherence protocol is hardcoded and its stats do not expose coherence traffic at the level of detail needed.

The other option is the Ruby memory system. It is a modeling framework for cache-coherence protocols written in the domain-specific language SLICC. We do not need to learn the details of the language, as Ruby ships with several protocols out of the box, including MESI two-level (private L1, shared L2) and MOESI.

For simplicity, we will not switch the models and perform all experiments in this chapter using Ruby with the MESI two-level protocol.

13.1.2 MESI Two-Level Hierarchy

The MESI two-level hierarchy in Ruby consists of a private L1 data cache and a private L1 instruction cache per core. The L2 cache is shared across all cores and backed by a directory controller. Coherence is maintained at the L1 level via the standard MESI states (Chapter 11). Table 13-1 lists the main parameters we use in this chapter.

Table 13-1. *MESI Two-Level Parameters*

gem5 Parameter	Value	Relevant Concept
l1d_size / l1i_size	32 KiB, 8-way	Private L1 caches
l2_size	1 MiB, 16-way	Shared L2
num_l2_banks	1	Single shared LLC
coherence protocol	MESI two-level	Coherence protocol
clk_freq	3 GHz	Fixed for cross-run comparability
cpu_type	O3CPU	Back-end model

The default Ruby topology connects L1 controllers, L2 controllers, and the directory via a simple point-to-point network.

13.1.3 Configuration Script

Listing 13-2 shows the baseline script used throughout this chapter. It is similar to the one we used for Chapter 12, adapted for multicore runs with the Ruby memory system. The script follows the current gem5 standard-library tutorial pattern for Ruby-based SE simulations in gem5 v25.1.0.0.

Listing 13-2. Baseline Configuration Script (in $CHAPTER_DIR/configs/ch13_multicore.py)

```
import argparse, os
from gem5.components.boards.simple_board import SimpleBoard
from gem5.components.cachehierarchies.ruby \
    .mesi_two_level_cache_hierarchy import (
    MESITwoLevelCacheHierarchy,
)
from gem5.components.memory import SingleChannelDDR4_2400
from gem5.components.processors.cpu_types import CPUTypes
```

```
from gem5.components.processors.simple_processor import
SimpleProcessor
from gem5.isas import ISA
from gem5.resources.resource import BinaryResource
from gem5.simulate.simulator import Simulator
from gem5.utils.requires import requires

requires(isa_required=ISA.X86)

parser = argparse.ArgumentParser()
parser.add_argument("--binary", type=str, required=True)
parser.add_argument("--num-cores", type=int, default=1)
args = parser.parse_args()

cache_hierarchy = MESITwoLevelCacheHierarchy(
    l1d_size="32KiB", l1d_assoc=8,
    l1i_size="32KiB", l1i_assoc=8,
    l2_size="1MiB", l2_assoc=16,
    num_l2_banks=1,
)

memory = SingleChannelDDR4_2400(size="512MiB")

processor = SimpleProcessor(
    cpu_type=CPUTypes.O3, isa=ISA.X86, num_cores=args.
num_cores,
)

board = SimpleBoard(
    clk_freq="3GHz", processor=processor,
    memory=memory, cache_hierarchy=cache_hierarchy,
)

board.set_se_binary_workload(
```

```
    BinaryResource(local_path=os.path.abspath(args.binary)),
    arguments=[str(args.num_cores)],
)

Simulator(board=board).run()
```

Note that we use a --binary flag to specify the workload and a --num-cores flag to set the core count. The script automatically passes the core count as argv[1] to the workload so that it spawns a matching number of threads. For simplicity, we will use the same number of cores as the number of threads we intend to run.

Other parameters are hardcoded to prevent their variation from interfering with our studies.

13.1.4 Ruby Statistics Output

In Chapter 12, you read per-core statistics directly from gem5's stats.txt output file. Ruby produces the same per-core fields but adds message buffer counters on each cache controller. The full stat strings now include a numeric index (cores0, cores1, and so on) to specify each core's counters separately. Listing 13-3 shows an excerpt from a 2-core stats.txt with minimal inter-core sharing.

Listing 13-3. Sample Ruby Statistics Excerpt

```
board.processor.cores0.core.
ipc                                      1.92
board.processor.cores1.core.
ipc                                      1.90
board.processor.cores0.core.commitStats0.
numInsts                         150234
board.processor.cores1.core.commitStats0.
numInsts                         148891
```

```
simSeconds                                        0.000039
board.cache_hierarchy.ruby_system.l1_controllers0.L1Dcache.
m_demand_hits      50123
board.cache_hierarchy.ruby_system.l1_controllers0.L1Dcache.
m_demand_misses    312
board.cache_hierarchy.ruby_system.l1_controllers0.
requestToL1Cache.m_msg_count    8
board.cache_hierarchy.ruby_system.l1_controllers0.
responseToL1Cache.m_msg_count  320
board.cache_hierarchy.ruby_system.l1_controllers1.L1Dcache.
m_demand_hits      49876
board.cache_hierarchy.ruby_system.l1_controllers1.L1Dcache.
m_demand_misses    298
board.cache_hierarchy.ruby_system.l1_controllers1.
requestToL1Cache.m_msg_count    6
board.cache_hierarchy.ruby_system.l1_controllers1.
responseToL1Cache.m_msg_count  304
```

The Ruby-specific fields appear as the message buffer counters on each L1 controller. Table 13-2 lists the ones most relevant to this chapter and what each one means in terms of coherence protocol behavior.

Table 13-2. Key Ruby Message Buffer Statistics

Stat Field	Protocol Meaning
requestToL1Cache.m_msg_count	Inbound forwarded requests from the directory (or the shared L2) to this L1. Increments when another core's miss forces invalidation or data transfer from this L1.
responseToL1Cache.m_msg_count	Inbound data responses from the L2 or directory. Roughly tracks demand misses + coherence-triggered fills.
requestFromL1Cache.m_msg_count	Outbound requests from this L1 to the directory.

Note that a high value of requestToL1Cache can indicate inter-core interference due to coherence, and the experiments in this chapter use it to that extent. Since Ruby reports this statistic per L1 controller, you should sum the requestToL1Cache.m_msg_count values across the active controllers when you want a single run-level total.

13.2 Experimental Design

Before running any experiments, you should carefully plan what to run and what to measure. Let's take a look at the workloads, metrics, and the general experimental process.

13.2.1 Workload Selection

Following the trend we have established, the workloads used in this chapter are specifically designed to expose multicore behavior while keeping other effects negligible to the best extent. Table 13-3 lists each workload and the intended use.

Table 13-3. *Custom Workloads for Multicore Experiments*

Workload	Access Pattern	Working Set	Purpose
parallel_reduce	Per-thread private array summation, final reduction at the end	16 KiB total	Exposes clean multicore scaling when negligible sharing exists
serial_bottleneck	90% of work serial on thread 0, 10% split across all threads	16 KiB	Exposes the parallel speedup ceiling due to serialization
false_share	N threads increment adjacent counters in the same cache line	64 B total (single line)	Exposes the cost of coherence traffic from cache-line granularity
padded_share	Same as false_share but each counter padded to its own cache line	64 B per thread	Control for false_share: identical compute, but no inter-thread sharing
atomic_contend	N threads do atomic RMW on one shared counter	8 B (single line)	Exposes the cost of synchronization on a contended location
atomic_private	Same atomic RMW but each thread operates on its own counter on its own line	8 B per thread	Control for atomic_contend: same atomic instruction, no contention

These six workloads can be thought of as 3 pairs organized by the mechanism they target. parallel_reduce versus serial_bottleneck isolates workload-level parallelism. false_share versus padded_share isolates data layout. atomic_contend versus atomic_private isolates synchronization overheads.

13.2.2 Key Metrics

In Chapter 12, you used per-core IPC as the primary metric, sufficient for single-core experiments. With multiple cores, the more useful metric is execution time (simSeconds). It captures the time it takes the entire multithreaded workload to complete. This conveys the complete bottom-line performance that is hard to judge from individual cores' IPC values. With this metric, the speedup can be conveniently expressed as the ratio of single-core execution time to N-core execution time. We will also use the count of inbound coherence messages at each L1 to uncover how coherence traffic influences performance.

To summarize, the statistics most relevant to this chapter are listed below. In each path, the trailing number (0, 1, ...) selects the core or controller, matching the format shown in Listing 13-3.

- simSeconds: total simulated execution time. This is the primary performance metric for all experiments. It includes thread creation, the parallel kernel, joining, and other setup/teardown overhead.
- board.processor.coresN.core.ipc: per-core instructions per cycle.
- board.cache_hierarchy.ruby_system.l1_controllersN.requestToL1Cache.m_msg_count: inbound coherence messages at each L1.

13.2.3 Experimental Process

We will follow the familiar methodology used in earlier chapters to maintain a clear view of the cause-and-effect relationship. For each experiment, you start with workloads that differ only in sensitizing the mechanism under study and compare what you hypothesized vs. what you observe in the results.

13.2.4 Companion Repository Setup

The configuration script and workloads for this chapter are located in the companion repository at ch13-multicore-sim/. Set the environment variables as shown below before running the experiments:

```
export CHAPTER_DIR=/path/to/ch13-multicore-sim
export GEM5_ROOT=/path/to/gem5
```

The workloads/ directory contains pre-built binaries of the workloads we use in this chapter for convenience, so you can run the experiments directly without compilation.

With the setup in place, let's begin with the first experiment that illustrates the effect of increasing the core counts for multithreaded workloads.

13.3 Multicore Scaling

As you already know, adding cores helps when independent work exists in the absence of bottlenecks caused by shared resources. We will verify this in the current experiment and measure the effect of sweeping core count from 1 to 8 on parallel_reduce and serial_bottleneck workloads.

The Experiment

For this experiment, no source code modifications or rebuilds are required. You only need to pass the core count from the command-line flag (--num-cores) that we exposed in the config script (Listing 13-2). Before running, predict which workloads will scale and which will plateau based on their descriptions in Table 13-3. Listing 13-4 shows how to run the experiment succinctly with a bash for loop. If the loop syntax doesn't work in your shell, each individual command can be run separately.

Listing 13-4. Multicore Scaling Sweep

```
cd $CHAPTER_DIR

# Sweep core count on parallel_reduce
for N in 1 2 4 8; do
    $GEM5_ROOT/build/X86_MESI_Two_Level/gem5.opt \
        -d results/parallel_reduce_n${N} \
        configs/ch13_multicore.py --num-cores $N \
        --binary workloads/parallel_reduce
done

# Sweep core count on serial_bottleneck
for N in 1 2 4 8; do
    $GEM5_ROOT/build/X86_MESI_Two_Level/gem5.opt \
        -d results/serial_bottleneck_n${N} \
        configs/ch13_multicore.py --num-cores $N \
        --binary workloads/serial_bottleneck
done
```

After the runs complete, note down the simulation time for each workload from stats.txt (simSeconds) and compute the speedups relative to the single-threaded case (Section 13.2.2). For example, open results/parallel_reduce_n4/stats.txt and record the simSeconds line.

Results and Explanation

Table 13-4. Multicore Scaling Reference Values

Cores	parallel_reduce simSec (ms)	parallel_reduce Speedup	serial_bottleneck simSec (ms)	serial_ bottleneck Speedup
1	2.83	1.00x	0.44	1.00x
2	1.48	1.92x	0.43	1.02x
4	0.80	3.56x	0.42	1.04x
8	0.46	6.14x	0.42	1.03x

For parallel_reduce, execution time drops significantly from 2.83 ms with one core to 0.46 ms with eight cores, yielding a roughly 6.14x speedup with an 8x increase in cores. This is precisely because of having independent work to utilize multiple cores without significant serialization overhead. Note that, in addition to serialization (at the final reduction point), thread creation, joining, other setup code, etc., also incur minor overheads, preventing perfect scaling.

As you might expect, for serial_bottleneck, the execution time barely changes. Since 90% of the work runs serially on thread 0, the small parallel segment (10%, divided among all threads), combined with other overheads, has no meaningful effect on performance.

The contrast clearly shows that core count is only part of the story, and to extract maximum parallelism for performance, the workload must be amenable to it as well.

While we covered a simple, directed case, sometimes even when the workload is designed to be parallelism-friendly, pathologies creep in and nullify the intended gain. Let's conduct an experiment that demonstrates a common issue known as false sharing.

13.4 False Sharing

If two threads modify independent variables, there should be no coherence issues, ideally. However, if these variables naively map to the same cache block, the coherence protocol will keep moving the cache line back and forth between them, even though there is no need to share the data. This is commonly referred to as false sharing. This experiment measures how the performance cost of this unintentional coherence traffic grows with core count if left unchecked.

From Section 13.2.1, the two workloads sensitize the issue and the solution. false_share packs N counters into a single 64-byte cache line, while padded_share pads them into separate lines. The computation is kept identical to avoid it from influencing the results. Listing 13-5 shows how the shared variables are laid out in both cases.

Listing 13-5. Data Layout (from false_share.c and padded_share.c)

```
// false_share.c: all counters packed into one cache line:
static volatile uint32_t shared_counters[16]
    __attribute__((aligned(64)));

static void do_work(int idx, int iters) {
    for (int i = 0; i < iters; i++)
        shared_counters[idx]++;
}

// padded_share.c: each counter padded to its own cache line:
typedef struct {
    volatile uint32_t counter;
    uint8_t pad[60];
} padded_counter_t;

static padded_counter_t counters[MAX_THREADS]
    __attribute__((aligned(64)));
```

```
static void do_work(int idx, int iters) {
    for (int i = 0; i < iters; i++)
        counters[idx].counter++;
}
```

The Experiment

In this experiment, you will sweep the core count from 2 to 8 on both workloads. Before running, think about what state restrictions a coherence protocol would impose for incrementing counters and what it implies as the number of cores increases. Listing 13-6 shows the commands to run the experiment.

Listing 13-6. False Sharing Sweep

```
cd $CHAPTER_DIR

# Sweep core count on padded_share (baseline)
for N in 2 4 8; do
    $GEM5_ROOT/build/X86_MESI_Two_Level/gem5.opt \
        -d results/padded_share_n${N} \
        configs/ch13_multicore.py --num-cores $N \
        --binary workloads/padded_share
done

# Sweep core count on false_share
for N in 2 4 8; do
    $GEM5_ROOT/build/X86_MESI_Two_Level/gem5.opt \
        -d results/false_share_n${N} \
        configs/ch13_multicore.py --num-cores $N \
        --binary workloads/false_share
done
```

When the runs complete, compare execution times (simSeconds) and the requestToL1Cache counts for each core count. To recap, this can be done by opening each run directory's stats.txt, recording simSeconds, and summing the per-controller requestToL1Cache.m_msg_count values.

Results and Explanation

Table 13-5. *False Sharing Reference Values*

Cores	padded_ share simSec (ms)	padded_ share Speedup	false_ share simSec (ms)	false_ share Speedup	requestToL1Cache (false_share, total across all cores)
2	1.42	1.00x	1.80	1.00x	318,950
4	0.76	1.87x	1.80	1.00x	319,972
8	0.44	3.25x	1.80	1.00x	320,035

As you may have expected, even though the two workloads commit nearly identical total instructions (since they divide the same fixed work among threads), their execution times diverge sharply. padded_share speeds up from 1.42 ms with 2 cores to 0.44 ms with 8 cores (3.25x), while false_share stays at 1.80 ms regardless of the core count.

In the false_share workload, each write requires exclusive ownership of the shared line, forcing an ownership transfer whenever another core last wrote to it. Contrary to this, for padded_share, each thread's line is private, and no ownership transfer is required regardless of core count. The requestToL1Cache statistic further corroborates the story. It is consistently high for false_share, indicative of heavy coherence traffic. The total stays nearly constant because the total work is fixed and preserves the same shared-line contention pattern.

Note that a single-core simulator would exhibit identical behavior for both workloads and encounter no issues with either approach. When parallel code fails to scale, as a modeler, you should look at coherence message counts rather than relying on statistics about individual core behavior.

Let's now look at the impact of coherence when multiple threads explicitly and intentionally need to share data with each other.

13.5 Synchronization Cost

In the previous experiment, we covered a problem that can occur unintentionally and is fixed with a simple layout change. The work remains the same in both cases. In this experiment, we will examine a case where threads genuinely need to share a variable and update it atomically. An example of this is the global atomic counter mechanism, which counts total events across all threads and uses an atomic read-modify-write instruction to ensure each update is indivisible. In other words, between reading and updating the global counter from one thread, no other thread should change it. Different platforms offer mechanisms to achieve this, and on x86, __atomic_fetch_add is a commonly used example for this pattern.

To illustrate the performance impact of this, we will use the atomic_contend workload and atomic_private strictly as a control, where this problem doesn't exist but the work remains the same (albeit private). The control case doesn't offer a solution to the problem, but it clearly highlights it as a baseline. Listing 13-7 shows the hot loops from each workload.

Listing 13-7. Worker Loops (from atomic_contend.c and atomic_private.c)

```
// atomic_contend.c - all threads target the same counter:
static uint64_t shared_counter
    __attribute__((aligned(64))) = 0;

static void do_work(int iters) {
    for (int i = 0; i < iters; i++)
        __atomic_fetch_add(&shared_counter, 1, __ATOMIC_
        RELAXED);
}

// atomic_private.c - each thread targets its own counter:
typedef struct {
    uint64_t counter;
    uint8_t pad[56];
} padded_counter_t;

static padded_counter_t counters[MAX_THREADS]
    __attribute__((aligned(64)));

static void do_work(int idx, int iters) {
    for (int i = 0; i < iters; i++)
        __atomic_fetch_add(&counters[idx].counter, 1, __ATOMIC_
        RELAXED);
}
```

The Experiment

In this experiment, you will sweep the core count from 1 to 8 on both workloads. No source or configuration changes are required beyond selecting the binary. Before running, you should predict and reason about the behavior of the shared-counter and private-counter versions as the core count increases. Listing 13-8 shows the commands to run the experiment.

Listing 13-8. Synchronization Cost Sweep

```
cd $CHAPTER_DIR

# Sweep core count on atomic_contend (shared counter)
for N in 1 2 4 8; do
    $GEM5_ROOT/build/X86_MESI_Two_Level/gem5.opt \
        -d results/atomic_contend_n${N} \
        configs/ch13_multicore.py --num-cores $N \
        --binary workloads/atomic_contend
done

# Sweep core count on atomic_private (per-thread counters)
for N in 1 2 4 8; do
    $GEM5_ROOT/build/X86_MESI_Two_Level/gem5.opt \
        -d results/atomic_private_n${N} \
        configs/ch13_multicore.py --num-cores $N \
        --binary workloads/atomic_private
done
```

After the runs, note down and compare the execution times (simSeconds) and the requestToL1Cache metric across each core count for both workloads, similar to the last experiment.

Results and Explanation

Table 13-6. *Synchronization Cost Reference Values*

Cores	atomic_ private simSec (ms)	atomic_ private Speedup	atomic_ contend simSec (ms)	atomic_ contend Speedup	requestToL1Cache (atomic_contend, sum across all threads)
1	13.94	1.00x	13.94	1.00x	0
2	7.02	1.99x	11.55	1.21x	1,599,268
4	3.56	3.92x	8.62	1.62x	1,599,962
8	1.84	7.60x	8.62	1.62x	1,600,034

Starting from a single core, both workloads have identical execution times of 13.94 ms. This communicates that the rest of the story is primarily driven by contention.

atomic_private scales cleanly, and the execution time drops from 13.94 ms to 1.84 ms at eight cores (7.60x speedup). This is predictable, as each thread's counter remains in its L1 in the modified state, avoiding the inter-core ownership transfers that dominate in atomic_contend.

atomic_contend, the primary focus of the experiment hits a ceiling. Execution time plateaus at 4 cores (at 8.62 ms) and doesn't improve as the core count increases. The coherence message count stays at approximately 1.6 million across all multicore configurations. This highlights that coherence traffic is an important barrier to performance scaling with increasing core counts. Each thread's atomic update forces a line transfer through the directory and serializes updates globally. The throughput, instead, is bounded by the speed at which a single line can transfer between the cores.

This experiment highlights the unavoidable costs associated with some common algorithms and the need to be aware of them when interpreting simulation results. This, in turn, can lead you to find relevant mitigation strategies programmatically or architecturally.

13.6 Summary

This chapter used gem5 with a Ruby MESI two-level memory system to illustrate the three-pronged effects of workload parallelism with three directed simulation experiments.

The first experiment evaluated the effects of increasing the core count from 1 to 8 on an extremely parallel workload and contrasted it with a heavily serialized workload. It demonstrated how the fraction of parallelizable work bounds the achievable speedup.

The second experiment demonstrated the detrimental effect of unintentional interaction between independent threads strictly attributable to suboptimal data layout. A simple change completely removed the bottleneck and allowed workload parallelism to improve the performance as intended.

The third experiment demonstrated a real issue arising from workload parallelism that cannot be avoided with a simple layout change. The primary goal was to quantitatively assess the detrimental effect of synchronization, even when the algorithm is otherwise perfectly parallelizable.

In each experiment, the requestToL1Cache coherence message count was invaluable for confirming the hypothesis and further validating the decision to use the Ruby memory system in this chapter.

The next chapter shifts to GPU modeling, where the execution model significantly alters architectural implications. We will start with a quick coverage of essential concepts in Chapter 14, followed by hands-on experimentation in Chapter 15.

Review Questions

1. In the first experiment, why do the speedups of parallel_reduce and serial_bottleneck differ so much, despite both using the same number of cores and the same hardware configuration?

2. Explain why it is easy to recover performance through a single change in Experiment 2, but not in Experiment 3. Why do Experiment 3's changes not achieve the same outcome?

3. Explain the reason the Ruby memory model was needed for this chapter, as opposed to the regular gem5 build used in the last one.

Exercises

Exercise 1: Implement a common mitigation for the atomic_contend workload by accumulating locally for K iterations and issuing a single atomic add of the accumulated value. As an example, copy atomic_contend.c to atomic_batched.c and modify the worker loop to accumulate locally for BATCH_SIZE iterations before each atomic add. Sweep K = 1, 4, 16, 64, 256 at 4 cores. Explain your observations.

Exercise 2: Repeat the experiment in Section 13.4 for higher core counts, i.e., 16, 32, etc. Does the performance gap between false_share and padded_share grow, shrink, or stay the same as you increase the core count? Use the observed inbound L1 message count to help with interpretation.

PART V

GPU Modeling

CHAPTER 14

GPU Architecture

Part V shifts the focus from CPU to GPU architecture and simulation. This chapter covers the foundations needed to understand GPU systems you will model in Chapter 15. GPUs started as efficient graphics processors. Today, they are used everywhere for high-throughput computing, thanks to their unique execution model. This chapter focuses on general-purpose compute (GPGPU) execution, which is what GPU performance simulators like Accel-Sim target.

Staying with the book's common theme, the chapter takes the modeler's perspective and does not aim to serve as a GPU programming guide or rederive the theory found in architecture textbooks. You are encouraged to follow external resources to go deeper into the topics covered.

We will first look at the execution model, followed by how it is implemented in the compute units. Then we'll examine warp scheduling and how it enables latency hiding. Next, we will cover the memory hierarchy from on-chip memory to high-bandwidth memory (HBM). Finally, we will discuss occupancy and the resources that limit it, as well as common performance pathologies resulting from misalignment between kernel behavior and hardware design assumptions.

This chapter is vendor-neutral. The two major GPU vendors use the same fundamental model, but their terminology and internal organization differ. Both are noted when differences matter. "Warp" refers to the SIMT execution unit (called wavefront in AMD) and "compute unit" to the

A. Pareek, *Performance Modeling of Computer Systems*, Maker Innovations Series,
https://doi.org/10.1007/979-8-8688-2476-0_14

hardware block (called SM by NVIDIA or CU by AMD). "Matrix engine" covers dedicated hardware (called tensor core or matrix core). Graphics features and vendor-specific settings are outside this book's scope.

14.1 GPU Execution Model

Contrary to the CPU, which is designed with deep pipelined machinery to execute a single instruction stream as fast as possible, a GPU devotes its hardware budget to execution capacity and relies on the programmer to provide thousands of threads to keep it busy. This is achieved through programming abstractions and hardware architectural choices that this section covers.

14.1.1 SIMT and Warps

GPUs do not execute individual threads. They are grouped into bundles of fixed size that execute the same instructions together across parallel execution lanes. This bundle is called a warp (or wavefront), and the execution model is called SIMT (single instruction, multiple threads). Warps are typically 32 or 64 threads wide in the current architectures.

The warp is the unit of scheduling for GPUs. When the scheduler selects work, it selects a warp and all lanes advance together with the same instruction but using different data. Warp sizes determine the scope of memory coalescing (Section 14.3), the scope of penalties from divergence (Section 14.5), and the minimum useful parallelism a kernel must expose. Due to its significant implications for performance, it is usually a first-order configuration parameter in simulators.

14.1.2 Thread Blocks and Grids

The programmer does not create warps directly; instead, GPU computation is organized into thread blocks and grids.

A thread block, also called a cooperative thread array or workgroup, is a group of threads that can cooperate with shared memory and barrier synchronization. Thread blocks are set at kernel launch with configurable dimensions (1D, 2D, 3D). The typical maximum size is 1024 threads. The hardware splits each block into warps. For example, a block of 512 threads contains 16 warps. If the block size isn't a multiple of the warp size, the last warp is padded with inactive threads, which still use hardware resources.

From the hardware's perspective, thread blocks are independent. In the default execution model, they can execute in any order, on any available hardware unit, without any guarantee of coresidence. Threads within the same block, however, can use barrier instructions to synchronize and wait for completion.

A grid is the next higher abstraction level. It is the collection of all thread blocks in a single kernel (the GPU function that all threads execute) launch. Its dimensions determine the total number of thread blocks and, hence, the total thread count for the kernel. The hardware distributes thread blocks from the grid to execution units as resources become available. Figure 14-1 shows the hierarchy described above.

```
                              Grid
+-------------------------------------------------------------------+
|                                                                   |
|  Block (0,0)             Block (1,0)             Block (2,0)      |
| +-----------------+     +-----------------+     +-----------------+ |
| | Warp 0          |     | Warp 0          |     | Warp 0          | |
| |  t0 t1 ... t31  |     |  t0 t1 ... t31  |     |  t0 t1 ... t31  | |
| | Warp 1          |     | Warp 1          |     | Warp 1          | |
| |  t0 t1 ... t31  |     |  t0 t1 ... t31  |     |  t0 t1 ... t31  | |
| |  ...            |     |  ...            |     |  ...            | |
| | Warp N          |     | Warp N          |     | Warp N          | |
| |  t0 t1 ... t31  |     |  t0 t1 ... t31  |     |  t0 t1 ... t31  | |
| +-----------------+     +-----------------+     +-----------------+ |
|                                                                   |
|  Block (0,1)             Block (1,1)             Block (2,1)      |
| +-----------------+     +-----------------+     +-----------------+ |
| |  ...            |     |  ...            |     |  ...            | |
| +-----------------+     +-----------------+     +-----------------+ |
|                                                                   |
+-------------------------------------------------------------------+

                   Block scheduler distributes
                     blocks to compute units
                              |
                              v

  Compute Unit 0          Compute Unit 1          Compute Unit 2
 +-----------------+     +-----------------+     +-----------------+
 | Block (0,0)     |     | Block (1,0)     |     | Block (2,0)     |
 | Block (0,1)     |     | Block (1,1)     |     | Block (2,1)     |
 | (if resources   |     | (if resources   |     | (if resources   |
 |  permit)        |     |  permit)        |     |  permit)        |
 +-----------------+     +-----------------+     +-----------------+
```

Figure 14-1. *Thread, Block, and Grid Hierarchy*

14.1.3 The Compute Unit

The compute unit is the GPU's analog to the CPU core. However, unlike a CPU, the compute unit is designed to keep many warps resident and relies on switching between ready ones to hide latency. A GPU contains multiple compute units organized in different ways depending on the architecture, generation, etc.

A compute unit typically contains the following core components internally:

Register File: This is a large group of registers (~ 128–512 KB), shared by all threads on an SM. Each thread gets a private allocation from this pool. All resident threads' register needs must fit within it. Organization differs across vendors: AMD uses fewer, wider vector registers; NVIDIA uses more scalar registers. Total storage is usually similar.

Execution Units: Each compute unit contains a set of execution units organized by functionality. This includes an integer and floating-point (FP) unit for standard arithmetic, special-function units for transcendental functions (sine, cosine, etc., at lower throughput), load/store units for memory access, and other architecture-specific dedicated units, such as FP64. These are shared across all resident warps. The throughput for FP instructions depends on their precision as well. Typically, FP16 instructions run at twice the rate and FP64 at a fraction of the FP32 rate, depending on the architecture.

Warp Scheduler: The hardware logic block that selects eligible warps and issues their instructions to execution units each cycle. The exact architecture varies between vendors and generations, but the fundamentals remain the same. For example, some architectures use multiple independent schedulers that work on statically assigned subsets of warps, while others use a single scheduler that cycles across execution units.

L1 Data Cache: Used for hardware-managed caching of global memory accesses. Generally, the capacity is around 16–128 KB per compute unit.

Shared Memory: This is a software-managed scratchpad that threads within a thread block use for fast inter-thread communication. The capacity (generally in tens to hundreds of KBs) and organization vary across architectures. Some use physically shared partitioned space with L1 cache, while others use separate physical locations.

Matrix Engines: These are dedicated units for matrix multiply-accumulate operations found in modern GPUs. A matrix engine instruction computes D = A x B + C (where A, B, C, and D are small matrix tiles) by sourcing the operands from the register file and writing the results back to it. Note that this is fundamentally different from the SIMT lane path in that, instead of one scalar operation per thread per lane, the matrix engine processes the full tile multiply-accumulate across the warp with a single instruction. Instruction throughput through these engines scales with operand precision, and the chip's specification usually lists multiple peak throughputs.

Figure 14-2 shows the typical high-level organization of the compute unit.

```
                         Compute Unit
+------------------------------------------------------------+
|                                                            |
|  Warp Scheduler                                            |
|  +----------------------------------------------------+   |
|  |  Eligible warp pool                                |   |
|  |  [W0] [W1] [W2] [W3] [W4] ... [Wn]                 |   |
|  |                                                    |   |
|  |  Select eligible warp --> Issue one instruction    |   |
|  +------+--------+----------+-----------+-------------+   |
|         |        |          |           |                  |
|         v        v          v           v                  |
|     +------+ +------+ +--------+ +---------+              |
|     | INT/ | | SFU  | | Matrix | | LD / ST |              |
|     | FP   | |      | | Engine | |  Unit   |              |
|     +------+ +------+ +--------+ +---------+              |
|         |        |          |           |                  |
|         +--------+----------+-----------+                  |
|                     |                                      |
|                     v                                      |
|  +----------------------------------------------------+   |
|  |            Register File  (128 - 512 KB)           |   |
|  |      Per-thread private allocation from pool       |   |
|  +----------------------------------------------------+   |
|                                                            |
|  +-------------------------+ +------------------------+   |
|  |  Shared Memory          | |  L1 Data Cache         |   |
|  |  (software-managed)     | |  (hardware-managed)    |   |
|  +-------------------------+ +------------------------+   |
|              |                          |                  |
+------------------------------------------------------------+
               |                          |
               +------------+-------------+
                            |
                            v
                       To L2 / HBM
```

***Figure 14-2.** Compute Unit Block Diagram*

A GPU contains multiple compute units, and the count varies by SKU and generation. When a kernel is launched, the block scheduler distributes thread blocks across compute units, and each unit holds multiple thread blocks simultaneously as long as the aggregate resource demand (registers, shared memory, warp slots) fits within its limits. Table 14-1 shows representative parameters for a modern GPU compute unit. The values are from publicly documented data and represent ranges rather than a single product.

Table 14-1. *Representative GPU Compute Unit Parameters*

Parameter	Typical Range	Description
Warp Size	32–64 threads	Threads per warp (32 on NVIDIA; 32 or 64 on AMD depending on architecture family)
Max Threads per Block	1,024	Maximum threads in a single thread block
Max Warps per Compute Unit	32–64	Maximum concurrent warps resident on a compute unit
Max Thread Blocks per Compute Unit	8–32	Maximum concurrent thread blocks
Warp Schedulers per Compute Unit	1–4	Scheduling units selecting warps for execution
Register File	128–512 KB	Total register storage shared across all resident threads
Shared Memory	48–228 KB	Software-managed scratchpad; fixed or configurable depending on architecture
L1 Data Cache	16–128 KB	Hardware-managed cache per compute unit
L2 Cache (chip-wide)	10s–100s MB	Shared across all compute units

With the execution model's static structure and the relevant hardware structures covered, the next section examines the dynamic behavior.

14.2 Warp Scheduling

The key to high throughput in GPUs is keeping the compute unit's execution resources busy. On the CPU, the out-of-order machinery is designed to achieve the same with available instructions within a window. For the GPU, the warp scheduler plays the corresponding role. This section will cover the scheduling mechanism, the latency spectrum it aims to address, and the conditions for effective latency hiding, which are essential for accurate performance modeling.

14.2.1 Scheduling Mechanics

In Section 14.1.3, you learned about the warp scheduler as a component of the compute unit that selects eligible warps and issues their instructions. Let us now understand the eligibility and how the scheduler makes decisions.

A warp is eligible to be issued upon four conditions being met. (1) Its next instruction has been fetched, (2) its source operands are ready, (3) the functional unit needed for it is available, and (4) it is not waiting on a barrier synchronization. The scheduler examines the pool of such warps each cycle and selects one to be issued.

Once a warp is selected, the scheduler issues one instruction from it to the appropriate path, such as the SIMT lanes, the matrix engine, or the memory unit. A scoreboard mechanism tracks when the instruction is issued and marks the destinations pending. This information is used to select the eligibility of subsequent instructions from the same or different warps. Some architectures optimize this further by recording short- and long-latency operations separately and allowing the scheduler to distinguish between the two when making decisions.

If several warps are eligible, the scheduling policy determines which one is selected. While exact policies in real hardware are not often publicly documented, some high-level examples are listed below:

Greedy-Then-Oldest (GTO): This favors the currently running warp until it stalls, then picks the oldest ready.

Loose Round-Robin (LRR): This cycles through the warps in an approximate round-robin order.

Two-Level Scheduling: This partitions warps into active and pending groups and schedules only among the active group until they all stall. At that point, pending and active groups are swapped for issuing.

14.2.2 Instruction and Memory Latencies

The completion times for GPU operations can vary vastly. This influences how many warps the scheduler needs to track and how the scheduling policy should balance them to achieve the best throughput. The three primary categories are listed below:

Standard Arithmetic on SIMT Lanes: Operations such as FP32 and INT32 add, multiply, and FMA complete in around four cycles on modern architectures.

Special Function Unit Operations: Transcendental functions such as sine, cos, etc., take longer, approximately 20–28 cycles. FP64 operations have similar latencies as FP32, but at a much lower throughput (Section 14.1.3).

Memory Operations: These span a much wider range. Shared memory accesses complete in 20–30 cycles, depending on the microarchitecture. L1 and L2 cache hits are around 25–40 and 100–500 cycles, respectively. An access that goes all the way to HBM costs 250–700 cycles.

Table 14-2 summarizes representative latencies of recent architecture generations. Specific latencies are best confirmed via microbenchmarking on the target device.

Table 14-2. Representative Instruction and Memory Latencies

Operation	Latency (cycles)	Notes
FP32/INT32 arithmetic	~4	Pipelined
FP64 arithmetic	~4–8	Similar latency, lower throughput (Section 14.1)
SFU/transcendentals	~20–28	
Shared memory access	~20–30	Varies by architecture; subject to bank conflicts
L1 cache hit	~25–40	Per compute unit
L2 cache hit	~100–500	Chip-wide shared cache
HBM (off-chip DRAM)	~250–700	

14.2.3 Latency Hiding

To effectively hide the latency, if a scheduler issues one instruction per cycle and the issued warp is blocked for L cycles, it may need as many as L other eligible warps, in the worst case, to avoid a bubble. Hence, for arithmetic-bound code with 4-cycle dependencies, a handful of warps are fine, but for a memory-bound kernel with dominant latency in hundreds of cycles, due to HBM accesses, the scheduler needs hundreds of warps to keep up. In practice, the actual number lies between these two extremes. Note that a single compute unit holds at most 32-64 warps, so warp count alone may not fully hide the latency. In practice, several mechanisms help close the gap, such as efficient caching, memory coalescing, and overlapping compute and memory operations.

Some factors can limit this mechanism's effectiveness and expose latency. The kernel may not expose enough total parallelism, i.e., the grid is too small, or the blocks are too few. The kernel's per-thread resource requirements may limit how many warps can fit on a compute unit, for example, using many registers per thread or a large shared memory allocation.

As you can see, the order-of-magnitude variation in memory latencies is an important factor to consider when tuning the scheduler design and algorithm. Let's turn to the memory hierarchy to understand how this variation comes about.

14.3 Memory Hierarchy

This section walks through memory system tiers from the compute unit outward. We will cover the access patterns that determine effective bandwidth and mechanisms to overlap between compute and memory transfers effectively.

14.3.1 Shared Memory and L1 Cache

Earlier, we covered shared memory and L1 data cache as two distinct on-chip storage mechanisms for data. Shared memory is software-managed storage that the programmer explicitly loads data into to enable cooperative data reuse across threads within a block. The L1 data cache, however, is a hardware-managed storage, similar to the traditional caches we have seen in earlier chapters, that stores global memory accesses based on access patterns with no programmer intervention. A kernel can use both at the same time.

Shared memory uses bank organization to enable parallel access. Accesses from a warp's thread to different banks are complete in a single transaction. If the accesses are made to the same bank, however, they get serialized. In other words, if N accesses conflict on a bank at a time, it costs N times the single-access latency. Typically, the usage pattern involves threads loading data from global memory into shared memory, synchronized through barriers to ensure all loads have completed, and then reading from it to perform cooperative computation. This enables data reuse across threads within a block without repeated accesses to the global memory. In some architectures, shared memory and the L1 data cache share a single physical SRAM partition, with a configurable split per kernel based on data sharing and performance needs. The combined pool ranges from around 80–256 KB per compute unit on modern hardware.

Modeling Perspective: On architectures with shared memory and L1 cache on the same partition, changing shared memory allocation simultaneously changes L1 cache capacity. This coupling can create effects that can be misattributed to cache configuration when the root cause may be the shared memory allocation.

14.3.2 L2 Cache and HBM

The L2 cache sits outside the compute units and is shared across all. It is the first chip-wide shared resource in the memory hierarchy. The L2 is partitioned across memory channels, with each partition connected to a local memory controller. Compute units and L2 partitions are connected via an on-chip interconnect, mostly a crossbar or a mesh network. This means that a compute unit accessing a non-local partition will incur additional latency, making L2 cache access time non-uniform across the chip. This non-locality is an important factor to consider while modeling, as the results will vary significantly if the simulator doesn't use the same partitioning.

In the general case, the L2 handles atomic operations on global memory. An atomic update from any compute unit travels to the appropriate L2 slice, executes there, and returns the result. This can make L2 a serialization point and a bottleneck for workloads with high atomic contention.

Further away from the core, HBM (High Bandwidth Memory) provides the GPU's primary storage capacity. A modern data center GPU has multiple HBM stacks that enable aggregate bandwidth of multiple TB/s. HBM is the dominant constraint for most modern GPU workloads, especially in the AI/ML world. Its capacity determines the largest problem that can fit on the device, its bandwidth sets the ceiling for memory-bound kernels, and its latency is the longest stall the scheduler must hide.

Figure 14-3 shows the high-level block diagram of the memory hierarchy, including the above components.

```
       Per Compute Unit                          Chip-Wide
 <--------------------------->      <---------------------------->

 +----------------------------+
 |      Register File         |      128-512 KB per CU
 |      (1 cycle)             |      Private per thread
 +----------------------------+
              |
 +----------------------------+
 | Shared Memory |  L1 Cache  |      ~256 KB combined per CU
 | (software     | (hardware  |      20-30 cycles
 |  managed)     |  managed)  |
 +----------------------------+
              |
 - - - - - - -|- - - - - - - - - - - - - - - - - - - - - -
              |     Compute unit boundary
              v
 +--------------------------------------------+
 |            L2 Cache                        |
 |  Partitioned across memory channels        |  A few to ~50 MB
 |  Non-uniform access latency                |  80-200 cycles
 |  Hosts global atomic operations            |
 +--------------------------------------------+
              |
              v
 +--------------------------------------------+
 |            HBM                             |
 |  Multiple stacks                           |  Tens to hundreds of GB
 |  Multi-TB/s aggregate bandwidth            |  250-500 cycles
 +--------------------------------------------+
```

Figure 14-3. *GPU Memory Hierarchy*

14.3.3 Memory Coalescing

Each thread comprising a warp produces an address with load and store instructions. The hardware combines these per-thread addresses into the smallest set of memory transactions to reduce traffic. In the worst case, it can still be one transaction per thread; in the best case, if the threads access consecutive locations within an aligned region, they can all be combined into a single transaction.

The difference in bandwidth between a well-coalesced access and an uncoalesced one can be an order of magnitude or more, despite transferring the same number of bytes. The pattern is determined by the interaction of the kernel's data layout and indexing with the hardware's coalescing machinery. This emphasizes the need to tune the memory layout properly to achieve the best memory bandwidth for a workload.

14.3.4 Asynchronous Data Movement

Recent GPU architectures have added a dedicated mechanism for moving data asynchronously between different tiers of the memory hierarchy. This primarily addresses the need to feed the matrix engines at full throughput, as a warp can issue data transfer and continue executing computation on previously arrived data. This enables software pipelining, as data fetch and computation can overlap. The specific mechanism and programming interfaces vary by architecture, but the fundamental principle remains the same.

Let's summarize the memory hierarchy with representative data from modern data center GPUs in Table 14-3.

Table 14-3. *Representative Memory Hierarchy Characteristics*

Tier	Capacity per CU	Latency (cycles)	Notes
Registers	128-512 KB	1	Per-thread private allocation; no misses or replacement
Shared memory / L1	~80-256 KB combined	~20-30	Banked; configurable split on some architectures
L2 cache (chip-wide)	10s to 100s MB	~100-500	Partitioned across channels; hosts global atomics
HBM (chip-wide)	Tens to hundreds of GB total	~250-700	Multi-TB/s aggregate bandwidth

Ideally, a scheduler would simply keep as many warps as possible to maximize latency hiding. This is not possible in practice, and the next section covers the limits and how they affect performance.

14.4 Occupancy and Resource Limits

Occupancy is the ratio of the number of warps resident on a compute unit relative to the maximum that the hardware can place. It is determined by the kernel's resource demand on one hand and the compute unit's fixed limits on the other. This, in turn, can determine how effectively the scheduler hides latency. In this section, we will discuss what limits occupancy and see how that relates to performance.

14.4.1 Resource Limits

Occupancy is determined by the resources available in the compute unit. Each independent resource imposes an upper bound on the number of resident warps, and the most constrained one determines the overall possibility. The primary independent resource limits are listed below:

Warp Slots: Each compute unit's hardware structure can hold a fixed maximum number of warps regardless of any resource usage. For current-generation architectures, it is typically 32–64.

Register File: The register pool available to a compute unit is divided among all resident threads. Thus, a kernel that uses fewer registers per thread can fit more threads, and vice versa. For example, for a compute unit with 65,536 32-bit registers and a maximum of 64 warps, if the kernel needs 64 registers per thread, the occupancy is 50%, as it can accommodate 65,536/64 = 1024 threads, or 32 warps.

Important Note: The example above divides the register count evenly for clarity. In practice, registers are not allocated individually; both major vendors allocate them in fixed-size blocks. This means that the per-thread register count and achievable occupancy are step functions rather than smooth curves. In other words, a small increase in register usage can cross a block boundary, leading to a disproportionate drop in occupancy. The exact allocation granularity varies by architecture, and both vendors provide tools to calculate the actual achievable values for a given kernel and target device combination.

Shared Memory: The shared memory pool is divided among the resident thread blocks, and hence, the memory needed per block can constrain occupancy. For example, if the compute unit has 228 KB of shared memory and the kernel needs 96 KB per block, only two blocks can fit. If each block contains 8 warps, the occupancy is only 25% if the maximum number of warp slots is 64.

Block Slots: In addition to warp slots, each unit also has a hardware-defined limit of the maximum number of blocks it can track concurrently, typically 8–32. As an example, if a kernel has small blocks of 64 threads (2 warps), it can hit the limit even if the other resources are underutilized.

These independent resource constraints highlight the importance of careful tuning to balance kernel demand and hardware limits and achieve the best performance and fairness across all. In practice, optimal design points are determined through empirical tuning, highlighting the importance of simulation once again.

Modeling Perspective: Occupancy doesn't communicate how many warps are eligible to issue at any given cycle. A kernel can achieve a high occupancy and still leave the scheduler idle if all resident warps are simultaneously blocked. You must check the warp issue efficiency (the fraction of cycles where the scheduler found an eligible warp) along with the occupancy ratio.

With an understanding of the hardware-imposed limits on occupancy, let's now look at specific ways GPU throughput breaks down when kernel behavior works against the hardware's design assumptions.

14.5 Performance Pathologies

In practice, many conditions need to be met to allow the GPU throughput model to achieve the best results; else, the performance can suffer severe degradation. This includes uniform control flow within warps, aligned memory access patterns, balanced execution resource use, and so on. This section covers common scenarios that lead to suboptimal performance. For each of these, mitigation techniques are extensively documented in vendor programming guides and the references listed at the end of the chapter.

14.5.1 Warp Divergence

Since the hardware can only issue one instruction across the warp's lanes at a time, if threads within a warp take different control paths on branch instructions or have loops with differing iteration counts, each distinct path must be executed separately, with only the threads on that path doing useful work. The cost is proportional to the number of distinct paths within the warp. For example, a two-way branch roughly doubles execution time for that code section. A data-dependent loop, where threads execute different counts, costs as much as the maximum iteration count in the warp.

This is typically caused by data layout issues where the work assigned to threads sharing a warp varies in type or amount. This is commonly fixed by arranging the work so that threads in the same warp follow the same path, and there are numerous software-level techniques to achieve it. This problem is worse for architectures with higher warp sizes, e.g., 64-wide.

14.5.2 Uncoalesced Memory Access

If a warp's constituent threads access scattered addresses, the hardware issues many small transactions instead of a few large coalesced ones. This results in data wastage as transactions fetch aligned blocks only to discard most of it.

This usually results in a high reported memory bandwidth utilization with low useful throughput. In common profiling tools, this is reported as low memory transaction efficiency or a high ratio of sectors transferred vs. sectors used by the kernel.

14.5.3 Bank Conflicts

As we covered before, shared memory is organized in banks to enable parallel access. This means that memory access patterns will serialize if they are not well aligned with the bank structure. For example, a 2D array stored in row-major order and accessed by column with a stride equal to the bank count will likely cause each access to hit the same bank and incur the worst-case serialized cost.

You should note that if multiple threads access the same exact address within a bank, hardware typically broadcasts the value in a single transaction rather than serializing.

14.5.4 Atomic Contention

Since global atomics to the same address are serialized at the L2 partition (in common cases) that owns the address, when many threads across the chip contend for the same address, throughput can drop sharply. Some examples of such patterns are shared counters or histogram updates.

14.5.5 Execution Throughput Bottlenecks

If the arithmetic work in an execution kernel is concentrated on a single unit type, it can hit the unit's throughput ceiling even with other units sitting idle. Some examples are heavy transcendental use or FP64 work on consumer hardware, or using only SIMT lanes while the matrix engine sits idle.

14.6 Summary

This chapter covered essential GPU architecture concepts necessary for conducting simulation experiments. The key takeaways are the following:

First, GPUs execute work through the SIMT model. Threads are grouped in fixed numbers, called warps, and execute the same instruction together. The programmer organizes threads into grids and blocks, which are mapped onto compute units by hardware. The primary components of a compute unit are the register file, execution units, warp scheduler, shared memory, L1 cache, and matrix engines.

Second, the warp scheduler is responsible for keeping the execution units busy by switching among resident warps whenever the current one encounters a stall. This requires enough warps to be present in the eligible pool and an effective scheduling policy to optimally use them when needed.

Third, the memory hierarchy consists of small per-compute storage, such as registers, shared memory, and L1 cache; and chip-wide storage, including L2 cache and HBM. Shared memory is software-managed and enables cooperative data reuse in a block, whereas L1 cache is hardware-managed.

Fourth, occupancy depends on constraints imposed by four independent resource limits. These are warp slots, register files, shared memory, and block slots. Performance depends on balancing these limits with kernel demand.

Fifth, performance pathologies, such as warp divergence, uncoalesced memory accesses, and bank conflicts, result from kernel behavior that violates architectural assumptions. Recognizing these is essential for resolving common performance issues.

With the basic concepts covered, the next chapters put them into practice through simulations. We will use Accel-Sim as the simulator of choice due to its widespread adoption in the research community.

Review Questions

1. You observe high memory bandwidth utilization with low kernel throughput in a simulation run. What are the two possible causes that we covered, and how would you distinguish between them using profiling data?

2. Consider a compute unit with 65,536 32-bit registers running a kernel with 96 registers per thread and blocks of 256 threads. What is the maximum number of resident warps considering the register limit exclusively (assuming simple register division, and ignoring allocation granularity)? What would be the binding constraint if the kernel requests 96 KB of shared memory per block and the compute unit has 228 KB available to use?

3. Explain the effect of warp size on memory coalescing efficiency and divergence cost. In what sense do these two push in opposite directions?

Further Reading

W. W. Hwu, D. B. Kirk, and I. El Hajj, *Programming Massively Parallel Processors: A Hands-on Approach*, 4th Edition, Morgan Kaufmann, 2022. The standard textbook on GPU programming and architecture.

T. M. Aamodt, W. W. L. Fung, and T. G. Rogers, *General-Purpose Graphics Processor Architectures*, Synthesis Lectures on Computer Architecture, Morgan & Claypool, 2018. A focused architectural treatment of GPU hardware.

M. Khairy, Z. Shen, T. M. Aamodt, and T. G. Rogers, "Accel-Sim: An Extensible Simulation Framework for Validated GPU Modeling," ISCA 2020. Describes the GPU simulator used in Chapter 15, including its execution-driven and trace-driven modes.

V. Narasiman, M. Shebanow, C. J. Lee, R. Miftakhutdinov, O. Mutlu, and Y. N. Patt, "Improving GPU Performance via Large Warps and Two-Level Warp Scheduling," MICRO 2011. Introduced the two-level warp scheduling policy discussed in the chapter.

NVIDIA Corporation, "NVIDIA H100 Tensor Core GPU Architecture" whitepaper, and the corresponding Hopper Tuning Guide. Primary source material for current data center GPU microarchitecture and relevant resource limits.

CHAPTER 15

GPU Simulation

In this chapter, we will apply the familiar hands-on simulation workflow to the GPU. Building on the concepts from Chapter 14, you will run focused experiments with intentionally designed GPU workloads and draw architectural conclusions from them. Each experiment will follow the same step-by-step approach you have applied earlier.

By the end of the chapter, you will develop an understanding of how memory coalescing, warp divergence, and per-warp latency tolerance affect GPU throughput. Reiterating an essential point, you should focus on the directional changes observed in the experiments, not on replicating the printed values.

We will use Accel-Sim as the simulator for the experiments in this chapter, given its widespread adoption in the GPU research community and validated performance on modern NVIDIA hardware. It is a trace-driven front-end on top of GPGPU-Sim that uses per-warp sequences of SASS instructions as traces. The traces to be used in this chapter are supplied pre-generated in the companion repository, so you do not need GPU hardware to produce any.

Recall that PTX is NVIDIA's virtual GPU ISA, whereas SASS is the native machine instruction set executed by the hardware. Accel-Sim uses the latter in trace-driven mode. While we have covered trace-driven simulation before, in this chapter, the trace format is GPU-specific and records warp-level execution information rather than a CPU-style instruction stream we saw earlier.

A. Pareek, *Performance Modeling of Computer Systems*, Maker Innovations Series,
https://doi.org/10.1007/979-8-8688-2476-0_15

Prerequisites

This chapter assumes you are familiar with

- GPU architecture concepts from Chapter 14
- Basic modern C++ programming

A Note on Accel-Sim Version: The code listings, configurations, and commands in this chapter are based on Accel-Sim at commit 3016c65 with GPGPU-Sim 4.2.0 at commit 6c3cf4ff. For brevity, only the core logic is shown, and the file path is listed.

Tool Setup

Accel-Sim can be built from source and automatically pulls the required GPGPU-Sim 4.x performance model during configuration. To use the simulator, you need the NVIDIA CUDA Toolkit and make sure it is available at /usr/local/cuda. If not, set CUDA_INSTALL_PATH to your actual CUDA installation directory. Listing 15-1 walks through the setup process.

Listing 15-1. Installing Accel-Sim

```
# Install build dependencies (Ubuntu 24.04)
# Install the equivalent dependencies for your Linux
distribution if not Ubuntu
sudo apt-get install -y build-essential bison flex \
  libboost-all-dev libxml2-dev libssl-dev zlib1g-dev \
  xutils-dev libglu1-mesa-dev

# Accel-Sim expects a CUDA toolkit on the system
# Use the appropriate path below if it is not installed at /
usr/local/cuda
export CUDA_INSTALL_PATH=/usr/local/cuda

# Clone the framework; GPGPU-Sim is pulled in during setup
```

```
git clone https://github.com/accel-sim/accel-sim-framework.git
cd accel-sim-framework

# Keep a handle to the top-level framework directory for
this chapter
export ACCELSIM_FRAMEWORK_ROOT=$PWD

# Source the environment helper (clones GPGPU-Sim the
first time)
source ./gpu-simulator/setup_environment.sh

# Build the simulator
make -j$(nproc) -C ./gpu-simulator
```

Note This listing assumes you are running in a shell with sudo privileges for package installation and that a CUDA toolkit is already installed at /usr/local/cuda. The run commands in this chapter rely on the runtime environment set by the setup_environment.sh script. Hence, if you quit your shell, make sure to source this script each time you run the experiments.

The build produces the simulator binary at gpu-simulator/bin/release/accel-sim.out. Unless the source code is modified, no rebuild is needed if you only change the configuration files and the traces to be simulated.

15.1 Simulator Configuration

In this section, let's look at how Accel-Sim is organized and how the configuration files and traces are formatted.

15.1.1 Accel-Sim Organization

Accel-Sim contains two main parts. The first, or the front-end, is responsible for parsing SASS traces, handing warps to the timing models, and tracking statistics. The second, or the back-end, is the GPGPU-Sim performance model, which implements the detailed microarchitecture, including the SM, memory hierarchy, interconnect, and DRAM timing. A simulation run using the binary accel-sim.out has both pieces linked into a single process.

Practically, the split implies that the knobs you need to configure live in two places. Trace-level parameters, such as the per-kernel register count or instruction mix, are set at trace generation, whereas microarchitectural parameters, such as cache geometry or DRAM timing, are set in the GPGPU-Sim config. This further means that source code modifications are usually in the GPGPU-Sim tree, while launch-time configuration modifications are in the Accel-Sim tree.

In this chapter, we will use the SM7_QV100 configuration, which is modeled after NVIDIA's Volta V100 GPU. Accel-Sim distribution ships a tuned, validated configuration for this GPU, and its parameters are well documented. Table 15-1 summarizes the relevant hardware parameters.

Table 15-1. SM7_QV100 Configuration Summary

Parameter	Value	Notes
SMs	80	Compute units (clusters x cores)
Warp size	32 lanes	SIMT execution width
Max warps per SM	64	Warp-slot limit
Max thread blocks per SM	32	CTA-slot limit
Registers per SM	65,536	32-bit registers
Shared memory per SM	96 KB	Unified with L1
L1 data cache per SM	32 KB	128 B line, 4 sets, 64 ways
L2 cache	6 MB	Shared, 64 sub-partitions
HBM2 bandwidth	900 GB/s	4,096-bit bus
Warp scheduler (default)	LRR	Loose round-robin

15.1.2 Configuration Files

Accel-Sim takes two configuration files as input. Listing 15-2 shows the command-line pattern.

Listing 15-2. Running Accel-Sim

```
$ACCELSIM_FRAMEWORK_ROOT/gpu-simulator/bin/release/accel-
sim.out \
  -trace <trace_dir>/kernelslist.g \
  -config $ACCELSIM_FRAMEWORK_ROOT/gpu-simulator/gpgpu-sim/
configs/tested-cfgs/SM7_QV100/gpgpusim.config \
  -config $ACCELSIM_FRAMEWORK_ROOT/gpu-simulator/configs/
tested-cfgs/SM7_QV100/trace.config
```

In the listing, the first config file, gpgpusim.config, sets microarchitectural parameters, and the second config file, trace.config, binds the SASS opcode table for the selected SM generation (SM_70 for Volta) and controls some trace-reader options. In this chapter, we will not modify its content and hence will not explore it in detail. Listing 15-3 shows the fields relevant to the experiments you will perform in this chapter.

Listing 15-3. Key Fields in gpgpusim.config

```
# Shader core
-gpgpu_n_clusters 80                     # number of SMs
-gpgpu_shader_core_pipeline 2048:32      # max threads/SM :
                                         warp size
-gpgpu_shader_registers 65536            # register file
                                         size per SM
-gpgpu_shader_cta 32                     # max CTAs
                                         resident per SM
-gpgpu_scheduler lrr                     # warp scheduler policy

# Caches
-gpgpu_cache:dl1 S:4:128:64,...          # L1D geometry
-gpgpu_cache:dl2 S:32:128:24,...         # L2 partition geometry
```

15.1.3 Trace Format

Traces are plain-text files that list a kernel's instruction stream, grouped by thread block and warp. Listing 15-4 shows an excerpt with one warp.

Listing 15-4. Trace Excerpt (One Warp)

```
-kernel name = _Z8exampleKv
-kernel id = 1
```

```
-grid dim = (80,1,1)
-block dim = (256,1,1)
-shmem = 0
-nregs = 16
-binary version = 70

#traces format = threadblock_x threadblock_y threadblock_z
warpid_tb PC mask dest_num reg_dests opcode src_num reg_srcs
mem_width mem_addresses

#BEGIN_TB
thread block = 0,0,0

warp = 0
insts = 2
0 0 0 0 0010 ffffffff 1 R3 IADD3 2 R3 R4 0
0 0 0 0 0020 ffffffff 1 R5 LDG.E 1 R6 4 1 0x7f0000000080 4
#END_TB
```

On each instruction line, the leading 0 0 0 0 is the thread block (x,y,z) and the warp ID within that block. The next field is the PC (program counter), followed by the 32-bit active mask (one bit for each lane of the warp). Following this, it lists the destination register count and the corresponding registers, the SASS opcode, the source register count and the corresponding registers, the memory width in bytes, which is zero for non-memory-related operations, and, finally, the per-lane addresses in one of three compressed forms. The traces used in this chapter are aimed at isolating specific GPU behaviors, and you do not need to modify any. You are encouraged to learn more about the format through documentation and create your own workloads to experiment further.

15.2 Experimental Design

This section covers the workloads, relevant metrics, and the general experimental process that we will follow, similar to the previous hands-on chapters.

15.2.1 Workload Selection

We will use small, targeted kernels as workloads for this chapter to expose specific architectural behaviors while keeping other effects small and predictable. Each workload uses a 640-CTA grid with 256 threads (8 warps per CTA) to keep comparisons on equal footing. Table 15-2 lists the workloads.

Table 15-2. *Custom Workloads for GPU Modeling*

Workload	Pattern	Purpose
coalesced_stream	LDG.E loads with stride-4 per lane	Baseline for coalescing experiment
strided_stream	LDG.E loads with stride-128 per lane	Uncoalesced contrast; each lane hits a different 128 B line
uniform_kernel	IADD3 chain, full 32-lane active mask	Baseline for warp divergence
divergent_kernel	Same IADD3 chain, split into 32 serial 1-lane paths	32-way divergence contrast
memory_bound	Coalesced LDG.E chain with per-warp dependency cycle, nregs = 16	High-occupancy case for latency experiment (64 warps/SM resident)
memory_bound_ regheavy	Same as memory_bound but nregs = 128	Low-occupancy case for latency experiment (16 warps/SM resident)
compute_bound	Pure IADD3 chain, no memory	Inert control for the latency experiment

15.2.2 Key Metrics

Relevant output fields from Accel-Sim, for the experiments you will conduct, are listed below:

- gpu_sim_cycle: Total simulated cycles
- gpu_sim_insn: Total active-lane instructions executed (already masked by the active-lane count)
- gpu_ipc: Active-lane instructions per simulated cycle
- L2_total_cache_accesses: L2 sector accesses, which reflect the coalescer's transaction count
- total DRAM reads: DRAM read requests issued

15.2.3 Experimental Process

We will follow the familiar process for each experiment, starting with one workload intended to expose the mechanism under study and using one or two other workloads for contrasting or control cases.

15.2.4 Companion Repository Setup

The traces and modified source files for this chapter are located in the companion repository at ch15-gpu-sim/. Set the environment variables as shown below, and make sure to source the setup_environment.sh file shown earlier before running:

```
export CHAPTER_DIR=/path/to/ch15-gpu-sim
export ACCELSIM_FRAMEWORK_ROOT=/path/to/accel-sim-framework
```

Note Each experiment in this chapter writes the simulator output (stdout) to a log file under $CHAPTER_DIR/results/, which is shown in the run commands. The metrics referenced are read from those log files.

With the setup in place, let's begin with the first experiment on memory coalescing. No local GPU hardware or trace-generation step is required for the main workflow in this chapter; the traces used here are the pre-generated ones supplied in the companion repository.

15.3 Memory Coalescing

As we covered in Chapter 14 on global loads, the memory coalescer inspects per-lane addresses and tries to service them with the fewest possible transactions. This experiment measures the effect of this coalescing on performance.

The Experiment

You will use the traces coalesced_stream and strided_stream for this experiment. They share the same instruction and warp count and differ only in the per-lane address stride inside each LDG.E load. In coalesced_stream, lane i reads the address base + 4i, so all 32 lanes fall within a single 128-byte cache line. This enables the coalescer to service the warp with the four 32-byte sector transactions corresponding to that line. In strided_stream, on the other hand, lane i reads base + 128i, so every lane lands on a different 128-byte line. Hence, each LDG.E touches 32 lines, resulting in an 8x increase in sector transactions.

Before you run the simulation, predict how the statistics should move and how to see the cost of the sub-optimal striding pattern. Listing 15-5 shows the run commands for both variants. Recall that you should source setup_environment.sh in the shell you run the experiments from.

Note strided_stream can take dramatically longer wall-clock time than coalesced_stream. You should confirm if the process has stopped consuming CPU load before concluding that it has failed or hung.

Listing 15-5. Coalescing Experiment Run

```
cd $CHAPTER_DIR
mkdir -p results

# Coalesced baseline
$ACCELSIM_FRAMEWORK_ROOT/gpu-simulator/bin/release/accel-
sim.out \
  -trace traces/coalesced_stream/kernelslist.g \
  -config $ACCELSIM_FRAMEWORK_ROOT/gpu-simulator/gpgpu-sim/
configs/tested-cfgs/SM7_QV100/gpgpusim.config \
  -config $ACCELSIM_FRAMEWORK_ROOT/gpu-simulator/configs/
tested-cfgs/SM7_QV100/trace.config \
  > results/coalesced.log

# Strided contrast
$ACCELSIM_FRAMEWORK_ROOT/gpu-simulator/bin/release/accel-
sim.out \
  -trace traces/strided_stream/kernelslist.g \
  -config $ACCELSIM_FRAMEWORK_ROOT/gpu-simulator/gpgpu-sim/
configs/tested-cfgs/SM7_QV100/gpgpusim.config \
```

```
  -config $ACCELSIM_FRAMEWORK_ROOT/gpu-simulator/configs/
tested-cfgs/SM7_QV100/trace.config \
  > results/strided.log
```

After the runs complete, check the relevant metrics in each log (gpu_sim_cycle, gpu_sim_insn, gpu_ipc, L2_total_cache_accesses, total DRAM reads) and compare them against your prediction. Table 15-3 shows the reference values for a subset of metrics.

Table 15-3. *Coalescing Experiment Reference Values*

Workload	Cycles	IPC	IPC Ratio	L2 Sector Accesses	DRAM Reads
coalesced_stream	~26,781 (baseline)	~97.9	-	327,680	327,680
strided_stream	~297,569	~8.8	0.090x	2,621,440	2,621,440

Results and Explanation

As you may have expected, strided access produces an 8x increase in L2 sector accesses and DRAM reads, owing to the exact mechanism we sensitized. The total number of cycles, however, increases even more, about 11x. This is likely due to strided accesses saturating many structures, leading to heavy queueing delays. This is also reflected in the IPC noted.

This clearly shows that the coalescer is one of the most consequential hardware features and that suboptimal transaction patterns can ripple throughout the system.

After studying the cost of uncoalesced memory accesses, let's turn to understanding the cost of divergent control flow.

15.4 Warp Divergence

As we saw in Chapter 14, warp divergence causes serialization of the code path and results in suboptimal utilization at the warp level. The cost increases with the number of distinct paths within the warp, and this experiment measures it by forcing a fixed number of paths and comparing against a uniform baseline.

The Experiment

We will use the workloads uniform_kernel and divergent_kernel for this experiment. In uniform_kernel, each warp issues a chain of 16 IADD3 instructions with all 32 lanes active for each one. In divergent_kernel, however, the same 16 operations are replicated across 32 sequential paths, with each path masking in one lane. This causes the forced serialization we want to evaluate.

Before running, predict the direction and the relative magnitude of the expected performance change. Listing 15-6 shows the run commands. Remember to source the setup_environment.sh script if you run it in a new shell.

Listing 15-6. Divergence Experiment Run

```
cd $CHAPTER_DIR
mkdir -p results

# Uniform baseline
$ACCELSIM_FRAMEWORK_ROOT/gpu-simulator/bin/release/accel-
sim.out \
  -trace traces/uniform_kernel/kernelslist.g \
  -config $ACCELSIM_FRAMEWORK_ROOT/gpu-simulator/gpgpu-sim/
configs/tested-cfgs/SM7_QV100/gpgpusim.config \
```

```
  -config $ACCELSIM_FRAMEWORK_ROOT/gpu-simulator/configs/
tested-cfgs/SM7_QV100/trace.config \
  > results/uniform.log

# 32-way divergence
$ACCELSIM_FRAMEWORK_ROOT/gpu-simulator/bin/release/accel-
sim.out \
  -trace traces/divergent_kernel/kernelslist.g \
  -config $ACCELSIM_FRAMEWORK_ROOT/gpu-simulator/gpgpu-sim/
configs/tested-cfgs/SM7_QV100/gpgpusim.config \
  -config $ACCELSIM_FRAMEWORK_ROOT/gpu-simulator/configs/
tested-cfgs/SM7_QV100/trace.config \
  > results/divergent.log
```

After the runs complete, compare gpu_sim_cycle and gpu_ipc across the two result files. Table 15-4 lists the IPC and cycles taken to complete for reference.

Table 15-4. *Divergence Experiment Reference Values*

Workload	Cycles	Active-Lane Instructions	IPC	IPC Ratio
uniform_kernel	~5,554 (baseline)	2,621,440	~472.0	-
divergent_kernel	~21,660 (32-way)	2,621,440	~121.0	0.26x

Results and Explanation

As you may have predicted, the divergent kernel runs much slower, taking almost four times as long. However, you may have expected a 32x slowdown, since we execute each warp with only one thread enabled at a time, increasing serialization by 32x. To understand this, consider that at the SM level, the scheduler draws from the resident warp pool to keep the issue unit busy, absorbing some of the cost.

Let's now work on an experiment involving some source code modification related to latency tolerance.

15.5 Latency Tolerance

The warp scheduler hides memory latency by switching to other resident warps whenever the current one stalls on a long operation (longop). We will make the stall length configurable and observe how occupancy affects the resulting IPC penalty as we increase the stall time by a fixed amount.

The Experiment

GPGPU-Sim's scoreboard tracks which registers are written by long operations in the file $ACCELSIM_FRAMEWORK_ROOT/gpu-simulator/gpgpu-sim/src/gpgpu-sim/scoreboard.cc. It reserves a register when an instruction issues and records it as a longop destination if it is a global or local load. It is then released at writeback. The scheduler (in shader.cc) uses the checkCollision() function before issuing the warp's next instruction and prevents any warp from issuing if it depends on the reserved register. For this experiment, we will add a per-warp cooldown counter that can be configured and prevents the scheduler from issuing that warp until it decrements to zero. This achieves controllable stalling, which we will use for the experiment.

The modification involves five small changes across three files. Listings 15-7a to 15-7e show each to guide you through the full setup.

Listing 15-7a. Scoreboard State (in $ACCELSIM_FRAMEWORK_ROOT/gpu-simulator/gpgpu-sim/src/gpgpu-sim/scoreboard.h)

```
// In the public section, after islongop():
void tick();
bool is_longop_stalled(unsigned wid) const;
```

```
// In the private section, after longopregs:
std::vector<unsigned> m_longop_cooldown;
unsigned m_longop_cooldown_cfg;
```

Listing 15-7b. Scoreboard Init and Methods (in $ACCELSIM_FRAMEWORK_ROOT/gpu-simulator/gpgpu-sim/src/gpgpu-sim/scoreboard.cc, inside the constructor and at file scope)

```
// Inside Scoreboard::Scoreboard(), after longopregs.resize():
m_longop_cooldown.assign(n_warps, 0);
const char* env = getenv("GPGPU_LONGOP_COOLDOWN");
m_longop_cooldown_cfg = env ? (unsigned)atoi(env) : 0;

// At file scope:
void Scoreboard::tick() {
  for (unsigned w = 0; w < m_longop_cooldown.size(); ++w) {
    if (m_longop_cooldown[w] > 0) m_longop_cooldown[w]--;
  }
}

bool Scoreboard::is_longop_stalled(unsigned wid) const {
  return m_longop_cooldown[wid] > 0;
}
```

Listing 15-7c. Arm Cooldown on Longop Issue (in Scoreboard::reserveRegisters, inside the longop-detection if-block, after the longopregs insertion loop)

```
// Arm the post-longop cooldown for this warp.
if (m_longop_cooldown_cfg > 0) {
  m_longop_cooldown[inst->warp_id()] = m_longop_cooldown_cfg;
}
```

Listing 15-7d. Tick the Cooldown (in $ACCELSIM_FRAMEWORK_ROOT/gpu-simulator/gpgpu-sim/src/gpgpu-sim/shader.cc, inside shader_core_ctx::cycle() after m_stats->shader_cycles[...]++)

```
// Tick the per-warp longop cooldown once per shader cycle.
m_scoreboard->tick();
```

Listing 15-7e. Scheduler Guard (in shader.cc, inside scheduler_unit::cycle() just after "unsigned warp_id = (*iter)->get_warp_id();")

```
// Skip warps still in post-longop cooldown.
if (m_scoreboard->is_longop_stalled(warp_id)) {
  continue;
}
```

After applying these changes, rebuild Accel-Sim, and remember to source the setup_environment.sh script beforehand if you change your shell.

Once built, the cooldown value can be controlled at runtime through the GPGPU_LONGOP_COOLDOWN environment variable. In the experiment, we will run two cooldown values, 0 and 2000, across three workloads: memory_bound, memory_bound_regheavy, and compute_bound. Before running, you should reason about the expected observations and IPC movement across the three workloads, given their characteristics. Listing 15-7f shows the process to run the full matrix.

Listing 15-7f. Latency Tolerance Run Commands

```
cd $CHAPTER_DIR
mkdir -p results

# Baseline (cooldown = 0)
for wl in memory_bound memory_bound_regheavy compute_bound; do
  GPGPU_LONGOP_COOLDOWN=0 \
```

```
    $ACCELSIM_FRAMEWORK_ROOT/gpu-simulator/bin/release/accel-
sim.out \
    -trace traces/$wl/kernelslist.g \
    -config $ACCELSIM_FRAMEWORK_ROOT/gpu-simulator/gpgpu-sim/
configs/tested-cfgs/SM7_QV100/gpgpusim.config \
    -config $ACCELSIM_FRAMEWORK_ROOT/gpu-simulator/configs/
tested-cfgs/SM7_QV100/trace.config \
    > results/${wl}_d0.log
done

# Added latency (cooldown = 2000)
for wl in memory_bound memory_bound_regheavy compute_bound; do
  GPGPU_LONGOP_COOLDOWN=2000 \
    $ACCELSIM_FRAMEWORK_ROOT/gpu-simulator/bin/release/accel-
sim.out \
    -trace traces/$wl/kernelslist.g \
    -config $ACCELSIM_FRAMEWORK_ROOT/gpu-simulator/gpgpu-sim/
configs/tested-cfgs/SM7_QV100/gpgpusim.config \
    -config $ACCELSIM_FRAMEWORK_ROOT/gpu-simulator/configs/
tested-cfgs/SM7_QV100/trace.config \
    > results/${wl}_d2000.log
done
```

After the runs, compare IPC between the baseline and the cooldown=2000 case for each workload. Table 15-5 lists the observed values for reference.

Table 15-5. Latency Tolerance Reference Values

Workload	Cooldown	Cycles	IPC	IPC Ratio
memory_bound (64 warps/SM)	0	~26,781	~97.9	-
memory_bound	2000	~37,178	~70.5	0.72x
memory_bound_regheavy (16 warps/SM)	0	~19,615	~133.6	-
memory_bound_regheavy	2000	~133,048	~19.7	0.15x
compute_bound	0	~5,554	~472.0	-
compute_bound	2000	~5,554	~472.0	1.00x

Results and Explanation

You can see that compute_bound serves as a control and stays at the same value for both cooldown periods. This is intended as the mechanism only targets longops.

There are two important observations to be made. The first is that the baseline IPC of memory_bound_regheavy is higher than memory_bound, even though it has fewer warps per SM. The likely reason for this is that the extra available warps (being memory-bound) create more concurrent memory requests, causing contention and decreasing IPC relative to the "lighter" memory_bound_regheavy.

The second observation is that the same extra warps enable the memory_bound workload to hide latency much more effectively, and thus, as the longop latency increases, the IPC remains higher than memory_bound_regheavy. Two different pressure points favor each workload.

15.6 Summary

This chapter presented three focused simulation experiments related to the concepts covered in Chapter 14.

The first experiment evaluated the performance difference between coalesced and uncoalesced memory access patterns. It also showed the second-order effects on the IPC due to saturation and queueing delays.

The second experiment evaluated the cost of divergence by forcing one workload to serialize while keeping the other enabled on all lanes. It also demonstrated that the SM-level warp pool can absorb some of the cost of divergence.

The third experiment evaluated how three different (and intentionally chosen) workloads tolerate latency by making code changes to explicitly add controllable latency for long operations and evaluating the effects of making it large across the workload spectrum.

Together, the experiments illustrated some important first-order determinants of GPU throughput and how they interact with different workloads.

In the next chapter, we will shift the focus to domain-specific accelerators and how their architectures and corresponding simulation approaches change.

Review Questions

1. Explain why the number of cycles taken for strided_stream workload is more than 8x, which is the number of extra L2 sector accesses it issues compared to coalesced_stream. What does it imply about the regime of the workloads (compute or memory-bound)?

2. In the second experiment, explain why the performance loss you observed was much less than 32x, which is the serialization factor we introduced.

3. In the third experiment, memory_bound_regheavy had a higher baseline IPC than memory_bound, yet, with the longop cooldown enabled, it lost far more. Can you explain why?

Exercises

Exercise 1: Plot the IPC numbers observed while sweeping the GPGPU_LONGOP_COOLDOWN value from 0 to 2,000 in steps of 250 on the memory_bound workload. Note the shape of the curve that results and the reason why it is so.

Exercise 2: Extend the second experiment with an intermediate variant that only introduces an 8-way divergence. Run the experiment and reason about the IPC number you measure. Add a few more intermediate steps and check whether your reasoning holds.

PART VI

Accelerator Modeling

CHAPTER 16

Tensor Accelerator Architecture

In Part VI, we move from general-purpose architectures to specialized hardware structures known as tensor accelerators. These structures give up flexibility to spend their silicon (and energy) budget catering to specific patterns within a class of workloads and offer a massive performance boost on those patterns. Since these architectures must be tuned for specific types of workloads, they are fast-evolving and far more heterogeneous. Designs and feature sets differ between vendors and generations, and publicly available information can be sparse. Hence, the treatment in this chapter is correspondingly broader and shallower than other similar chapters, such as 11 (CPU) and 14 (GPU). The essential goal is to build a mental map that makes the hands-on work in Chapter 17 intuitive and to develop a vocabulary for self-guided research.

We will start by understanding why such accelerators exist in the first place. Next, we will cover the systolic-array organization found in many modern AI accelerators and examine the dataflow choices that determine the movement of operands through it. We will then turn to the memory hierarchy and the mapping problem of fitting workloads onto the hardware and what aspects to be mindful of for optimal performance.

A. Pareek, *Performance Modeling of Computer Systems*, Maker Innovations Series,
https://doi.org/10.1007/979-8-8688-2476-0_16

16.1 The Case for Tensor Accelerators

As you have seen with GPU and CPU architectures, branch predictors, schedulers, caches, and out-of-order engines keep execution efficient to a certain degree when the workload is unknown. In many specific domains, such as deep learning, computations tend to be highly similar (e.g., matrix multiplication), and data reuse is common. Other important aspects, such as precision tolerance, etc., are frequently well understood. This reduces the need for generic structures that cater to workload variation, as with a CPU or a GPU. Instead of dynamic instruction scheduling, accelerators can manage with fixed data flow. Similarly, software-managed scratchpads with lower hardware complexity can be used instead of complex caching systems. All these savings enable the addition of more targeted hardware structures, such as multiply-accumulate units.

As an example, numeric precision is one design freedom that specialization opens up. While general-purpose processors prioritize FP32 or FP64 for compatibility, neural networks tolerate much lower precision. With appropriate calibration, models could be run at INT8 or lower with known minimal accuracy loss. Since an INT8 multiplier is much smaller than an FP32 multiplier, lower precision can unlock higher throughput within the same silicon budget.

Several real-world examples address this specific tradeoff, including Google's TPU using BF16, INT8, etc., and NVIDIA Blackwell, which uses FP4 and FP8.

Modeling Perspective: Along with compute throughput, precision choice also affects the effective memory bandwidth, since a lower-precision tensor takes fewer bytes. When comparing simulator results across precisions, make sure to account for both the throughput multiplier and the bandwidth-per-element factor needed.

16.2 The Systolic Array

Many modern AI accelerators typically contain a two-dimensional array of small multiply-accumulate units, which is surrounded by a few software-managed SRAM buffers. Further, high-bandwidth channels are used to communicate with off-chip memory. This organization is based on a decades-old concept called the systolic array, which fits well with dense matrix multiplication workflows. You are encouraged to follow its development throughout history and its resurgence in the machine learning world.

In this section, we will examine this structure in three layers, i.e., the static structure, the rhythmic data movement (as the name suggests), and a real-world example.

16.2.1 Array Organization

A typical systolic array is a regular two-dimensional grid of identical processing elements (PEs). Each PE contains a multiplier, an accumulator register, and a few operand registers. Essentially, there is enough to perform a multiply-accumulate (MAC) and forward values to the neighbors that are connected in the four directions corresponding to the grid organization. Within the PE array, there is typically no global interconnect, or shared bus, and the locality makes this organization cheap to implement and easy to scale.

The on-chip SRAM buffers hold the immediate data needed, including the input buffer for activations, a weight buffer, and an output buffer for accumulated results. Off-chip memory, such as HBM or LPDDR, sits behind these with higher access latency but larger storage capacity. The entire data path, from the off-chip memory to the PEs and back, is largely orchestrated by the compiler, runtime, and DMA control mechanisms. Figure 16-1 shows the typical array organization.

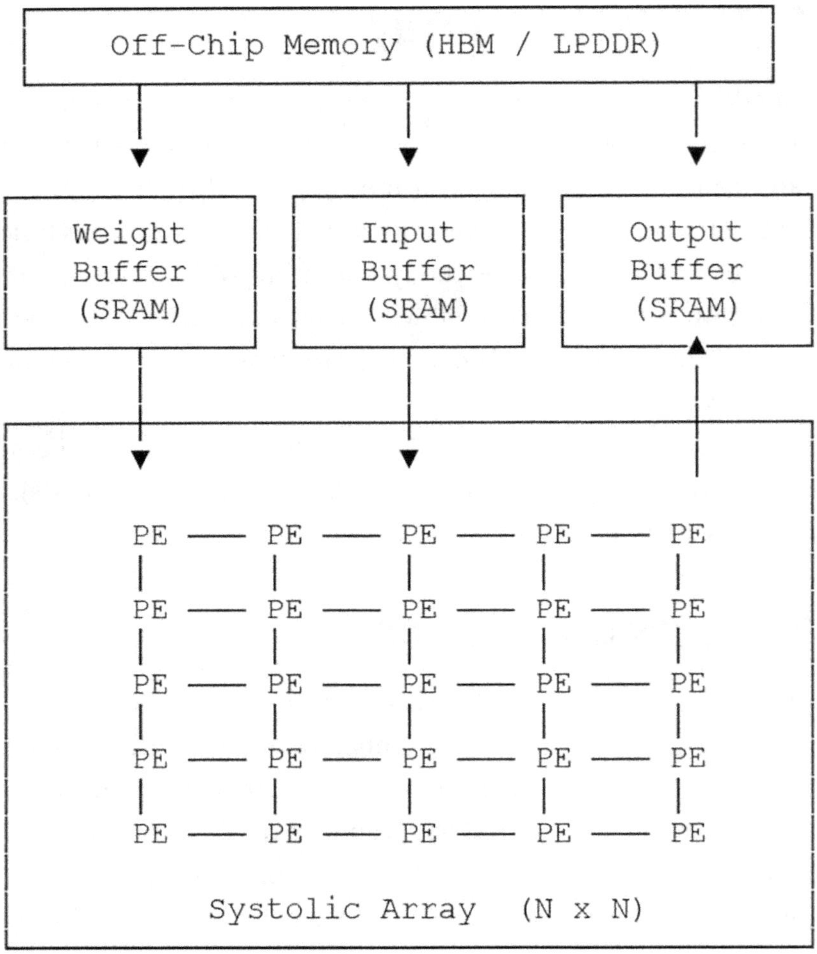

Figure 16-1. *Systolic Array Organization*

16.2.2 Data Movement Through the Array

The defining behavior of a systolic array is that data flows through the PEs in a rhythmic manner rather than being fetched on demand. The array works similarly to an assembly line, where each station does a fixed job on whatever arrives at its input.

Let's take a matrix multiplication operation as a more concrete example. In an arrangement where the weights stay put, on every cycle, each PE receives the partial sum from above and activation from the left. It then multiplies the activation by its preloaded weight, adds the product to the partial sum, and passes the updated partial sum downward and the activation to the right. Listing 16-1 shows the per-cycle behavior of one PE.

Listing 16-1. Per-Cycle Behavior of a Systolic PE (Weight-Stationary)

```
def pe_cycle(pe, in_top, in_left):
# weight is preloaded, and stays put
  psum_out  = in_top + (pe.weight * in_left)  # MAC, send
                                               partial sum down
  out_right = in_left                          # forward
                                               activation
                                               rightward
  return psum_out, out_right
```

In this way, a single weight or activation feeds many MACs before leaving the array, resulting in a high reuse. This results in memory bandwidth scaling sub-linearly with compute capacity and enables a systolic array to sustain high throughput at modest off-chip bandwidth.

16.2.3 The TPU Example

Google's first Tensor Processing Unit, described by Jouppi and colleagues in 2017, is the canonical academic example of a systolic array. It consists of a 256x256 systolic array of INT8 multiply-accumulators, which are 65,536 MACs, enabling a peak throughput of 92 tera-operations per second. It is complemented with 28 MiB of on-chip SRAM. The data flow involves loading the model weights into the array and streaming activations through it. This choice was primarily due to inference being the target of that generation. Since then, subsequent TPU generations have added support for training, mixed-precision arithmetic, and larger memory hierarchies.

As you may have noticed, dataflow choice directly determines which workloads run efficiently on a given array. Let's cover that in the next section.

16.3 Dataflow Choices

Dataflow, as the name suggests, defines the flow of data within the systolic array. It determines which operands see the most reuse, what influences bandwidth and storage pressure, and, in turn, which workloads run the most efficiently. For example, in matrix multiplication, the three operands are the inputs, the weights, and the outputs. With the PE array dimension and architecture fixed, the choice involves selecting which of the three remain in place within the PEs and which stream through. This section covers the three primary patterns relevant to the modeling experiments in the next chapter.

Weight Stationary (WS): In this organization, weights are loaded into the PEs once and remain fixed throughout a tile. Activation streams from one end of the array and partial sum streams out from the other. It works well when weights are large and stable across many inputs, which is common in inference.

Output Stationary (OS): In this organization, each PE accumulates a single element of the output matrix across multiple steps. Activations and weights flow in, and partial sums never leave the PE until the full computation is done. This matters when partial-sum traffic is dominant, e.g., in layers with large outputs.

Input Stationary (IS): Here, the activations are pinned to the PEs, and the weights and partial sums stream in and out of the array. It is suited to scenarios where activations are shared across many weight sets. An example of such a pattern is convolutional layers when the input tensor is small relative to the number of output channels.

While not supported in SCALE-Sim, the tool you will use in the next chapter, **Row Stationary (RS),** is another common dataflow variant. It keeps a row of convolutions stationary within each PE and relies on exploiting the convolutional structure instead of treating the operation as a generic matrix multiply.

The right choice depends on the layer's shape, array sizes, and the characteristics of the memory hierarchy, such as bandwidth and capacity, which we turn to in the next section.

16.4 Memory Hierarchy on Accelerators

As we have seen with other architectures as well, the compute throughput depends on how quickly operands can be supplied to the processing elements. In this section, we will walk through the memory hierarchy tiers from the PE outward and contrast the software-managed scratchpad model with the cache-based hierarchy we covered earlier. This will enable you to develop a mental model of how memory affects sustained performance.

16.4.1 Scratchpad Hierarchy

At the innermost tier, closest to the PEs, each PE holds a small set of registers, including an accumulator, which the multiplier uses directly. Further out is the local SRAM that feeds the array's edges. This contains the inputs, weights, and output buffers. One step further is the chip-level scratchpad that is shared across multiple arrays. The last level is the off-chip memory that holds the bulk of a model's weight and activation tensors (HBM or LPDDR). Table 16-1 lists typical representative capacity and bandwidth values for each level.

***Table 16-1.** Representative Accelerator Memory Hierarchy*

Tier	Capacity	Approximate Bandwidth (representative)
PE registers	A few bytes per PE	Effectively no bottleneck
Array-local SRAM (input/weight/output buffers, accumulators)	Several MiB total	Hundreds of GB/s to several TB/s
Chip-level scratchpad (e.g., TPU's VMEM, CMEM)	Tens to hundreds of MiB	Several TB/s
Off-chip HBM (data center)	Tens to hundreds of GB	Several TB/s
Off-chip LPDDR (mobile)	Several GB	Tens to hundreds GB/s

16.4.2 Software-Managed Data Movement

In contrast with the other units we covered, particularly the CPU, on an accelerator, most data movement between memory tiers is explicit. It is either issued by the compiler at code generation time or by a DMA engine following directions provided by the compiler.

This shift has two main implications you need to be mindful of. First, the compiler (or an accelerator mapping tool) is responsible for choosing sizes that fit the SRAM budgets at each tier. Poor choice can result in capacity overflows or stalls that the hardware cannot handle on its own. The second implication is that it makes modeling more direct. The simulator does not need to model cache or replacement policies. Data movement schedule and bandwidth limits at each tier largely suffice.

Modeling Perspective: When comparing simulator results against hardware measurements, discrepancies often result from the data-movement schedule rather than the array model. Tile sizes, buffering depth, and DMA queueing are important parameters to be mindful of.

Now that we have covered individual components, let's look at the full picture and cover how to lay a real workload on the hardware in the next section. We will also look at common bottlenecks that produce suboptimal performance.

16.5 Mapping and Performance Bottlenecks

For a given layer, specifications such as matrix dimension, precision, batch size, etc. must be translated into a concrete execution plan to be launched on the PE array. It is commonly referred to as the mapping and involves choosing tile sizes that fit the array and its SRAM buffers, selecting a dataflow for each tile, ordering the tiles, and finally staging data through the memory hierarchy so that the arrays stay fed. Note that in many accelerators, there is little or no runtime fallback in case of a suboptimal mapping choice, making it an extremely important piece of the whole execution.

Tiling is the most visible aspect of mapping. Most of the time, the layer dimensions and the array's fixed dimensions mismatch, necessitating partitioning the workload into blocks that fit on the PE arrays. As a concrete example, with a fully connected layer with a 384x512 weight matrix (384 input channels, 512 output channels) mapped onto a 256x256 weight-stationary array, the output dimension can be split into two tiles of 256 columns. Similarly, the input dimension also needs two tiles, one to cover the first 256 rows and the next for the remaining 128. This can be mapped to 4 tiles in total: 2 at full utilization and 2 at 50% utilization. This results in an average spatial utilization of around 75%, producing a noticeable gap between peak and sustained throughput in the simulator.

While we walked through one example of spatial underutilization that creates a gap between sustained and peak throughput, you may encounter many other factors in real runs. For example, if the SRAM buffers cannot refill from off-chip memory fast enough, PEs can stall waiting for data. This can usually be captured by the roofline model when the operation falls in the memory-bound regime. Examples where this is most pronounced are low-intensity layers such as the small GEMMs found in LLM decode.

Sparsity and precision can also create bottlenecks distinct from the two we discussed. In many trained models, zeroes can occur at a significant fraction of weight or activation values. This property, known as sparsity, can waste compute cycles if not optimized for. Typically, accelerators support handling structured sparsity, such as the 2:4 pattern, in which exactly two of every four consecutive values are non-zero. Quantization has a similar hardware dependency. Without native hardware units or mechanisms to handle model quantization, the expected speedups may not be realized.

16.6 Summary

This chapter covered the architectural concepts needed to conduct simulation experiments related to tensor accelerators. The key takeaways are:

First, the core principle behind accelerators is trading general flexibility for efficiency. Dynamic scheduling is reduced in favor of more fixed dataflow, memory movement is largely managed through software with minimal hardware machinery, and precision trade-offs are used to increase throughput.

Second, we covered the systolic array as a representative design pattern for modern deep learning accelerators. The core organization consists of a regular grid of small PEs whose data movement is primarily to immediate neighbors.

Third, the dataflow choice dictates which operand sees the most reuse, and that, in turn, determines the workload class suitable for each. There is no universally best dataflow choice.

Fourth, the memory hierarchy consists of mostly software-managed scratchpads, ranging from PE registers to main memory. Modeling explicit data movement is an important aspect of simulation accuracy and differs from the hardware cache-based mechanisms we saw earlier in the book.

Fifth, for an end-to-end run, mapping a real workload into the PE array involves tiling, dataflow selection, and dimension matching. We covered common bottlenecks that can arise in this process and produce a gap between achieved and peak throughput.

With these concepts in hand, in the next chapter, you will configure a systolic array in SCALE-Sim and measure the impact of dataflow, tiling, and sparsity on performance.

Review Questions

1. Despite each PE of a systolic array being capable of only one multiply-accumulate each cycle, what makes the systolic array efficient at matrix multiplication at scale?

2. Which operands see the most reuse and which are streamed for the three dataflow patterns we covered? Describe the best-fitting workloads for each case.

3. For an LLM decode inference workload with large weight matrices, a batch size of 1, and a growing KV cache, explain why peak TOPS is a poor predictor of achieved performance.

Further Reading

H. T. Kung, "Why Systolic Architectures?" IEEE Computer, 15(1), January 1982. The original paper about systolic design.

N. P. Jouppi et al., "In-Datacenter Performance Analysis of a Tensor Processing Unit," ISCA 2017. The TPU v1 paper and description of a weight-stationary inference accelerator.

Y.-H. Chen, T. Krishna, J. Emer, and V. Sze, "Eyeriss: An Energy-Efficient Reconfigurable Accelerator for Deep Convolutional Neural Networks," IEEE Journal of Solid-State Circuits 52(1), January 2017 (also ISSCC 2016). Introduces the Row Stationary dataflow.

V. Sze, Y.-H. Chen, T.-J. Yang, J. Emer, Efficient Processing of Deep Neural Networks, Morgan & Claypool, 2020. The standard reference textbook on DNN accelerator architecture.

A. Parashar et al., "Timeloop: A Systematic Approach to DNN Accelerator Evaluation," ISPASS 2019. Mapping, search, and analytical modeling are used widely in accelerator research.

H. Kwon et al., "MAESTRO: A Data-Centric Approach to Understand Reuse, Performance, and Hardware Cost of DNN Mappings," IEEE Micro, 2020. Alternative analytical cost model for dataflow analysis.

CHAPTER 17

Accelerator Simulation

This chapter walks you through hands-on experiments with SCALE-Sim as the platform to simulate systolic accelerator behavior. You will use concepts from Chapter 16 and observe how the dataflow choice, array geometry, and structured sparsity affect performance and utilization.

Each experiment follows the familiar workflow we carried out in previous hands-on chapters:

- Predict the effects of an architectural change.
- Implement the change.
- Run workloads that are sensitive to it.
- Check relevant metrics in the output.
- Reason about the performance change observed.

Prerequisites

This chapter assumes you are familiar with

- Accelerator architecture concepts from Chapter 16
- Basic Python familiarity and editing INI-style configuration files and CSV files

A. Pareek, *Performance Modeling of Computer Systems*, Maker Innovations Series,
https://doi.org/10.1007/979-8-8688-2476-0_17

A Note on SCALE-Sim Version: The configuration formats and run commands used in this chapter were validated against the public SCALE-Sim source tree corresponding to v3.0.0 from `https://github.com/scalesim-project/SCALE-Sim` repository. During the work, the current public tree also required a minor runtime workaround for completing the experiments.

Tool Setup

The setup process is straightforward. The simulator can be cloned and installed using pip from a local version of the repository, as shown in Listing 17-1.

Listing 17-1. Installing SCALE-Sim

```
# Clone the canonical repository.
git clone https://github.com/scalesim-project/SCALE-Sim.git
cd SCALE-Sim

# Create a virtual environment
python3 -m venv .venv
source .venv/bin/activate

# Install the package and its dependencies
pip install -U pip
pip install -e .

# Verify installation
python3 -m scalesim.scale --help
```

After installation, the python3 -m scalesim.scale entry point becomes available and is the command we use to run simulations throughout this chapter.

Important Note In the current public v3.0.0 release, experiments may crash due to an array-to-scalar reduction issue in the code. If you face this issue, as a fix, the companion repository includes replacement source files under listing-files/. You can copy them into your local SCALE-Sim checkout if needed using the following procedure:

```
export SCALE_SIM_ROOT=/path/to/SCALE-Sim
export CHAPTER_DIR=/path/to/ch17-accelerator-sim

cp $CHAPTER_DIR/listing-files/listing-17-runtime-workaround/
double_buffered_scratchpad_mem.py \
   $SCALE_SIM_ROOT/scalesim/memory/
cp $CHAPTER_DIR/listing-files/listing-17-runtime-workaround/
read_buffer.py \
   $SCALE_SIM_ROOT/scalesim/memory/
```

To revert to the public release later, copy the original files back from listing-files/original/.

17.1 Simulator Configuration

Before we begin running simulations, let's explore how SCALE-Sim models the accelerator hardware and the workload and how we run custom experiments.

17.1.1 SCALE-Sim Architecture Model

SCALE-Sim models a systolic array accelerator with the structure we covered in Chapter 16. It is a two-dimensional array of multiply-accumulate (MAC) units fed by three on-chip SRAM buffers: input (IFMAP), weights (Filter), and output (OFMAP). These buffers are connected to off-chip memory through a configurable bandwidth channel.

Table 17-1 lists the architectural parameters that come with the default configuration files in the repository. We will adjust them throughout the chapter.

Table 17-1. *Default Architecture Parameters*

Parameter	Default	Notes
Array dimensions	32 x 32	1,024 MACs total
IFMAP SRAM	64 KB	input feature map buffer
Filter SRAM	64 KB	weight buffer
OFMAP SRAM	64 KB	output buffer
Off-chip bandwidth	10 elements/cycle	DRAM interface
Dataflow	WS	weight-stationary
Memory banks	1	single-bank model

17.1.2 Configuration File

SCALE-Sim uses an INI-format configuration file to describe the architecture and runtime parameters. The file is organized in sections, and the most important ones for this chapter's experiments are [general] for naming the simulation run, [architecture_presets] for specifying array and SRAM dimensions, [layout] for specifying the buffer layout, and [sparsity] for the sparsity controls used in the last experiment. Listing 17-2 shows the baseline configuration we will work with.

Listing 17-2. Baseline Configuration File (in $CHAPTER_DIR/configs/baseline.cfg)

```
[general]
run_name = ch17_baseline_32x32_ws

[architecture_presets]
ArrayHeight: 32
ArrayWidth: 32
IfmapSramSzkB: 64
FilterSramSzkB: 64
OfmapSramSzkB: 64
IfmapOffset: 0
FilterOffset: 10000000
OfmapOffset: 20000000
Bandwidth: 10
Dataflow: ws
MemoryBanks: 1
ReadRequestBuffer: 32
WriteRequestBuffer: 32

[layout]
IfmapCustomLayout: False
IfmapSRAMBankBandwidth: 10
IfmapSRAMBankNum: 10
IfmapSRAMBankPort: 2
FilterCustomLayout: False
FilterSRAMBankBandwidth: 10
FilterSRAMBankNum: 10
FilterSRAMBankPort: 2

[sparsity]
SparsitySupport: false
```

```
SparseRep: ellpack_block
OptimizedMapping: false
BlockSize: 8
RandomNumberGeneratorSeed: 40

[run_presets]
InterfaceBandwidth: CALC
UseRamulatorTrace: False
```

Common adjustments for experimental analysis include the array dimensions (ArrayHeight and ArrayWidth), the SRAM sizes, and the dataflow specifier (ws, os, or is). For each experiment in this chapter, you will change one of these in isolation and keep the others fixed.

17.1.3 Topology File

The topology file contains the workload you will simulate on the hardware. It is described using CSV format. By default, SCALE-Sim accepts a convolution-oriented format in which each row corresponds to a single CNN layer. The fields are layer name, input feature map height and width, filter height and width, number of input channels, number of output filters, and stride. You can check some examples shipped with the repository under topologies/conv_nets/.

SCALE-Sim also accepts a more general M, N, K GEMM format for topology specification when invoked with the -i gemm option. To explore both types, we will use the convolution-style format for Experiments 1 and 3 and switch to the GEMM style in Experiment 2. We use a single layer to keep the experiments focused and easy to interpret.

Listings 17-3a and 17-3b show examples of both specification formats.

Listing 17-3a. Convolution-Style Single-Layer Topology (in $CHAPTER_DIR/topologies/midconv.csv)

```
Layer name, IFMAP Height, IFMAP Width, Filter Height, Filter
Width, Channels, Num Filter, Strides,
midconv, 56, 56, 3, 3, 64, 64, 1,
```

Listing 17-3b. GEMM-Style Single-Layer Topology (in $CHAPTER_DIR/topologies/midgemm_small.csv)

```
Layer Name, M, N, K,
midgemm_small, 3136, 24, 216,
```

17.1.4 Layout File

Along with the configuration and topology specification, SCALE-Sim v3 also expects a layout file that describes how tensor data is arranged across the SRAM banks. Since we will run the experiments with custom layout disabled, we only need to supply the fixed default layout file located at layouts/conv_nets/test.csv to satisfy the current SCALE-Sim v3 workflow. It carries no other meaning.

17.2 Experimental Design

Similar to previous hands-on chapters, let's take a look at the workload, metrics, and the general experimental process we will follow through the experiments.

17.2.1 Workload Selection

We will use two single-layer workloads for understanding the results clearly. For dataflow and sparsity, we will use the convolution-style topology shown in Listing 17-3a. For the array-size experiment, Section 17.4, we will switch to a GEMM-styled topology, as shown in Listing 17-3b. It lists the M, N, and K parameters of the GEMM kernel to be simulated.

17.2.2 Key Metrics

SCALE-Sim produces four CSV reports under the configured output directory. Some fields that convey important information are listed below:

- **Compute Cycles (COMPUTE_REPORT.csv)**: Total cycles taken to execute the layer on the configured array.
- **Mapping Efficiency (COMPUTE_REPORT.csv)**: Fraction of array cycles spent on useful compute. This captures spatial underutilization.
- **SRAM Bandwidth (BANDWIDTH_REPORT.csv)**: Per-buffer bandwidth in elements per cycle.
- **DRAM Bandwidth (BANDWIDTH_REPORT.csv)**: Off-chip bandwidth, capturing memory pressure.
- **Detailed Accesses (DETAILED_ACCESS_REPORT.csv)**: Total SRAM and DRAM accesses.
- **Time Estimate (TIME_REPORT.csv)**: Layer-wise runtime estimates derived from cycle counts.

17.2.3 Experimental Process

For each run, you will supply a configuration file, a topology file, and the default layout file as inputs. You also need to provide an output directory where simulation results will be written upon completion. Listing 17-4 shows an example of the command we will use.

Listing 17-4. Example SCALE-Sim Run Command

```
python3 -m scalesim.scale \
  -c $CHAPTER_DIR/configs/<config>.cfg \
  -t $CHAPTER_DIR/topologies/<topology>.csv \
  -l $SCALE_SIM_ROOT/layouts/conv_nets/test.csv \
  -p $CHAPTER_DIR/outputs
```

17.2.4 Companion Repository Setup

The configuration, topology, and listing files used in this chapter are available in the companion repository at ch17-accelerator-sim/. If not already done so, you should set the CHAPTER_DIR and SCALE_SIM_ROOT environment variables in the following way:

```
export CHAPTER_DIR=/path/to/ch17-accelerator-sim
export SCALE_SIM_ROOT=/path/to/SCALE-Sim
```

With the setup in place, let's begin with our first experiment comparing dataflow choices.

17.3 Dataflow Comparison

In this experiment, you will compare the three dataflow choices covered in Section 16.3. The workload will remain the same. Before running, recall that WS reuses weights, OS reuses outputs, and IS reuses inputs, and predict the outcome of the experiment.

The Experiment

We will use three config files supplied with the chapter repository. They differ only in the dataflow line (and the experiment names), while keeping the other parameters constant. Listing 17-5 shows the process for running the experiment using bash for-loop syntax. It should also work in other POSIX-compliant shells, such as zsh. If you use a shell that doesn't support it, you can run each command individually.

Listing 17-5. Dataflow Comparison Sweep

```
# $CHAPTER_DIR/configs/df_ws.cfg  (Dataflow: ws)
# $CHAPTER_DIR/configs/df_os.cfg  (Dataflow: os)
# $CHAPTER_DIR/configs/df_is.cfg  (Dataflow: is)

# Experiment Run Commands:
for df in ws os is; do
  python3 -m scalesim.scale \
    -c $CHAPTER_DIR/configs/df_${df}.cfg \
    -t $CHAPTER_DIR/topologies/midconv.csv \
    -l $SCALE_SIM_ROOT/layouts/conv_nets/test.csv \
    -p $CHAPTER_DIR/outputs_dataflow
done
```

After the runs complete, open the COMPUTE_REPORT.csv and BANDWIDTH_REPORT.csv files to compare the results using the metrics from Section 17.2.2. Table 17-2 shows the expected values.

Table 17-2. Dataflow Comparison Reference Values

Dataflow	Total Cycles	Total Cycles (relative)	Mapping Efficiency %	Filter SRAM BW	OFMAP SRAM BW
WS	108359	1.00x	100.00	0.34	31.00
OS	117391	1.08x	99.05	28.89	1.69
IS	261647	2.41x	99.05	12.96	12.84

Results and Explanation

As you may have predicted, WS completes the fastest, as shown by the Total Cycles column. This is because weights are loaded once and reused across many input activations. This can also be corroborated by looking at the Filter SRAM BW column, which shows that the bandwidth pressure for WS is the lowest of the three.

You can also see that different dataflows move pressure to different buffers. As we discussed in Chapter 16, there is no universally best dataflow, and the performance depends on the shape of the operation being launched on the systolic array. For layers with filters much larger than the input, results can easily shift, and IS or OS can outperform WS. You will explore this in this chapter's exercises.

The next experiment walks you through observing how workload topology and array geometry interact, specifically when there is a deliberate mismatch.

17.4 Array Size and Mapping Efficiency

This experiment varies the PE array dimension (with SRAM scaled to match) while keeping the workload and all other architectural parameters constant. To offer a more general, matrix-oriented view rather than the convolutional style elsewhere in the chapter, we will use a GEMM workload. The dimensions are chosen specifically for illustrative purposes, to make spatial underutilization easy to observe.

The Experiment

The configurations you will use differ only in ArrayHeight, ArrayWidth, and the SRAM sizes (which scale with the array size). The dataflow is fixed to WS, and the M, N, and K topology (also fixed) is chosen such that one dimension is smaller than the array dimension for some configurations (M=3136, N=24, K=216). Note the extra flag in the run command that enables the GEMM input mode. Listing 17-6 shows the sweep command.

Listing 17-6. Array Size Sweep

```
# sz_16x16.cfg: ArrayHeight: 16, ArrayWidth: 16, SRAM
32 KB each
# sz_32x32.cfg: ArrayHeight: 32, ArrayWidth: 32, SRAM
64 KB each
# sz_64x64.cfg: ArrayHeight: 64, ArrayWidth: 64, SRAM
128 KB each
# Experiment Run Commands:
for sz in 16x16 32x32 64x64; do
  python3 -m scalesim.scale \
    -c $CHAPTER_DIR/configs/sz_${sz}.cfg \
    -t $CHAPTER_DIR/topologies/midgemm_small.csv \
    -i gemm \
    -l $SCALE_SIM_ROOT/layouts/conv_nets/test.csv \
    -p $CHAPTER_DIR/outputs_array
done
```

Once complete, compare cycles and mapping efficiency from the output CSV files across the three runs. Table 17-3 shows the expected values.

Table 17-3. *Array Size Sweep Reference Values*

Array	PE Count	Total Cycles	Total Cycles (relative)	Mapping Efficiency %	Overall Utilization %
16 x 16	256	89095	3.94x	72.32	71.28
32 x 32	1024	22609	1.00x	72.32	70.22
64 x 64	4096	13303	0.59x	31.64	29.84

Results and Explanation

As you can see, even though 64x64 completes the fastest, the mapping efficiency and utilization drop sharply compared to the other two. The smaller 16x16 and 32x32 arrays are slower in absolute cycle counts but waste less array space.

This experiment illustrates the spatial underutilization problem from Chapter 16. Overall Utilization captures the achieved compute rate as the fraction of the array's peak capacity. As the array grows beyond what the workload can keep fed, realized utilization drops. This highlights the importance of matching tensor dimensions to the array geometry.

Let's move to the third and final experiment of the chapter that exercises one of v3's signature features: structured sparsity.

17.5 Sparsity

In this experiment, you will enable 2:4 sparsity, which is the pattern where two of every four contiguous values in the weight tensor are non-zero. The goal is to observe its effect on compute cycles and the storage required for the weight tensor.

The Experiment

The changes needed to enable sparsity are shown in Listing 17-7. The topology file needs a sparsity column to specify the N:M ratio for each layer, and the configuration file's [sparsity] section needs to be enabled with the corresponding block size (4 in this case).

Listing 17-7. Sparse Topology, Configuration, and Run Commands

```
# $CHAPTER_DIR/topologies/midconv_sparse.csv
Layer name, IFMAP Height, IFMAP Width, Filter Height, Filter
Width, Channels, Num Filter, Strides, Sparsity,
midconv, 56, 56, 3, 3, 64, 64, 1, 2:4,

# $CHAPTER_DIR/configs/sparse_2_4.cfg  (excerpt)
[sparsity]
SparsitySupport: true
OptimizedMapping: false
SparseRep: ellpack_block
BlockSize: 4
# Experiment Run Commands:
# Dense baseline
python3 -m scalesim.scale \
  -c $CHAPTER_DIR/configs/baseline.cfg \
  -t $CHAPTER_DIR/topologies/midconv.csv \
  -l $SCALE_SIM_ROOT/layouts/conv_nets/test.csv \
```

```
  -p $CHAPTER_DIR/outputs_sparse

# Sparse
python3 -m scalesim.scale \
  -c $CHAPTER_DIR/configs/sparse_2_4.cfg \
  -t $CHAPTER_DIR/topologies/midconv_sparse.csv \
  -l $SCALE_SIM_ROOT/layouts/conv_nets/test.csv \
  -p $CHAPTER_DIR/outputs_sparse
```

Once complete, in addition to the other reports you are now familiar with, the sparse run produces an extra SPARSE_REPORT.csv that contains the storage savings from compressing the sparse filter (original filter storage, new storage, filter metadata storage). Table 17-4 shows the expected values of relevant metrics.

Table 17-4. *Dense vs. 2:4 Sparse Comparison*

Configuration	Total Cycles	Total Cycles (relative)	Total Filter Storage	Metadata Storage
Dense (baseline)	108359	1.00x	36864	0
2:4 sparse	54179	0.50x	19584	1152

Results and Explanation

As you can observe, with sparsity support, both the number of cycles required to complete and the storage needed for weights (filters) drop to about 50% of the original values. This benefit, however, is only achievable when the sparsity pattern is supported by the hardware. Note that the 50% storage reduction is approximate since it does not include the metadata storage overhead. In general, real accelerators may realize smaller speedups than what models predict because activation and output traffic do not scale with weight sparsity. Other overheads such as metadata decode, operand routing, and load balancing across PEs also incur extra cost in practice.

17.6 Summary

This chapter connected concepts from Chapter 16 to three focused simulation experiments on SCALE-Sim.

The first experiment compared the three dataflows on the same workload and array dimensions. WS ran the fewest cycles and consumed the least Filter SRAM bandwidth due to reuse.

The second experiment varied the array dimension on a GEMM workload, keeping everything else constant. It illustrated that spatial utilization can fall drastically even with faster runtime.

The third experiment exercised SCALE-Sim v3's structured-sparsity feature with a 2:4 pattern and displayed the possible advantages of hardware-supported sparsity.

With accelerator simulations covered, in the next chapter, let's briefly discuss the importance of power and energy modeling and demonstrate how it can be achieved with some of the simulators we have used in this book.

Review Questions

1. Reason about how the ranking of different dataflow choices would change if we were to use a layer with 256 input channels and 16 output filters instead of 64 and 64.

2. If you were to use a 256 x 256 systolic array to run the midgemm_small workload, think of ways the workload could be reshaped or batched to improve efficiency without changing the array.

3. Explain which property of array execution enables structured sparsity to be exploited.

Exercises

Exercise 1: Repeat the array-size sweep experiment from Section 17.4 with the midgemm_small topology. Run all array configurations with OS or IS dataflow, and compare and reason about your findings.

Exercise 2: Change the midconv workload to reduce the number of output filters to 16. Run the workload with WS, OS, and IS dataflow on the baseline 32 x 32 array, and explain your findings.

PART VII

Power Modeling

CHAPTER 18

Power Modeling – A Walkthrough

So far in the book, we have focused on performance as the singular goal in evaluating the effects of the architectural changes through simulation experiments. We have largely ignored power and energy, which are important aspects with their own modeling disciplines. While detailed treatment and experimental demonstration are outside the scope of the book, this chapter aims to introduce the basics and provide a starting point if you decide to research it further. To that end, the chapter offers a basic walkthrough of the power analysis tools available for use with the performance simulators we used earlier. The guidance offered is at a high level, and you are encouraged to consult the respective tools' documentation for more information. You are not expected to run the experiments straight by copying the example code snippets.

18.1 Why Model Power

The performance numbers we have used thus far, such as IPC, latency, bandwidth, or throughput, do not communicate the cost of the work done in terms of the energy consumed. Energy efficiency is increasingly important at both ends of the spectrum, from ultra-low-power mobile devices to full-scale data centers. It is more common to report performance-per-watt than bare performance numbers.

A. Pareek, *Performance Modeling of Computer Systems*, Maker Innovations Series,
https://doi.org/10.1007/979-8-8688-2476-0_18

Power is defined by two main components. Dynamic power is associated with transistor switching and corresponds to the chip's activity. Static power (or leakage power) is the power consumed continuously regardless of transistor activity. It scales with chip area, voltage, and temperature. While power simulators report both, dynamic power is often the more interesting part from the architectural viewpoint.

Let's quickly cover how to enable power modeling for the CPU and GPU simulation workflows you learned before.

18.2 CPU Power with McPAT

For CPU architecture research, McPAT (Li et al., MICRO 2009) is a commonly used power modeling tool. It takes a hierarchical processor description (cores, caches, memory controller, etc.) at a configurable technology node and estimates the per-access energy cost of each component. It combines this with activity counts from a performance simulator (e.g., cache reads, ROB accesses, etc.) to estimate dynamic power consumption. Static power is derived from the technology node, structure sizes, etc., without considering activity.

Note that McPAT is a standalone tool and is not tied to any particular simulator. To use it with gem5, you need a bridging tool that takes gem5's stats.txt and config.json files and produces an XML file in McPAT's expected format, with the information filled in. While gem5 doesn't supply such a tool out of the box, several community-maintained scripts are available. You can use either depending on your needs. Some examples are Hardik44/Gem5toMcPat_parser and saideeptiku/Gem5McPatParser on GitHub. Listing 18-1 shows a typical workflow example.

Listing 18-1. Example McPAT Workflow on a gem5 Run

```
# 1. A gem5 run produces two files needed by McPAT:
ls <gem5_output_dir>/
```

```
  config.json         # architectural configuration
  stats.txt           # runtime activity counts

# 2. Run a community gem5-to-McPAT parser to produce the McPAT
input XML.
#    The script name and CLI vary by parser; this is an
     example.
python3 <parser>.py \
    <gem5_output_dir>/stats.txt \
    <gem5_output_dir>/config.json \
    <mcpat_template>.xml \
    -o <output>.xml

# 3. Run McPAT on the generated input
$MCPAT_ROOT/mcpat \
    -infile <output>.xml \
    -print_level 5 > <power_report>.txt
```

The output file contains the hierarchical breakdown of energy and area. McPAT reports the peak and average runtime dynamic power for each entry (unit). This breakdown can serve as guidance for optimizing your architectural feature for power efficiency or for identifying any non-trivial effects caused by your changes.

Let's look at how to perform power analysis for GPU simulations next.

18.3 GPU Power with AccelWattch

AccelWattch (Kandiah et al., MICRO 2021) provides the corresponding power model for Accel-Sim and can be run with the timing simulator. Along with a runtime flag to enable it, you need to supply an additional configuration file (shipped with the code) that describes the needed parameters for the target GPU. The results are reported in a separate file named accelwattch_power_report.log. Listing 18-2 shows how to enable AccelWattch on an experiment from Chapter 15.

Listing 18-2. Example of Running AccelWattch on an Experiment from Chapter 15

```
# Re-run the divergent_kernel experiment with
AccelWattch enabled
$BIN -trace traces/divergent_kernel/kernelslist.g \
     -config $GCFG \
     -config $TCFG \
     -power_simulation_enabled 1 \
     -accelwattch_xml_file $ACCELSIM_FRAMEWORK_ROOT/
     gpu-simulator/gpgpu-sim/configs/tested-cfgs/SM7_QV100/
     accelwattch_sass_sim.xml \
     > results/divergent_timing.log
```

The generated report contains per-kernel power (average, max, and min) and per-component average power fields covering integer units, floating-point units, tensor cores, register files, schedulers, L2 cache, etc. It also contains some cumulative fields that summarize power across all kernels.

18.4 Looking Further

This chapter provided a brisk walkthrough of an increasingly important aspect of modeling. The approach we covered is still the first layer of a deeper subject and extends in various directions. Some of these are listed below:

Full-System Power: The IP-level power estimation tools we covered offer only part of the picture and ignore many important components, such as DRAM modules, voltage regulators, fans, and external interconnects. Full-system estimation is therefore a necessary step in scoping and understanding the potential benefits of intended architectural changes.

Thermal Modeling: Higher power consumption increases heat dissipation, often leading to throttling. Understanding this feedback is essential for understanding how performance depends on factors external to IP-level architectural changes.

ML-Driven Power Prediction: Recent work applies ML to calibrate or replace analytical power estimates, offering novel research opportunities for further exploration.

With a brief coverage of power modeling, let's now continue to the final chapter of the book and revisit the techniques and tools we covered for a unified perspective.

Closing Thoughts

In this book, we developed a layered simulation toolkit. We started with workload characterization through tracing and sampling and continued through understanding and simulating the memory hierarchy, CPU microarchitecture, GPU microarchitecture, and systolic accelerators. What carries forward from all the work is the methodology that ties the tools together.

The essential methodology, repeated across every experiment in the book, consists of five steps:

- Predicting the effects of architectural change
- Implementing the change through code or configuration
- Running workloads that are sensitive to the change or offer a control signal
- Checking relevant metrics in the output
- Reasoning about the observed changes versus the initial hypothesis

The final step is what the first four exist to enable and the actual muscle we intend to develop with the work done throughout. That is where real understanding happens and innovations follow.

For the next steps following the book, the most useful exercise is to apply this loop to a workload of your own choice. This can be a benchmark relevant to your work, or a GPU kernel from a paper you found interesting, and so on. You can also read documentation of the tools we covered to try deeper simulations.

A. Pareek, *Performance Modeling of Computer Systems*, Maker Innovations Series,
https://doi.org/10.1007/979-8-8688-2476-0

The tools and architectures we covered will continue to evolve, and some will get replaced over time. The methodology and understanding developed are durable, and the part you have actually been practicing throughout the book.

Index

A

Accel-Sim, 16–17
coalescing memory, 312
experiments, 312–314
reference values, 314
configuration files, 305
command-line pattern, 307
front-end/back-end, 306
gpgpusim.config, 308
hardware parameters, 306
thread block, 309
trace format, 308–309
trace-level parameters, 306
experimental process, 310
companion repository, 311–312
experimental process, 311
metrics, 311
workloads, 310
installation, 304
latency tolerance, 317
checkCollision() function, 317
reference values, 321
run commands, 319
scoreboard init and methods, 318
scoreboard tracks, 317-321
setup process, 304–305
traces, 303
warp level, 315
divergent kernel, 316
experiment, 315–316
reference values, 316–317
Address translation, 155–156
Architecture concepts, 21
bandwidth and latency, 27–29
categories, 22
compute-memory balance, 22–26
fundamental constraint, 22
parallelism, 30–36

B

Bandwidth constraints, 27–28
accurate representation, 28
factors, 27
memory channels, 27
memory technology, 27
numerical process, 28
wider buses, 27
Basic block vector (BBV), 98–99

A. Pareek, *Performance Modeling of Computer Systems*, Maker Innovations Series,
https://doi.org/10.1007/979-8-8688-2476-0

Branch predictor metrics
  MPKI reference ranges, 129
  Re-order Buffer (ROB), 128
  statistics, 127–129
Branch Target Buffer (BTB), 215

C

Cache management
  architecture, 143
    access flow, 144
    hierarchy parameters, 145
    inclusion policies, 149
    miss classification, 146
    parameters, 143
    prefetcher
      monitors, 147–148
    primary parameters, 144
    replacement
      policies, 146–147
    set-associative
      organization, 144–145
    VIPT addressing, 145
    write-read policies, 148
  LRU (least recently used), 147
  metrics
    accuracy, 126
    cross-level analysis, 125
    prefetcher statistics, 126–127
    statistics, 122–124
  pseudo-LRU (pLRU), 147
  shared resources, 148
Cache metrics
  MPKI reference ranges, 124
Central processing unit (CPU)
  CPU (*see* CPU core
    architecture)
  GPU (*see* Graphics processing
    unit (GPU))
  McPAT workflow, 360–361
  multicore (*see* Multicore
    simulations)
  parallelism, 34–36
  simulator, 231–253
ChampSim, 15
  cache metrics, 122
  output
    general structure, 116
    report, 116–120
    simulation pipeline, 120
    structure, 116
  sampling techniques, 108
  tool setup, 70–72
  traces
    collection parameters,
      81, 82
    compression ratio, 83
    Pin installation, 81
ChampSim models
  DRAM organization, 186
  version, 186
Chip structure and design, 3
Clustering, 50
  SimPoint methodology, 100
  and visualization techniques,
    50–51
Comparative analysis
  architectural features, 131

geometric *vs.* arithmetic
mean, 132
normalized speedup, 131
reporting checklist, 132–133
Compute-memory balance
computational resources,
24–25
equation, 22
fundamental level, 22
hardware system, 24
matrix multiplication, 23
memory-bound, 25
numerical operation, 24
operational intensity, 23–24
platform comparison, 26
resources, 23
roofline model, 24
work rate, 23
CPU core architecture, 209
execution back end
architectural register, 218
arithmetic operations, 220
core-level studies, 219
in-order execution, 217
out-of-order execution, 217
physical register, 218
register renaming, 217–218
reorder buffer
(ROB), 218–219
representative
execution, 219–221
retirement stage, 221
scheduling stage, 219–221
sequential execution, 216
front-end
and back-end, 209
branch prediction, 214–216
branch target prediction, 215
direction prediction, 215
fetch/decode
stages, 213–214
instruction TLB (I-TLB), 213
ISA-level instructions, 214
L1 instruction cache
(L1-I), 213
modern processors, 214
return target prediction, 216
memory interface, 222
load-store queue (LSQ), 222
parallel load
opportunities, 223
store buffer, 223
multicore execution, 223
capacity contention, 224
coherence protocols, 224–226
directory-based
protocols, 225
exclusive, 225
false sharing, 226
interconnect topology, 226
memory bandwidth
contention, 224
modified state, 225
on-chip interconnect,
226–227
shared/invalid, 225
shared resources/
contention, 224

CPU core architecture (*cont.*)
snoop-based protocols, 225
state transitions, 225
synchronization cost, 227
topology options, 227
pipeline, 210–213
CPU simulator
configuration scripts, 233
baseline script, 234–236
branch misprediction, 238
fetch loop, 237
key control points, 237–239
models, 233
O3CPU parameters, 236–237
retirement loop, 237
squash recovery transition, 239
execution unit bandwidth
functional-unit pool, 245
IntALU definition, 245
reference values, 247, 248
run simulations, 246
experimental process, 239
companion repository, 242
environment variables, 242
gem5 statistics, 241
methodology, 242
metrics, 241
workloads, 240
gem5 version, 232, 233
Reorder Buffer (ROB), 242–245
experiment, 243
reference values, 244
size/instruction, 242
setup process, 232
squash recovery delay, 248
constructor initialization, 249
delay argument, 250
parameter, 249
reference values, 252–253
run commands, 251
source code modifications, 249
stall recovery, 250
trigger recovery, 250
workflow, 231
Cycle-accurate simulation, 9
Cycles per instruction (CPI), 122

D

Data-level parallelism (DLP), 33
Data version control (DVC), 89
DCPerf benchmark, 52
Dynamic random access memory (DRAM), 185
abstraction level, 150
architecture, 150
configuration, 186–187
experimentation, 189
key metrics, 190
modifications, 190
repository setup, 190
RQ (Read Queue)/WQ (Write Queue), 190
workload selection, 189
fine-grained level, 151

metrics, 129–130
organization/bank structure, 150–151
parameter modification, 188
refresh overhead, 153
row buffer management, 195–204
scenarios, 152
steps, 185
timing configurations, 191
access latency, 191
experiment, 191–193
results/explanation, 193–195
timing constraints, 151–152

E

Execution-driven (PTX), 17

F

False sharing
data layout, 268
definition, 268
experiment, 269
reference values, 270
single-core simulator, 271
workloads, 270

G

Generalization problem
applicability, 43
backward working, 44
benchmarks, 42
cache replacement policy, 45–46
claims, 40, 43, 44
evidence requirement, 44
neglecting phases, 42
over-representation, 42
production-scale applications, 42
representativeness, 41–42
research claims, 44
research questions, 43
selection bias, 41
statistical sampling, 40
target applications, 45
temporal mismatch, 42
warning signs and remedies, 41
General-purpose compute (GPGPU), 279
Graphics processing unit (GPU)
Accel-Sim (*see* Accel-Sim)
AccelWattch, 361–362
architecture, 279
compute/memory transfers, 290
asynchronous, 293–294
characteristics, 294
L2 cache/HBM, 291–292
memory coalescing, 293
shared memory/L1 data cache, 290–291
execution model, 280
block diagram, 285
compute unit, 282–286
cooperative thread array, 281

Graphics processing unit (GPU) (*cont.*)
execution units, 283
high-level organization, 284
L1 data cache, 283
matrix engine instruction, 284
register file, 283
representative parameters, 286
shared memory, 283
SIMT/warp, 280
thread block/grids, 281–282
warp scheduler, 283
high-bandwidth memory (HBM), 279
occupancy/resources, 294
parallelism, 34–36
performance pathologies, 296
atomics, 298
bank structure, 298
execution kernel, 298
memory access, 297
warp divergence, 297
register pool, 295
resources, 295–296
shared memory pool, 295
vendor-neutral, 279
wrap scheduling, 287–290

H

Hyperthreading, 32

I

Instruction-level parallelism (ILP), 217
implementation, 31
meaning, 30
out-of-order execution, 31
pipelining, 30
speculation, 31
superscalar execution, 31
Instruction per cycle (IPC), 51, 121
Instructions per clock cycle (IPC), 86
Intel Pin, 70
Intel Processor Trace (PT), 76

J

Just-in-time (JIT), 79

K

k-means clustering, 100

L

Latency constraints, 28–29
access mechanics, 29
cache hierarchy, 29
factors, 28
identification, 29
physical distance, 28
scenarios, 29
Load-store queue (LSQ), 222

M

Machine-learning accelerators, 17
Main memory, *see* Dynamic random access memory (DRAM)
McPAT, 360–361
Memory system architecture
- address translation, 155–156
- caches, 143–149
- DRAM architecture, 150–153
- FCFS (first-come first-served), 154
- FR-FCFS (first-ready FCFS), 154
- memory controller, 153
  - byte-offset bits, 154
  - mapping physical addresses, 154
  - row buffer, 155
  - scheduling policies, 154–155
- virtual address, 156

Memory-level parallelism (MLP), 135
Methodology, 365–366
Mispredictions per kilo-instruction (MPKI), 91
Miss status holding registers (MSHRs), 148, 222
MLPerf (MLCommons) client, 53
Modeling techniques
- abstractions, 10
- accuracy/speed/flexibility
  - academic research, 12
  - accuracy *vs.* speed, 11
  - analytical reasoning, 13
  - design possibilities, 11
  - detailed confirmation, 13
  - fast/detailed simulation methods, 14
  - flexibility *vs.* accuracy, 11
  - gem5, 13
  - prefetcher evaluation, 12–14
  - rapid exploration, 13
  - recommendation, 13
  - tape-out, 12
  - tradeoffs, 10–11
- analytical models, 7
- approaches, 7
- balancing strategies, 5
- computational representations, 5
- cycle-accurate models, 9
- debugging, 6
- development lifecycle, 6
- development process, 4
- economic/practical aspects, 4
- history, 7
- open-source simulation, 14–18
- researchers, 6
- roofline model, 8
- simulators, 7
- system optimization, 6
- testing, 5
- transactions, 8–9

Multicore simulations
- experimental process, 262
  - companion repository, 265
  - methodology, 264
  - primary metrics, 264
  - workloads, 262–263

Multicore simulations (*cont.*)
false sharing, 268–271
gem5 version, 256
scaling process
command-line flag, 265
experiment, 265
false sharing, 267
reference values, 267
serialization, 267
simulator configuration
baseline configuration script, 258–260
classic/ruby memory system, 257
concepts, 257
MESI two-level hierarchy, 257–258
message buffer counters, 261
ruby statistics, 260–262
synchronization cost
experiment, 272, 273
global atomic counter, 271
performance impact, 271
reference values, 274
worker loops, 272
tool setup, 256
two-level binary, 256
Multiply-accumulate (MAC) units, 342

N

Non-inclusive/non-exclusive (NINE), 149

O

OCI Artifact registries, 89
Online transactional processing (OLTP), 54
Open-source simulation
Accel-Sim, 16–17
ChampSim, 15
DRAM Simulators, 18
frameworks, 14
gem5, 16
learning curve, 16
Pin (Intel), 18
SCALE-Sim, 17
selected tools, 15
toolkit, 16–17

P

Parallelism, 30
accelerators, 34
approaches, 34–36
data-level parallelism, 33
ILP techniques, 30–31
TLP model, 32–33
PARSEC workloads, 52
Performance modeling
modelers lens, 21–36 (*see also* Modeling techniques)
Pintools
analysis callbacks, 80
architecture, 79
callback functions, 80
definition, 80
framework, 80

instrumentation callback, 80
steps, 79
Pipeline workflow
branch misprediction, 212
categories, 211
control hazards, 211
depth/frequency, 212–213
front-end/back-end split, 210
fundamentals, 210
instruction execution, 210
representative parameters, 211–212
stage processes, 210
structural hazards, 211
Power modeling
AccelWattch, 361–362
CPU architecture research, 360–361
definition, 360
full-system estimation, 363
ML-driven power prediction, 363
static power (leakage power), 360
thermal modeling, 363
Precise event-based sampling (PEBS), 77
Prefetchers
evaluation, 12–14
statistics, 126–127
Principal component analysis (PCA), 50

Q

Queuing theory, 8

R

Register Transfer Level (RTL), 5
Re-reference interval prediction (RRIP), 147
Return Address Stack (RAS), 216
Rodinia benchmark, 52–53
Roofline model, 8
Row buffer management, 195–204
access pattern, 200
adaptive policy, 202
build and run policy, 197
close-on-conflict, 201
close-page and open-page policies, 203
close-page modification, 197
conflict tracking, 200
detecting conflicts, 201
experiment, 197–198
explanation, 203
finish_dbus_request(), 195, 196
observations, 196
results, 199, 203
service_packet() functions, 195

S

Sampling Microarchitecture Simulation (SMARTS), 107
Sampling techniques
checkpoints, 109
combination forces, 96
functional warming, 108
insufficient warm-up, 110
low weight points, 111

Sampling techniques (*cont.*)
phase behavior, 97
pitfalls, 110
real-world applications, 96
scenarios, 106–107
short intervals, 110
SimPoint (*see* SimPoint methodology)
steady-state execution, 96
steady-state region, 97–98
strategies, 108
unweighted averaging, 111
warming length guidelines, 109–110
Sanity checks
cross-metric plausibility, 135–136
internal consistency, 134–135
reference data, 136
SCALE-Sim models, 17
accelerator simulation, 340
architectural parameters, 342
array size/mapping
architectural parameters, 349
experiments, 350
reference values, 351
baseline configuration, 342–344
concepts, 339
dataflow, 347
experiment, 348–349
reference values, 349
experimental process, 345
companion repository, 347
layout file, 347
metrics, 346
workloads, 346
installation, 340
layout file, 345
setup process, 340–341
sparsity, 352
reports, 353
sparse comparison, 353, 354
topology file, 352, 353
topology file, 344–345
SIMD Instructions (CPUs), 33
SimPoint, 95
SimPoint methodology
basic block execution, 98–99
clustering, 100
intervals, 104, 105
representative intervals, 99–100
sampling pipeline parameters, 101–103
scenarios, 106–107
source, 100
tracing workflow, 103–105
weighted results, 105–106
Simulations
cache tag lookup, 64
CPU workflow, 231–253
DRAM access, 65
entry structure, 61
execution-driven, 75
last level cache (LLC), 64
memory access, 63–65
output, 115
branch statistics, 127–129

cache subsystem, 122–127
ChampSim, 116–120
comparative analysis, 131–133
DRAM statistics, 129–130
sanity checks, 133–136
throughput metrics, 120–122
pipeline, 120
sampling (*see* Sampling techniques)
statistics, 61
subsequent phases, 69
total latency, 65
trace-driven simulator, 61–63
Simultaneous Multithreading (SMT), 32
Single instruction, multiple threads (SIMT), 280
Stall budget, 122
Standard benchmarks, 51
CPU architecture research, 51–52
GPU and accelerator benchmarks, 52–53
limitations, 54
production workloads, 54
server/cloud workloads, 53–54
TPC benchmarks, 54
Statistical profiling extension (SPE), 77
Synthetic microbenchmarks, 55
System simulation (gem5), 77
Systolic array
definition, 329
grid organization, 329
matrix multiplication, 331
organization, 329–330
per-cycle behavior, 331
tensor processing unit, 331

T, U

Tensor accelerators, 327
dataflow
definition, 332
input stationary (IS), 332
output stationary (OS), 332
row stationary (RS), 333
weight stationary (WS), 332
domains, 328
mapping, 335
matrix dimension, 335
memory hierarchy tiers, 333
chip-level scratchpad, 333–334
components, 335
data movement, 334–335
representative capacity, 333
numeric precision, 328
on-chip SRAM buffers, 329
precision tolerance, 328
real-world, 328
sparsity and precision, 336
spatial underutilization, 335
systolic array, 329–332
Tensor Processing Unit (TPU), 331
Thread-level parallelism (TLP), 32–33

Throughput metrics, 120
TorchBench, 53
Trace collection
  ChampSim, 70–72, 81–83
  collection approach, 76
    DBI tracing, 76
    hardware tracing, 76
    Pin and DynamoRIO, 76
    system simulation (gem5), 77
  contents, 72–73
  factors, 89
  formats, 74–75
  GitHub page, 70
  high-level characterization, 78
  Intel Pin, 70–72
  interpretation, 72
  ISA-level instructions, 73
  kernel activity, 73
  kernel fraction, 90
  kernel-inclusive analysis, 77
  micro-operations, 73
  multi-threaded execution, 74
  organization/management, 86
    git-annex, 89
    metadata template, 87–88
    naming convention, 87
    storage, 88
    version control systems, 88–89
  Pin (*see* Pintool)
  PT and DBI tracing, 77–78
  SimPoint methodology, 103–105
  speculative execution, 73
  subsequent phases, 69
  validation, 83
    end-end process, 86
    hardware counters, 85–86
    instruction mix, 84–85
    Intel Processor Trace (PT), 86
    memory-intensive application, 85
    sanity checks, 84
  wrong path execution, 90–91
Trace-driven (SASS), 17
Trace-driven methodology, 9
Transaction level models (TLM), 8–9
Translation Lookaside Buffer (TLB), 155–156

V

Version control systems, 88–89
Virtual memory randomization, 189

W, X

Walk-through, *see* Power modeling
Warp execution (GPUs), 33
Workload selection
  characterization techniques, 46
    cache and memory system, 49–50
    clustering/visualization, 50–51

compute utilization, 48
distinct phases, 50
hardware performance counters, 47–48
memory bandwidth utilization, 48
operational intensity, 48–49
primary purposes, 46–47
reuse distance, 50
stride analysis, 49
working set estimation, 49
coverage-based approach, 56
DRAM experimentation, 189
gap identification, 51
generalization (*see* Generalization problem)
hardware prefetcher, 39
heuristics, 56
history of, 39
key principles, 57
practical factors, 56–57
real-world scenarios, 56
sources, 55
standard benchmarks, 51–54
standardized benchmarks, 55
trade-offs/pitfalls, 55
valid justifications, 56
Wrap scheduling
instruction and memory latencies, 288–289
latency hiding, 289–290
performance modeling, 287
primary categories, 288
representative latencies, 288
scheduling mechanics, 287
transcendental functions, 288

Y, Z

Yahoo Cloud Serving Benchmark (YCSB), 53

www.ingramcontent.com/pod-product-compliance
Lightning Source LLC
Chambersburg PA
CBHW070313180826
50013CB00022B/393
* 9 7 9 8 8 6 8 8 2 4 7 5 3 *